What Can U.S. Government
Information Do for Me?

What Can U.S. Government Information Do for Me?

Librarians Explain the Discovery and Use of Public Data, Documents, Maps and Images

Edited by Tom Diamond *and* Dominique Hallett

McFarland & Company, Inc., Publishers
Jefferson, North Carolina

ISBN (print) 978-1-4766-8949-4
ISBN (ebook) 978-1-4766-4958-0

LIBRARY OF CONGRESS AND BRITISH LIBRARY
CATALOGUING DATA ARE AVAILABLE

Library of Congress Control Number 2023038009

On the cover: *top left to right down* The McNary Dam Spilling, on the
Columbia River Bordering Oregon and Washington (U.S. Department
of Energy); Genealogy and Family History (MeganBrady/Shutterstock); Hubble
Space Telescope showcases an edge-on view of the majestic spiral galaxy UGC
11537 (ESA/Hubble & NASA, A. Seth); Colorized scanning electron micrograph
of a cell infected with a variant strain of SARS-CoV-2 virus particles, isolated from
a patient sample. Image captured at the NIAID Integrated Research Facility (IRF)
in Fort Detrick, Maryland. (NIAID); statue of Justice (© r.classen/Shutterstock)

Printed in the United States of America

*McFarland & Company, Inc., Publishers
Box 611, Jefferson, North Carolina 28640
www.mcfarlandpub.com*

Acknowledgments

The editors would like to thank Christopher C. Brown, reference librarian and coordinator of government documents at the University of Denver, for his valuable insights in current publishing practices and assisting the editors in preparing the proposal for this book. We would like to thank GODORT for its 2021 panel discussion, Writing & Publishing for Information Professionals, which sparked the ideas for this book. Special thanks to all the authors for their excellent contributions.

Table of Contents

Part VII. Science

Introduction

TOM DIAMOND *and* DOMINIQUE HALLETT

The U.S. federal government serves as one of the country's largest publishers. To assist it in its publishing goals, the Government Publishing Office serves as the government's "official, digital, secure resource for producing, procuring, cataloging, indexing, authenticating, disseminating, and preserving the official information products" (U.S. Government Publishing Office, n.d.a.). Government documents is a blanket term used to categorize any information produced and disseminated by a government agency. The mission of the GPO is "Keeping America Informed as the official, digital, and secure source for producing, preserving, and distributing official Federal Government publications and information products for Congress, Federal agencies, and the American public" (U.S. Government Publishing Office, n.d.b.).

The government's publications and data collection activities are astonishing. The value of this information cannot be underestimated. Bill Brantley, United States Patent and Trademark Office, addresses the value question and that citizens tend to underestimate its monetary impact. He writes about the need to create "methods for better measuring and managing the value of information" to realize its full potential (2018). Nicholas Eberstadt and others address the value of data collected by the federal government. The government plays a vital role in collecting data for the citizenry to use in conducting commerce and in their daily activities. The government's role as an impartial data collector is crucial for businesses, policymakers, and families to use in making well-informed decisions (2017). Ellen Hughes-Cromwick and Julia Coronado take a similar approach in documenting the value of data collected by the U.S. government and its impact on business decision-making. This includes its importance to parties such as researchers and nonprofits and industries such as the automotive industry (2019). The federal government collects and disseminates a massive treasure trove of information including

1

budgets, regulations, bills and laws, and the founding documents of our country.

The library community, and particularly government document librarians, are long-standing advocates, recognizing the value of government information and its importance to a well-informed citizenry. These individuals have published books and articles about accessing these materials. Arizona State University's CJ Garcia, Scholarly Communication Intern, views government information as an "overlooked gem." He writes of its importance in areas such as space research and the humanities. Garcia notes that the U.S. Census Bureau collects, produces, and disseminates a unique collection of population statistics, and nearly all this data is available for free (2022). Government document librarians have written articles about efforts to unlock collections and make them accessible to the public. For example, Sierra Laddusaw and Garret Littlejohn write about a project Texas A&M University Libraries undertook to unlock World War II map collections housed within the library's Map & GIS department. These are maps produced by the Army Map Service, the military's World War II printing agency. One of the project's goals is to provide digital access to the collection online (2019). William Sleeman writes about a project to unlock and make accessible unexplored maps published in U.S. Supreme Court's *Records and Briefs of the Supreme Court of the United States*. This project is using the materials housed in the library of the Supreme Court of the United States. As of this writing, the Court's online catalog provides access to records documenting maps contained in the nineteenth-century volumes. A review of the twentieth-century volumes is planned for 2022 (Sleeman 2022). These are a few examples of government resources, or hidden treasures, waiting to be discovered by the public. U.S. government publications are an incredible resource waiting to be used and discovered by the public.

Purpose of This Book

The purpose of this volume is to provide information to the reader about U.S. government resources, how to use these resources to answer different questions, and provide practical applications the reader can implement and adapt in one's library environment. Library personnel must remain knowledgeable about critical agencies and departments of the U.S. government and its websites, how to navigate the websites, what basic information each provides, and how to discover "hidden" resource treasures. Library personnel need to understand how to apply this information in the performance of their duties and learn from the experiences of colleagues. This includes answering various types of patron questions, performing community outreach, engaging in civic activities, serving business patrons, and providing classroom instruction. This is a practical, "hands-on" volume to guide people to resources they might not have ever discovered.

Librarians and library professionals from academic, public, school, federal, and special libraries will find this book useful as a learning tool and as a resource to consult when assisting patrons. This will be valuable when assisting, for example, high school, college, and graduate students who are conducting research or looking to build their resumes and learn about job opportunities with the federal government. These individuals may never have considered investigating the federal government for such information.

Organization of This Book

This book is organized into seven parts. Part I focuses on an assemblage of government departments and agencies that provide access to an eclectic group of resources. Claudene Sproles and Amy Laub delve into the critical collection known as the Serial Set, an often overlooked and misunderstood resource. The authors cover what is and is not included and, more importantly, how to unlock its contents through print and online resources. Elisabeth Pearson Garner unlocks a treasure of information offered by the Department of State. The everyday citizen can learn about topics such as geography, foreign policy issues, and opportunities for students and travelers. Ariana Baker and Allison Faix review crime and justice data collected and distributed by various federal agencies. They discuss the challenges in finding this data and offer strategies for successful searching. Amanda McLeod addresses the topic of policy research and analysis. Freely available government resources, along with practical and useful examples, are provided by McLeod for individuals and community-based organizations. Part I concludes with Jennifer Castle's exploration of a wide-ranging collection of public domain and copyrighted images offered by various government departments and agencies.

Parts II through VII address topical government resources. Part II explores the topic of education. Nicole Wood explores census data resources provided by the U.S. Census and census data provided by aggregators such as the IPUMS National Historical Geographic Information Systems. She provides two practical examples of how the Woodward Library's librarians bring alive census data through classroom instructions. High school teachers and university instructors will find this essay to be very useful. Emily Rogers and Laurie Aycock mine education resources provided by federal government departments, including the Department of Education. Resources such as quizzes, games, lesson plans, and videos, in addition to the traditional website resources, are freely available for all educators to use in the classroom. Caterina M. Reed discusses education resources addressing financial literacy. Her topics include budgeting and money management, student loans, and filing taxes. These resources are highly important for librarians to use when working with high school and college or university students.

Part III highlights genealogical resources. Jennifer Crowder Daugherty and Andrew Grace review an expansive, though not exhaustive, collection of federal genealogical resources. These resources cover topics such as land records, immigration and naturalization records, and military records. Departments explored include the Bureau of Land Management and the Social Security Administration. Kelly Bilz spotlights historic maps and aerial images used in genealogical research. She shares her experiences in using tools as a local history associate in a public library and as a librarian-in-residence in the Geography and Map Division at the Library of Congress.

Part IV highlights health and social programs. Angela L. Bonnell discusses key government sources about social service programs. Individuals working in fields such as social work, health care, and education will find these resources to be practical and informative for their research. Emily Alford focuses on a selection of key U.S. government digital resources concerning public health. Users will discover practical resources through websites such as My Healthfinder and MyPlate. Isabella Folmar and Blake Robinson explore federal resources for disabled individuals. These resources provide practical and relevant information concerning healthcare, employment, and education. Their essay covers relevant federal legislation, including the 1990 Americans with Disabilities Act.

Part V highlights military resources. Heather Seminelli and Lauren B. Dodd concentrate on military-related publications that are available from federal sources such as the Army, Department of Defense, and the National Archives and Records Administration. Sources include digitized materials from the archives and special collections of the United States Military Academy Library. Topics covered include Army resources, genealogical information, and military research from the USMA's Record Group 404. Michelle Shea discusses military-related research to help answer queries dealing with topics such as scholarships and financial aid, military and civilian jobs, databases for accessing peer-reviewed research articles, and military documentation and service benefits. Veterans, military families, and active-duty personnel will benefit from the knowledge shared by these authors.

Part VI focuses on Native American resources. Brandon R. Burnette reviews government resources that inform users about topics such as treaties, land cessions, legislation, and executive orders. These documents are published by government departments such as the Bureau of American Ethnology and the U.S. Bureau of Census. Connie Strittmatter takes a deeper look at government resources detailing the working relationship between Native Americans and the United States government. This narrative takes place through documents detailing the working relationship from 1776 to the early 1900s, the United States' evolving policy toward Native Americans, and canons of treaty construction and abrogation of treaties. The discussions provided by both authors will enhance research conducted by individuals in disciplines such as political science, anthropology, history, and Native American studies.

Part VII focuses on science resources. Claudene Sproles and Angel Clemons spotlight the weather data collecting activities of the National Weather Service and other departments and agencies such as the Federal Emergency Management Agency and the U.S. Geological Service. Topics addressed include dissemination of weather warnings, disaster preparedness, hurricanes, and earthquakes. Connie Hamner Williams discusses treasures and other resources provided by the National Park Service. Topics include trails and hiking, historical markers, and teaching and lesson plans. Mark Love uncovers excellent resources provided by the U.S. Department of Energy and the department's U.S. Energy Information Administration. His essay reviews resources for clean energy, ways to save energy, and science, technology, engineering, and math (STEM). The book concludes with an excellent discussion by Nathan A. Smith concerning science images copyright issues. He includes pertinent examples of science questions he has received via the Library of Congress's Ask a Librarian service and also from phone calls, emails, and mailed letters.

REFERENCES

Brantley, Bill. 2018. "The Value of Federal Government Data." Last updated February 15, 2020. https://digital.gov/2018/03/14/data-briefing-value-federal-government-data/.

Eberstadt, Nicholas, Ryan Nunn, Diane Whitmore Schanzenbach, and Michael R. Strain. 2017. "'In Order That They Might Rest Their Arguments on Facts': The Vital Role of Government-Collected Data." American Enterprise Institute. https://www.brookings.edu/wp-content/uploads/2017/02/thp_20170227_govt_collected_data_report.pdf.

Garcia, CJ. 2022. "Government Information: An Overlooked Gem." Arizona State University. Published April 25. https://lib.asu.edu/news/research/government-information-overlooked-gem.

Hughes-Cromwick, Ellen, and Julia Coronado. 2019. "The Value of US Government Data to US Business Decisions." *Journal of Economic Perspectives* 33, no. 1 (Winter): 131–46. https://www.aeaweb.org/articles?id=10.1257/jep.33.1.131.

Laddusaw, Sierra, and Garrett Littlejohn. 2019. "'Hidden Collections' in Your Collection: World War II Depository Maps at Texas A&M University Libraries." *DttP: Documents to the People* 47, no. 1 (Spring): 15–21. https://journals.ala.org/index.php/dttp/article/view/6982.

Sleeman, William. 2022. "Cartographic Treasures in the Records of the Supreme Court of the United States." *DttP: Documents to the People* 50, no. 1 (Spring): 7–11. https://journals.ala.org/index.php/dttp/article/view/7774.

U.S. Government Publishing Office. n.d.a. "About U.S. Government Publishing Office (GPO) Publications." Accessed August 3, 2022. https://www.govinfo.gov/collection/gpo.

U.S. Government Publishing Office. n.d.b. "GPO FY18–22 Strategic Plan." Accessed August 7, 2022. https://www.gpo.gov/docs/default-source/mission-vision-and-goals-pdfs/gpo-strategic-plan-fy2018-2022#.

APPENDIX: REFERENCES CONSULTED

Brown, Christopher C. 2020. *Mastering United States Government Information: Sources and Services*. Santa Barbara, CA: Libraries Unlimited.

Caro, Suzanne, ed. 2018. *Government Information Essentials*. Chicago: ALA Editions.

Hartnett, Cassandra J., Andrea L. Sevetson, and Eric J. Forte. 2016. *Fundamentals of Government Information: Mining, Finding, Evaluating, and Using Government Resources*. Chicago: ALA Neal-Schuman.

Hernon, Peter, et al. 2002. *United States Government Information: Policies and Sources*. Westport, CT: Libraries Unlimited.

Latham, Bethany. 2018. *Finding and Using U.S. Government Information: A Practical Guide for Librarians*. Lanham, MD: Rowman & Littlefield.

Part I
General

The United States Congressional Serial Set

A Rich Primary Resource of American History

CLAUDENE SPROLES *and* AMY LAUB

Introduction

The United States Congressional Serial Set, first published in 1817, serves as a rich resource of American history and primary source documents covering a wide variety of topics. Contained within its volumes one can find the history of legislation and legislative intent, detailed information on expeditions into the American West, conflicts, our growth as a country, annual reports, statistical sources, congressional reports, and presidential vetoes. One can locate materials such as maps, images, genealogical resources, House and Senate documents and reports, and other materials of historical significance.

The Serial Set remains an overlooked resource, due to users' lack of knowledge and understanding of its existence and organization. In this essay, the authors intend to help familiarize the reader with the Serial Set by covering multiple aspects of its content and organization. This includes information about the Serial Set, a brief history of why it exists, what materials it contains, both expected and unexpected, and, just as importantly, what it does not contain. The essay concludes with a discussion of how to access the Serial Set through print and online resources, both commercial and free online access.

History

The United States Congressional Serial Set is the bound collection of over 17,000 House and Senate documents and reports, along with some executive and legislative branch publications. Remaining unnamed until 1981, the collection became officially designated as the "United States Congressional Serial Set." Historically, the collection possessed a variety of colloquial names including the "Congressional Set," the "Serial Number Set," and the "Sheep Set," due to being bound in sheep leather (Saunders 1998).

The *American State Papers* consist of legislative and executive materials from the first fourteen Congresses and issued between 1789 and 1838. Although these papers are not officially part of the Serial Set, they are closely associated with it and considered its precursor (McKinney 2006, 5). The *American State Papers* are divided into ten topics, which mirror topics covered in the Serial Set through the early twentieth century:

I. Foreign Relations	VI. Naval Affairs
II. Indian Affairs	VII. Post Office
III. Finances	VIII. Public Lands
IV. Commerce and Navigation	IX. Claims
V. Military Affairs	X. Miscellaneous

As of this writing, the Library of Congress provides free access to the *American State Papers* online through its website "A Century of Lawmaking for a New Nation" at https://memory.loc.gov/ammem/amlaw/lwsp.html.

Beginning in 1895, responsibility for the Serial Set transferred from the Department of the Interior to the newly formed Government Printing Office (GPO) (McKinney 2006, 6). Directed by the Joint Committee on Printing, each volume is assigned a number using the system devised by Dr. John G. Ames, who served as superintendent of documents from 1869 to 1908. Beginning with volume 1, issued in 1817 (15th Congress, 1st Session), the Serial Set volumes continue to be issued numerically, and the Set grows with each Congress (Saunders 1998).

Currently, only reports and documents of Senate and House committees are added to the Serial Set (Saunders 1998). House and Senate *reports* consist of committee reports, miscellaneous reports on public bills, and special reports, whereas House and Senate *documents* include presidential vetoes and messages, reports from executive branch departments, and some reference works (Clark 1988, 213).

What Is in the Serial Set?

The Serial Set documents our growth as a country. Subject areas represented in the Serial Set include health studies, social issues and conditions, foreign affairs, exploration of the West, and policies affecting Native Americans and Chinese immigrants.

Due to a desire to reduce costs and duplication of departmental publications, the government reduced the scope of what is included in the Serial Set in the twentieth century (deLong 1996, 131). Until the early to mid-twentieth century, the Serial Set contained executive branch publications such as annual reports of some government agencies, the *Statistical Abstract of the United States, Foreign Relations of the U.S., Bulletin of the United States Bureau of Labor Statistics*, reports of the Geological Survey of the United States, *Foreign Commerce and Navigation of the United States*, the *Agricultural Yearbook*, Geological Survey *Water Supply Papers*, the *Minerals Yearbook*, American Ethnology Bureau *Bulletin*, and the *Pocket Data Book*. The Serial Set included the House and Senate journals and the daily record of activity on the floor of each chamber until 1953. Since 1979, the Serial Set included the Senate Executive documents and reports, but in 1981, the Senate Executive documents became the Senate Treaty documents. Additionally, the Serial Set included public reports, private reports, and special reports, which did not accompany legislation. (Saunders 1998).

The Serial Set volumes from the nineteenth century and early twentieth century included miscellaneous materials such as Court of Claims reports and motions, which cover claims actions against the federal government, and can be a useful resource in biographical or genealogical research (Quinn 2005, 184). These volumes also include petitions and memorials from private citizens, eulogies, and reports from non-governmental organizations, for example, the *Annual Report of the Boy Scouts of America* (Imholtz, Jr., 1999, 10).

The Backbone of the Serial Set

House and Senate reports can be valuable resources for determining the legislative intent of statutes. House and Senate documents have been an integral part of the Serial Set since 1817 (Saunders 1998). Reports contain committee reports and discussions on proposed bills and legislation (deLong 1996, 124), whereas House and Senate documents are wider ranging. House documents included publications such as annual reports of all departmental branches of government and agricultural and scientific reports. In 1907, the scope narrowed and now these publications contain only documents originating in the House of Representatives. Senate documents included accounts of surveys and explorations, scientific research, foreign relations, Indian affairs, and annual reports. Like the House documents, in 1907, the scope narrowed to include only publications created by the Senate (deLong 1996, 124–25). House and Senate journals, included in the Serial Set until 1953, contain minutes of the proceedings of each body in addition to presidential messages (124).

Genealogical Resources, Reports of Historical Significance, Maps, and Illustrations

The volumes of the Serial Set prior to the mid-twentieth century can contain useful genealogical resources for those willing to delve into them. Court of Claims reports and motions contain the names of people bringing monetary claims against the United States government and details of their cases. The Official Register lists current federal employees of the time. The Serial Set also includes petitions and memorials from private citizens. Additionally, genealogists can locate War of the Rebellion records, patents, land grants, private claims for military service, military registers, and Daughters of the American Revolution (DAR) grave registers.

Many documents of historical significance are contained within the Serial Set. Reports of survey expeditions in the West, for example, expeditions to the Rocky Mountains, the Hayden geological survey of 1872 to the area that would become Yellowstone National Park, and John Wesley Powell's expedition down the Colorado River are included in Serial Set volume 1805; Commodore Matthew Perry's report from Japan is in the Serial Set volume 803 (Quinn 2005, 184). These surveys included detailed information on Native Americans, botany, geology, zoology, and geology; detailed maps and illustrations often accompanied these survey reports (Ross 1994, 211). Other examples of historically significant events that can be traced through the Serial Set include petitions of suffragist Susan B. Anthony, the uses of Alcatraz Island, the sinking of the Titanic, the Armenian Genocide, and the 1918–19 influenza pandemic.

An important part of any survey expedition report is the maps accompanying the report. Overall, the Set contains over 55,000 maps. These maps, which range from lithographic images to woodcuts and line drawings (Bergen 1986, 18), are a rich resource of the varying historical means of producing maps and the physical space itself. Some examples of maps include John C. Fremont's 1845 maps of the West (Serial Set volume 467), the 1846 map of Florida (Serial Set volume 504), the Louisiana Purchase (Serial Set volume 4002), a map of the Choctaw Nation in Oklahoma, 1910 (Serial Set volume 5649), and maps of North America, 1830–1855 (Serial Set volume 2432).

Seavey notes that thousands of images and illustrations contained in the Serial Set range from photographs to hand-colored representations of silk worms (1990, 122) to reports from expeditions and surveys in the American West. The Serial Set is particularly rich in its illustrations of Native Americans, vistas, fossils, flora, fauna, and hieroglyphics (1990, 126). Additionally, reports from the Patent Office in the nineteenth century include many detailed drawings (1990, 135). Other examples of illustrations include drawings of Amazon explorations (Serial Set volume 678), a proposed drawing of the new Union Station in Washington, D.C. (Serial Set volume 4258), Ojibwe bead work (Serial Set volume 8819), detailed illustrations of geographic wonders in Yellowstone Park (Serial Set volume 2056), and for something strange, an 1871 drawing of entozoa found in the Beurre Langelier Pear (Serial Set volume 1522).

Annual Reports of the Commissioner of Indian Affairs are a useful source to document the activities of the War Department and the Department of the Interior in relating to Native Americans in the nineteenth and early twentieth centuries (Bernholz and Carr 2009, 543). For example, the 1891 Annual Report (Serial Set volume 2934) details the U.S. Army massacre of over 300 Lakota people at Wounded Knee, South Dakota. The *Bulletin of the United States Bureau of Labor Statistics* provide insight into working conditions in general, but a number focus specifically on women and children (Wondriska 1990, 153–56). Serial Set volume 7288 (Labor Statistics Bulletin 223) provides statistics of the employment of British women and children during World War I. Additional reports in the Serial Set include Pacific Railroad Reports; U.S. Navy explorations; Army Corps of Topographical Engineers reports; Census reports; Patent reports; and annual reports of the Smithsonian Institution, the Commissioner of Education, and the National Academy of Science (deLong 1996, 127).

Finding Aids to the Serial Set

Due to the random nature of Serial Set compilation, coupled with its enormous size, unlocking the contents of the Serial Set is no easy feat. The user is faced with a daunting and tricky challenge to use the Serial Set efficiently and effectively. Good indexing is key to discovering and locating Serial Set items. Historically, indexing the Serial Set has been a complicated and uneven process. For those accessing paper or microfiche Serial Set collections, there are several print indexes available. Often these print indexes can supplement electronic resources and indexing to locate tricky subjects or double-check search results.

From 1817 to 1897, individual volumes included a subject index. Early Serial Set indexes include:

- *Papers Relating to Early Congressional Documents: Public Documents of the First Fourteen Congresses, 1789–1817.* [GP 3.2: P 9612/Serial Set 3879] (Greely 1900).

This compilation selectively indexes materials in the *American State Papers*. Arranged in chronological order, the document includes a name index but lacks subject indexing. The *Papers* are supplemented in: *Annual Report of the American Historical Association for the Year 1903: In Two Volumes.* (p. 343–406). (Annual Report 1904).

- *Tables of and Annotated Index to the Congressional Series of U.S. Public Documents.* [GP 3.2:P 96] (U.S. Superintendent of Documents 1902).

This source indexes the Serial Set from the 15th through the 52nd Congresses. The tables can also be found in the *CIS Serial Set Index* and the *1909 Checklist*.

- *Index to the Reports and Documents of the 54th Congress, 1st Session—72d Congress, 2d Session, December 2, 1895–March 4, 1933, with Numerical Lists and Schedule of Volumes.* [GP 3.7: 1–43] (U.S. Superintendent of Documents 1897).

This subject index complements the *Tables of and Annotated Index to the Congressional Series of U.S. Public Documents*. It is also known as the Documents Index.

- *Checklist of United States Public Documents, 1789–1909.* [GP 3.2: C 41/2] (U.S. Superintendent of Documents 1911). Also available at https://digital.library.unt.edu/ark:/67531/metadc1029/.

Also known as the "1909 Checklist," this publication covers Serial Set volumes 1–5561. Per the U.S. Superintendent of Documents, this is "an approximately complete checklist of all public documents issued by the United States Government during the first century and a quarter of its history." (U.S. Superintendent of Documents 1911, vii).

Beginning with the 73rd Congress, 1933, the GPO printed the

- *Numerical Lists and Schedule of Volumes of the Reports and Documents of the 73d- Congress … 1933/34–.* [GP 3.7/2:] (U.S. Superintendent of Documents 1934–1980).

Popularly known as the "Numerical List," it gives the Serial Set number for each report issued by Congress. Unfortunately, it does not include a subject or name index. In 1985, it was issued as the *United States Congressional Serial Set Supplement: 97th Congress, 1981–1982: Numerical*

Lists of the Documents and Reports. [GP 3.8/6:], (U.S. Superintendent of Documents 1985) as a supplement to the *Monthly Catalog of United States Publications.*

For the years 1983–1990, the title changed again to the *United States Congressional Serial Set Catalog: Numerical Lists and Schedule of Volumes.* [GP 3.34:], (U.S. Superintendent of Documents 1983–1990).

After 1990, lists and scheduled volumes were intermittently issued through the *Administrative Notes: Technical Supplement* [GP 3.16/3–3:]. The *Technical Supplement* was discontinued in 2008. This title is available at govinfo.gov.

Commercial Print Index

For the most complete print Serial Set index, the best source to consult is the commercially produced *CIS US Serial Set Index.* (Congressional Information Service, 1975–b). CIS created the *Index* to accompany the CIS Serial Set on microform, available at many large depository and law libraries. It covers the years 1789–1969, including the *American State Papers.* It contains multiple indexes, including report and document numbers, Serial Set numbers, and subject and name indices. Part XIV of the index includes a listing of maps within the Serial Set that can be searched by area, name, or title. From 1969 to 2001, the *CIS Annual* (Congressional Information Service, 1975–a) covered all congressional publications for the year. It is searchable by keyword, title, and number.

Online Electronic Access to the Serial Set

- Congressional Serial Set, https://www.govinfo.gov/app/collection/serialset.

Govinfo.gov partnered with the Law Library of Congress to create a digital Serial Set. Launched in 2021, it is not yet complete but is being continually updated. The GPO plans to provide long-term access and preservation of this digital collection. The Serial Set volumes as well as the individual documents will be issued as PDF files. The files are also downloadable as ZIP files. Information about using the govinfo.gov version of the Serial Set can be found at https://www.govinfo.gov/help/serial-set. The help page explains the Serial Set, along with its contents and a variety of tutorials and handouts. In addition, the site provides search tips, tutorials, sample searches, and information for searching metadata fields. The help page also lists Congressional Serial Set Finding Aids, such as the

Numerical List of Documents and Reports and the Schedule of Serial Set Volumes. The help page links directly to the Serial Set search page.

- HathiTrust, https://www.hathitrust.org.

The HathiTrust has a Serial Set collection, largely based on the holdings of the University of California. Government resources and materials out of copyright are freely available at HathiTrust, although documents cannot be printed from non-member libraries. Due to limitations in scanning and indexing, searching can be tricky, especially when looking for specific documents within a Serial Set volume. Users should probably consult a Serial Set print or online index for in-depth searching. The coverage is incomplete.

- Internet Archive, https://archive.org/.

Many Serial Set volumes as well as the older indexes can be found in the Internet Archive. Searching limitations for the Internet Archive are similar to the HathiTrust, and it is best to use additional Serial Set indexes. The coverage is incomplete.

Commercial Sources for the Serial Set

- Readex U.S. Congressional Serial Set, 1817–1994.

This online collection covers the 15th through the 103rd Congress. Readex scanned approximately 14,000 volumes and 74,000 maps from the original Serial Set volumes for this collection. The maps are scanned as high-resolution TIFFs. Readex provides rich, expansive indexing, enhanced metadata, open URLs, and MARC catalog records for the collection. Of special note is that every individual named in the Serial Set is indexed, making this version excellent for genealogists. The map collection also possesses enhanced search capabilities and thorough indexing separate from the main index.

- ProQuest U.S. Congressional Serial Set.

Probably the most user-friendly commercial version of the Serial Set is the ProQuest U.S. Congressional Serial Set, formerly known as *Lexis-Nexis Congressional*. The online version is scanned from the CIS Serial Set microfiche set. The indexing is based on the print *CIS US Serial Set Index* with the thesaurus from *Executive Branch Documents, 1789–1909* as the base for the subject indexing, rather than examining individual volumes. Documents are available as searchable PDFs, and ProQuest employs "durable URLs" that remain constant. The ProQuest Serial Set is divided into two parts. Part I includes the *American State Papers* and covers 1789–1969. Part II, subdivided into four sections, covers 1970–2010.

The ProQuest Serial Set map collection contains more than 55,000 maps dating from the *American State Papers* until 2007. The maps and illustrations are in high-quality color, with many scanned at high resolution. The set includes robust indexing and descriptions.

- HeinOnline's U.S. Congressional Serial Set.

HeinOnline is releasing its new subscription version of the Serial Set in phases. As of this writing, this collection contains more than 17,000 volumes and is 95 percent complete. Phase two of the project will add maps and foldouts contained in the Serial Set. The record links to the HathiTrust for volumes not yet scanned to the HeinOnline database. This version includes the *American State Papers*. Documents are PDF images. The database continually adds current and newly released congressional reports and documents.

Additional Serial Set Resource

- U.S. Congressional Serial Set Inventory, https://digital.library.unt.edu/govdocs/ssi/index.php.

Relatively few libraries house a complete or near-complete set of the bound volumes and access may be an issue due to the fragile binding or brittle paper of older volumes. Based at the University of North Texas, the Serial Set Inventory lists Serial Set holdings for United States libraries, beginning with Vol. 1–Vol. 12880. The database lists bibliographic and holdings information for each volume.

Conclusion

The United States Congressional Serial Set is an often overlooked resource of primary source materials relating to American history, featuring maps, statistics, illustrations, and reports. The Serial Set can provide first-hand accounts of significant historical events, results from scientific inquiry, and results of expeditions and explorations as examples. Due to the random nature of its organization, users need to understand the types of materials it contains and how it is organized. Employing indexes and finding aids will unlock its vast contents. The Serial Set is a must for locating primary source material relating to American history.

REFERENCES

Annual Report of the American Historical Association for the Year 1903: In Two Volumes. 1904. Washington, D.C.: Government Printing Office. https://www.historians. org/about-aha-and-membership/aha-history-and-archives/annual-reports/annual-reports-1895-1909.

Bergen, Kathleen. 1986. "Hidden Cartographic Archives: Maps of the United States Serial Set." *Special Libraries Association Geography and Map Division Bulletin* no. 143 (March): 15–28. https://archive.org/details/sim_special-libraries-association-geography-map-bulletin_1986-03_143.

Bernholz, Charles D., and Anthony G. Carr. 2009. "The Annual Reports of the Commissioner of Indian Affairs: Revisiting the Key to the United States Congressional Serial Set, 1824–1920." *Government Information Quarterly* 26, no. 3: 540–45. https://doi. org/10.1016/j.giq.2008.01.008.

Clark, Suzanne M. 1988. "Use of the U.S. Serial Set in an Academic Institution: A Collection Management Tool." *Government Publications Review* 15, no. 3: 213–23. https://doi. org/10.1016/0277-9390(88)90059-3.

Congressional Information Service. 1975–a. *CIS Annual.* Washington, D.C.: Congressional Information Service.

Congressional Information Service. 1975–b. *CIS US Serial Set Index.* Washington, D.C.: Congressional Information Service.

deLong, Suzanne. 1996. "What Is in the United States Serial Set?" *Journal of Government Information* 23, no. 2: 123–35. https://doi.org/10.1016/1352-0237(95)00046-1.

Greely, Adolphus W. 1900. *Papers Relating to Early Congressional Documents: Public Documents of the First Fourteen Congresses, 1789–1817.* Washington, D.C.: Government Printing Office.

Imholtz, August A., Jr. 1999. "Some Problems in the Early U.S. Congressional Serial Set." *Documents to the People* 27, no. 2 (Summer): 10–15. https://searchworks.stanford.edu/ view/489643.

McKinney, Richard J. 2006. "An Overview of the U.S. Congressional Serial Set." Law Librarians' Society of Washington, D.C. Last revised October 2006. https://www.llsdc. org/assets/sourcebook/serial-set.pdf.

Quinn, Aimée C. 2005. "Cataloging the Congressional Serial Set." *Cataloging & Classification Quarterly* 41, no. 1: 183–205. https://doi.org/10.1300/J104v41n01_09.

Ross, Rodney A. 1994. "Using the U.S. Congressional Serial Set for the Study of Western History." *Western History Quarterly* 25, no. 2: 209–13. https://doi.org/10.2307/9714 63.

Saunders, Virginia. 1998. "U.S. Congressional Serial Set: What It Is and Its History." Federal Depository Library Program. Last updated December 16, 2021. Accessed January 14, 2022.

Seavey, Charles A. 1990. "Government Graphics: The Development of Illustration in U.S. Federal Publications, 1817–1861." *Government Publications Review* 17, no. 2: 121–42. https://doi.org/10.1016/0277-9390(90)90097-W.

U.S. Superintendent of Documents. 1897. *Index to the Reports and Documents of the 54th Congress, 1st Session—72d Congress, 2d Session, Dec. 2, 1895–March 4, 1933 with Numerical Lists and Schedule of Volumes. Being No. 1–43 of the "Consolidated Index" Provided for by the Act of January 12, 1895.* Washington, D.C.: Government Printing Office.

U.S. Superintendent of Documents. 1902. *Tables of and Annotated Index to the Congressional Series of U.S. Public Documents.* Washington, D.C.: Government Printing Office.

U.S. Superintendent of Documents. 1911. *Checklist of United States Public Documents, 1789–1909.* Third Edition Revised and Enlarged. Washington, D.C.: Government Printing Office.

U.S. Superintendent of Documents. 1934–1980. *Numerical Lists and Schedule of Volumes of the Reports and Documents of the 73d- Congress ... 1933/34.* Washington, D.C: Government Printing Office.

U.S. Superintendent of Documents. 1983–1990. *United States Congressional Serial Set*

Catalog: Numerical Lists and Schedule of Volumes. Washington, D.C.: Government Printing Office.

U.S. Superintendent of Documents. 1985. *United States Congressional Serial Set Supplement: 97th Congress, 1981–1982: Numerical Lists of the Documents and Reports.* Washington, D.C.: Government Printing Office.

Wondriska, Rebecca. 1990. "Women and the American Dream, 1900–1925: An Annotated Bibliography of Selected Documents from the U.S. Serial Set." *Government Publications Review* 17, no. 2: 143–57. https://doi.org/10.1016/0277-9390(90)90098-X.

Department of State and the U.S. Citizenship and Immigration Services

ELISABETH PEARSON GARNER

Introduction

Where can one learn about United States relations with Afghanistan and apply for a passport, all on the same day? Look no further than the Department of State website, https://www.state.gov. Thomas Jefferson, the nation's first Secretary of State, managed a very small staff that included only one language translator. Today, the Department employs almost 70,000 people at over 270 diplomatic missions worldwide (U.S. Department of State, n.d.a.).

The Department of State offers a treasure trove of information for the everyday citizen, all easily accessible from its website. Historically, the Department published the U.S. Census and handled copyright issues. Today, the Department has responsibility for dealing with issues as broad as worldwide terrorism, protecting U.S. interests abroad, and implementing foreign policy initiatives. Practically speaking, U.S. citizens can utilize all information from the Department's website to learn more about the geography, politics and society of various countries and areas, foreign policy issues, the Department's various bureaus and offices, job opportunities, and opportunities for students and travelers.

"Countries & Areas"

The "Countries & Areas" tab on the Department of State website leads visitors to information about the geography, politics, and society of various countries around the world as well as how the United States interacts with those countries. The website is especially useful for travelers seeking information on a specific country, students researching for an assigned class project, or researchers seeking up-to-date news regarding a particular country. Each country's website follows the same structure, including a fact sheet, names of embassies and consulates, and names of regional bureaus. Each country's website also includes current travel advisories and highlights State Department activities concerning that country. For example, selecting "Afghanistan" in the "Countries & Areas" drop-down menu reveals that the country is under a Level 4 Current Travel Advisory, meaning "Do Not Travel." This has been the case for several years in Afghanistan due to "civil unrest, armed conflict, crime, terrorism, and kidnapping" (U.S. Department of State, n.d.b.).

For projects from grade school to graduate school, researchers can use this same list to learn about U.S. relations with a specific country. For example, by selecting the country of Germany and clicking on the "View Fact Sheet" link, the user will find a page highlighting the historical relations between Germany and the U.S. In addition, users can learn about U.S. economic relations with Germany. This page even includes links to other government publications: *Library of Congress Country Studies*, the Central Intelligence Agency's "World Factbook Germany Page," and the U.S. Census Bureau's foreign trade statistics.

Finally, clicking on a country allows users to see the latest news headlines from that country. For example, clicking on the country of Moldova and scrolling down to find the word "Highlights" leads to the latest national news story in that eastern European country. News updates might include State Department press briefings or information on national holidays celebrated in that country. The example of these three countries, Afghanistan, Germany, and Moldova, provides just a glimpse of the wealth of information available.

"Policy Issues"

The "Policy Issues" collection allows users to learn about various subjects that the Department of State handles on a day-to-day basis. For example, the website currently provides access to more than twenty policy issues, including "Climate and Environment," "Countering Terrorism," "Global Health," and "Human Trafficking." Under the "Climate and Environment" option for "Policy Issues," https://www.state.gov/policy-issues/climate-and-environment/, the reader will learn that the State Department actively works with other agencies around the world to address climate change issues such as conserving nature, water security, and combating wildlife trafficking.

Another option under "Policy Issues" is "Countering Terrorism," https://www.state.gov/bureau-of-counterterrorism-programs-and-initiatives/. Here, the reader discovers how the Bureau of Counterterrorism, acting under the auspices of the Department of State, engages with global partners to "counter sources of violent extremist messaging, narratives, and recruitment." In fact, according to U.S. law (22 U.S.C. 2656f), the Secretary of State must provide Congress a full report, titled "Country Reports on Terrorism," by April 30 of each year. This report covers "developments in countries in which acts of terrorism occurred, countries that are state sponsors of terrorism, and countries determined by the Secretary to be of particular interest in the global war on terror." Other pieces of information included in this report deal with "information on terrorist groups responsible for the death, kidnapping, or injury of Americans" (U.S. Department of State, n.d.c.).

Under "Global Health" in the "Policy Issues" section, https://www.state.gov/policy-issues/global-health/, readers will learn how the Office of the U.S. Global AIDS Coordinator and Health Diplomacy (OGAC) and the Office of International Health and Biodefense (IHB) work to prevent millions of "new HIV infections" and control "the HIV/AIDS epidemic in more than 50 countries worldwide" while also "advancing foreign policy on international health issues." The State Department is also involved in efforts to protect the U.S. from the threat of infectious disease. By scrolling down the page, the reader finds links to related top stories, with articles that address numerous global health topics.

The State Department's "Policy Issues" about "Human Trafficking" addresses this ongoing, worldwide problem, and how the United States is at the forefront of tackling this issue. Because of the continued practice of human trafficking around the globe, the U.S. created the Office to Monitor and Combat Trafficking in Persons (TIP). This office works with partners worldwide, including those who have escaped and survived trafficking operations, to combat modern slavery in all its forms. For interested readers, the office's website includes the December 3, 2021, press statement, "Release of the National Action Plan to Combat Human Trafficking," https://www.state.gov/release-of-the-national-action-plan-to-combat-human-trafficking/, a government plan to address human trafficking over three years. There is even a fact sheet available titled "Understanding Human Trafficking" at https://www.state.gov/what-is-trafficking-in-persons/. In addition to reading this press statement, users can consult the annual report *United States Advisory Council on Human Trafficking*. The 2021 report is available at https://www.state.gov/united-states-advisory-council-on-human-trafficking-annual-report-2021/. This type of information can also prove useful for high school or college students who may be researching this topic.

"Bureaus & Offices"

Patrons and students wishing to learn more about how the Department of State functions can consult resources listed under "Bureaus & Offices." Users can, for example, learn more about the bureaus and offices that report directly to the Secretary of State. For instance, the Secretary of State's Office directly oversees the Office of Civil Rights, https://www.state.gov/bureaus-offices/secretary-of-state/office-of-civil-rights/. The Office's mission is to "propagate fairness, equity and inclusion at the Department of State." Key topics found in this section include the process for the filing of an Equal Employment Opportunity (EEO) Complaint, Harassment Policies, Reasonable Accommodation Policy, and Affirmative Action Plan for People with Disabilities.

Other "Bureaus & Offices" options include the Economic Growth, Energy, and Environment, https://www.state.gov/bureaus-offices/under-secretary-for-economic-growth-energy-and-the-environment/, where one can find several offices that pertain to environmental issues that could help students and researchers, including the Bureau of Oceans and International Environmental and Scientific Affairs. Examples of topics covered by the Bureau include, among others, "conservation and water," "global change," and "ocean and polar affairs." This is a great resource to show what our nation is doing to help with environmental issues worldwide.

Another area of interest might be the office of Civilian Security, Democracy, and Human Rights, https://www.state.gov/bureaus-offices/under-secretary-for-civilian-security-democracy-and-human-rights/, where one can learn more about the Bureau of Population, Refugees, and Migration, https://www.state.gov/bureaus-offices/under-secretary-for-civilian-security-democracy-and-human-rights/bureau-of-population-refugees-and-migration/, which serves as the Department's Humanitarian Bureau. Its mission is to provide "protection, ease suffering, and resolve the plight of persecuted and forcibly displaced people around the world." This is helpful for anyone who wants to learn more about the worldwide conditions of those suffering at the hands of corrupt governments and leaders, and how the United States is helping combat these ongoing problems. One section discusses "Refugee Admissions" in the United States, including the number of refugees allowed into the country each fiscal year. The reader can also explore the section titled "Overseas Assistance By Region," https://www.state.gov/overseas-assistance-by-region/, to learn how this bureau delivers assistance to refugees from various regions around the world. The Bureau provides helpful background information, if one clicks on a region link to learn why refugees from various countries may be fleeing their native land, a useful resource for those unfamiliar with the reasons underlying refugee migration. This brief historical background helps to explain the origins of these humanitarian problems around the globe.

Travel Resources

Practical information for travelers is readily available on the Department of State website. Few sites offer more valuable information regarding what travelers need to know when planning trips. The reader can access this information by visiting the website at https://www.state.gov/travelers/. The website contains two sections: "Emergency Information & Resources" and "Traveling Abroad: What You Need." Each section contains helpful suggestions and requirements listed for U.S. citizens traveling abroad. For example, the first option under "Emergency Information and Resources" is for "U.S. Citizen Travelers," and it contains information regarding the Smart Traveler Enrollment Program (STEP). This program allows travelers to sign up for travel alerts from the Department of State. The Department can better locate travelers enrolled in STEP in case of an emergency. The STEP website, https://step.state.gov/step, also lists useful phone numbers for U.S. embassies and consulates. The traveler must subscribe to receive these travel advisories.

The reader can scroll further down the travelers webpage, https://www.state.gov/travelers/, and find "Traveling Abroad: What You Need." This is a must-read before undertaking international travel. By clicking on the option for "Americans Abroad," travelers can find a list of instructions to help them if they lose their passports, face medical emergencies, encounter financial difficulties, or fall prey to criminal activity. The "Traveling Abroad: What You Need" section also lists travel tips for students. For those planning trips, the website contains information on local passport offices and instructions for obtaining your first passport or renewing an expired one. Another section pertains to visas for those interested in sponsoring someone who wants to visit the United States. For instance, spouses and children of lawful permanent residents can obtain nonimmigrant visas. Further down, under the "U.S. Government Resources" section, users will find a link to information on "Foreign Currency Exchange Rates."

Student Resources

The Department of State offers career opportunities in many different fields. For those just exploring careers, the website, https://www.state.gov/students/, details opportunities for "Interns & Fellows" and careers. This section is for undergraduates to post-graduate level students who are seeking to learn about U.S. interests abroad and how they may be able to build a career working for the Department of State. The "Interns & Fellows" section describes fellowships and internships in detail, allowing the student to decide which one may be of interest. These include the Charles B. Rangel International Affairs Program and the U.S. Department of State Student Internship Program. The "Other Student Programs" link leads to more information on other programs. These include the Council of American Ambassadors Fellowship and the Workforce Recruitment Program. Finally, there is a link for "Educational Resources" for students and educators. Students and educators planning to travel abroad will find even more examples of helpful information.

The "Careers" website is available at https://careers.state.gov/work and describes different career paths while working for the Department of State. The user will find lists of jobs currently available within the Foreign and Civil Services, a link to a list of available professional fellowships such as the Veterans Innovation Partnership Fellowship Program, as well as a list of benefits for working for the federal government. A link for "Related Careers and Links" is also available. There are also exchange programs that may be of interest to citizens/students at the "Bureau of Educational and Cultural Affairs Exchange Programs," found at https://exchanges.state.gov. This page offers a wealth of opportunities for those seeking to become involved in exchange programs, ranging from the arts, technology, youth/school programs, scholarships, sports, and leadership programs. There is an A-Z list of programs that one can peruse. Information for parents and families to help them prepare their child for travel, upcoming deadlines, and a "Know Before You Go" section are all included. Information on Travel and Living Arrangements is available along with Hosting and Volunteer Opportunities.

Additionally, one can visit https://studyabroad.state.gov to learn about the USA Study Abroad program. All types of resources abound at this website including sections on "The Value of Study Abroad," "Study Abroad Resources," and "U.S. Government Scholarships and Programs." Some subcategories of the above-mentioned sections include student stories from those who have studied abroad, country and regional profiles, financial resources, and travel health and safety information. This site offers opportunities for U.S. educators, scholars, undergraduate/graduate students, and K–12 students.

Immigration

There is a considerable amount of information related to the topic of "immigration" available at https://www.state.gov/visas. The webpage lists information regarding "Nonimmigrant Visas" and "Immigrant Visas." The Nonimmigrant Visa information is for short-term visitors to the country, and specific travel purposes only. Categories include Tourism & Visit, Study & Exchange, Business, Employment, and Other Visa Categories. For example, Tourism & Visit includes information on how to apply for a visa and the required documentation. For Immigrant Visas, the sections include information regarding Family-Based, Employment, and Diversity Visas.

U.S. Citizenship and Immigration Services

Stepping slightly away from the Department of State, but still very much related, one can find information related to the U.S. Citizenship and Immigration Services, https://www.uscis.gov/, an official website of the U.S. Department of Homeland Security. Some of the information listed below from this website is related to travel and can be invaluable for American citizens who may have family in foreign countries seeking citizenship in the United States.

The Green Card website, https://www.uscis.gov/green-card, provides information on becoming a permanent resident of the United States. The website is a one-stop resource to learn about how to apply for a green card, what processes and procedures to follow, steps to follow after being granted a green card, and steps to replace a lost green card. The website provides access to all the forms needed to apply for a green card, guidance on how to proceed, filing fees, and the ability to apply online. This is an excellent resource to keep in mind when working with international students and public library patrons.

The Citizenship Resource Center, https://www.uscis.gov/citizenship, is useful for those seeking information regarding becoming a U.S. citizen. The reader will find links to such topics as "Learn About Citizenship," "Apply for Citizenship," "Find Study Materials and Resources," and "Resources for Educational Programs." All of the information found on this page is managed by the Office of Citizenship, which is an office under the supervision of the Department of Homeland Security. The Department of Homeland Security mandated the Office of Citizenship in 2002 "to promote instruction and training on citizenship rights and responsibilities, including the development of educational materials." Those seeking naturalization in the United States can even take advantage of the "Naturalization Through Military Service" program, which can be found on the Citizenship Resource Center's homepage.

Freedom of Information Act and the No FEAR Act

Continuing with the U.S. Citizenship and Immigration Services site, the reader will find information related to requesting "records through the Freedom of Information Act (FOIA) or Privacy Act," https://www.uscis.gov/records/request-records-through-the-freedom-of-information-act-or-privacy-act. Step-by-step instructions are given to the reader to complete the request online. One can request immigration records, "whether your own or someone else's with their permission, and agency policies, data, communications, and other records." Additionally, the reader can find information regarding the No FEAR Act (Pub. L. 107-174), https://www.uscis.gov/about-us/equal-employment-opportunity/equal-employment-opportunity-data-posted-pursuant-to-the-no-fear-act, an Act that "increases federal agency accountability for acts of discrimination and reprisals against employees for whistleblowing." A toll-free number is listed for the Office of Equal Opportunity and Inclusion for those wishing to learn more about the Act, as well as a quarterly report that lists Equal Employment Opportunity data.

Conclusion

The Department of State website, https://www.state.gov, offers any member of the public the opportunity to learn about this vital part of the United States government. The duties carried out by the members of the Department are vast and varied, but all work together for the good of the American public. From learning about different countries around the world to learning about policy issues that are central to the United States government and other governments around the world, the reader can use http://www.state.gov as a great place for research.

Information on topics common in K–12 and university classroom assignments across all disciplines can be found on the website under "Policy Issues." The "Bureaus and Offices" link teaches the reader about the various departments within the Department of State that handle issues surrounding the use of energy, economic growth, and the environment, to name just a few. The information related to travel, and specifically to student travel and travel for leisure, is invaluable for staying abreast of conditions in other countries. The site's information for job-seekers is valuable for students who may be seeking internships and fellowships, or those who may be seeking employment with the Department of State.

Furthermore, the information found on the U.S. Citizenship and Immigration Services website, https://www.uscis.gov, is equally important and can offer American citizens the opportunity to learn more about how the U.S. government works with foreign citizens by issuing Green Cards. Information found on this site about the Citizenship Resource Center is also informative for immigrants who are interested in becoming U.S. citizens. Overall, the Department of State and the U.S. Citizenship and Immigration Service (under the Department of Homeland Security) are indeed great sources of information that are highly relevant to many of the things we do as citizens daily.

References

U.S. Department of State. n.d.a. "About U.S. Department of State." Accessed April 27, 2022. https://www.state.gov/about/.

U.S. Department of State. n.d.b. "Afghanistan Travel Advisory." Accessed April 27, 2022. https://travel.state.gov/content/travel/en/traveladvisories/traveladvisories/afghanistan-advisory.html.

U.S. Department of State. n.d.c. "Bureau of Counterrorism." Accessed April 27, 2022. https://www.state.gov/country-reports-on-terrorism/.

Discovering Crime and Justice Data on Government Websites

Ariana Baker *and* Allison Faix

Introduction

The U.S. government provides information related to crime and justice through many different agencies and websites. Navigating through this information can be a complicated process, especially without knowing where to start. The Federal Bureau of Investigation, the Department of Homeland Security, the Department of Justice, and other agencies have unique missions and collect and share valuable data in different formats that can often be difficult to locate and use.

Looking for data related to crime and justice can be challenging for everyone. Often there is a specific question in mind that might or might not be possible to answer exactly with the available data. For example, someone looking for a new house or apartment might want to know how safe different neighborhoods are, but depending on the area, Google searches on this may only retrieve news media articles about specific, isolated events. Google might also return descriptions of neighborhood life from real estate sites (whose main purpose is to get you interested in buying or renting in that location), or information designed for visitors or tourists, not necessarily locals. If you do not know anyone who already lives there, you might be left asking for advice from strangers on social media or other online forums (which could inspire a need for even more fact checking). The qualities that make a neighborhood safe might vary from person to person—one person might be worried most about robbery, while someone else worries more about hate crimes, illegal drugs, or even just whether there are enough sidewalks and crosswalks and streetlights. For example, a Google search for "how many houses were robbed in x city last year?" will most likely only find other news articles, if anything at all. This is because most crime data, like other kinds of data, live on what librarians call the "deep web." The deep web has been defined as "publicly accessible information available via the World Wide Web but not retrievable using search engines that rely on crawlers or spiders" (Reitz 2014). Searching the internet might not help an information seeker come away with a good idea of whether or not there is something to worry about. The data collected by law enforcement or other government agencies can be a better way to get a glimpse at the scope of the problem, but you must know where to look and realize that the exact data you expect might not be there at all. There may be other data you could take into consideration. A general search of Google does not do a good job finding it because to really work with it and use it, you need to go directly to the government agency that collects those statistics and start looking there instead.

This essay will outline different federal agencies that collect and distribute data related to crime and justice. It will offer some strategies for finding, navigating, and getting the most out of that data.

Department of Justice

The mission of the Department of Justice (DOJ), https://www.justice.gov/, includes law enforcement, public safety, crime prevention, punishment, and "fair and impartial administration of justice for all Americans." The DOJ oversees agencies such as the Federal Bureau of Investigation (FBI), the Drug Enforcement Agency (DEA), the Bureau of Alcohol, Tobacco, and Firearms (ATF), and the Federal Bureau of Prisons (BOP). These are all places where crime and justice data can be found. Some of this data is distributed through the Bureau of Justice Statistics, but in many cases can also be found on the agency website that collects the data. Figure 1 is a chart detailing the different types of statistical information that might be of interest from some of these agencies.

Federal Bureau of Investigation

The FBI, https://www.fbi.gov/, is an intelligence and law enforcement agency that gathers and disseminates data relating to terrorism, espionage, cyberattacks, and major criminal justice threats. Its website includes data sets on a wide variety of topics.

The FBI's Uniform Crime Reporting (UCR) Program, https://www.fbi.gov/services/cjis/ucr/, releases current data in its Crime Data Explorer, while historical data is kept on the UCR Publications page. FBI databases reporting this data include:

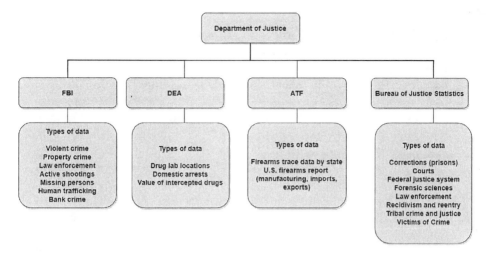

Figure 1: Flowchart showing the different agencies under the Department of Justice and the types of crime and justice data available from each.

- National Use-of-Force Data Collections, https://www.fbi.gov/ services/cjis/ucr/use-of-force, for death or serious injuries resulting from law enforcement use of force.
- Crime Data Explorer, https://cde.ucr.cjis.gov/LATEST/webapp/#/ pages/home, for

  ◊ Violent crime statistics
    Murder and nonnegligent manslaughter
    Rape
    Robbery
    Aggravated assault
  ◊ Property crime statistics
    Burglary
    Larceny/theft
    Motor vehicle theft
    Arson

Demographic information is provided about both the victims and the offenders.

- Hate Crime Statistics, https://www.fbi.gov/services/cjis/ucr/hate-crime, for crimes motivated by bias.

The FBI also publishes topical reports such as cargo theft, human trafficking, active shooter incidents, missing and unidentified persons, and bank crime statistics.

UCR provides current data, but the years vary by database. Historical data also varies. Its *Crime in the United States* report and *Hate Crime Statistics* data are available to the mid–1990s, while the National Incident-Based Reporting System only dates back to 2011. The FBI transitioned to a new data collection system in January 2021. While the intent is to provide more robust data, it may make comparing current and historic crimes difficult.

The FBI's website is easy to navigate. However, all agency data is reported together so users cannot search specifically by street or ZIP code but must read through larger data sets to retrieve the needed information. The Crime Data Explorer offers searching by location, dataset, reporting agency, and year. Depending on data type, the national, state, and local data may be available. To search for local crimes, choose the reporting agency closest to your neighborhood (there may be more than one) and the year.

Drug Enforcement Administration

The Drug Enforcement Agency (DEA), https://www.dea.gov/, is responsible for enforcing the nation's controlled substances laws. The Agency reports crime data related to drug labs and domestic arrests. The National Clandestine Laboratory Register Data (NCLRD), https://www.dea.gov/clan-lab, provides lists of locations where law enforcement agencies reported finding items indicating the presence of either clandestine drug laboratories or dumpsites. The Domestic Arrests database, https://www.dea.gov/data-and-statistics/domestic-arrests, is a single list that provides annual, national-level data on DEA arrests.

The DEA does not have much data, but what is available is easy to find through the Agency's Resources page. The NCLRD links to a downloadable CSV file with the raw data. Data in the NCLRD can be filtered by state or by year, but the reporting of this data varies widely by both categories. Some states have significant reporting going back to the twentieth century, while others have only a handful of recent incident reports. The Domestic Arrests data is reported annually from 1986 to the present.

Bureau of Alcohol, Tobacco, Firearms and Explosives

The Bureau of Alcohol, Tobacco, Firearms, and Explosive's (ATF) Resource Center provides data and statistics related to explosives and arson, firearms commerce, manufacture, trace data (national and international), and reported firearm thefts and losses. Highlights of both explosives and arson data are summarized in annual PDF reports, but the raw data for these categories is not available on the website. Data about firearms commerce, manufacture, trace data, and thefts and losses, however, are provided at the state and national levels.

The ATF website is easy to navigate. Most data is searchable by year, and by location within those years. While data does not go back very far, it is easy to compare data from the available years. Publication dates vary by database and location, but all data goes back at least five years.

Bureau of Justice Statistics

The Bureau of Justice Statistics (BJS) is the primary statistical agency of the DOJ, tasked with collecting, analyzing, publishing, and disseminating information about crime, criminal offenders, victims of crime, and the operation of justice systems at all levels of government. The website can be searched by topic:

- Corrections
  Courts
  Crime
  Federal justice system
  Forensic sciences
  Law enforcement
  Recidivism and reentry
  Tribal crime and justice
  Crime victims

- Database
  Arrests
  Parolees
  Prisoners
  Probation
  Juvenile justice
  Federal processing
  Crime victimization
  Prisoner recidivism

- Publications

Depending on the collection, data may be available at the national, state, and/or local level.

Topics and databases are both linked from the BJS's home page. Topical data links out to the National Archive of Criminal Justice Data (NACJD), https://www.icpsr.umich.edu/web/pages/NACJD/index.html, housed at the University of Michigan's Institute for Social Research. For example, each topic can be searched by subject term, data file format, and geography. Data analysis tools are located on the BJS website; data can be downloaded as XLS or CSV files, depending on the database. All of the data analysis tools include resource links with user guides, FAQs, and glossaries. Most data are collected annually and range from the late twentieth century to present, depending on the data set.

Federal Bureau of Prisons

The Federal Bureau of Prisons (BOP), https://www.bop.gov, provides for the welfare of prisoners. The Bureau conducts research about correctional topics such as drug treatment, vocational training, and prison management. The BOP's website includes a list of federal prison locations and a directory of past and present inmates.

Sourcebook of Criminal Justice Statistics

The *Sourcebook of Criminal Justice Statistics*, https://www.albany.edu/sourcebook/, is unique, but worth mentioning, even though it is not technically hosted by a federal government agency. It "brings together data from more than 100 published and unpublished sources about many aspects of criminal justice in the United States" (University at Albany, n.d.), many of which are from federal and state government agencies. Although this is not a government agency website but instead hosted by the University at Albany School of Criminal Justice, it is good to know about if you are looking for government data, especially as it includes more older, historical data than other sources. The Bureau of Justice Statistics previously published the *Sourcebook* in print, so many libraries may have older print copies of this source. While this is a good way to navigate older government data about crime and justice, unfortunately, it is not currently up to date on the data it includes, making it a better source for older information.

The *Sourcebook* is broken down into six different categories of information:

- characteristics of criminal justice
- public opinion
- crime and victims
- arrests and seizures
- courts, prosecution, and sentencing
- parole, jails, prisons, and the death penalty

For each broad category, the *Sourcebook* online dates back to 2003; an archive section covering 1994–2002 is temporarily unavailable at the time of this writing. The *Sourcebook* is further broken down into topical sections with links to tables of data within each section. The *Sourcebook* can also be searched by keywords, but there are no advanced search features other than sorting results by date. Tables are PDF files and easy to open in most internet browsers. Each table gives a citation for where the data came from, as well as the URL of the page in the *Sourcebook* displaying the data. This makes it easy for students to create citations.

National Crime Victimization Survey

An interesting data set related to crime and justice that might be easy to overlook is from the Bureau of Justice's *National Crime Victimization Survey* (NCVS), https://bjs.ojp.gov/data-collection/ncvs. The U.S. Census Bureau conducts this survey annually, starting in 1973 to the present. Each year, a nationally representative sample of people and households is surveyed on the "frequency, characteristics, and consequences of criminal victimization in the United States," including information on personal crimes like rape and sexual assault as well as property crimes like burglary, motor vehicle theft, and other types of crime both reported and unreported to authorities (U.S. Bureau of Justice Statistics 2009).

This survey data is valuable because it helps bridge the gap between what is known about crimes reported to authorities and what is not known about crimes never reported at all. It also gives insight into who are the victims of crimes, rather than focusing on who are the perpetrators of crime. Demographic data including age, race, and relationship to offenders is also collected as part of the survey. To help gain critical insights, questions are also asked about crime victims' experiences with the criminal justice system. The documentation for the survey, including the questionnaire, is also available on the website.

A general "Criminal Victimization" report is published each year the survey is conducted, but periodically reports will also be issued on specific topics or trends over time. For example, recent reports include *Crime against Persons with Disabilities, 2009–2019; Hate Crime Victimization, 2005–2019; Report on Indicators of School Crime and Safety, 2020;* and *Financial Fraud in the United States, 2017.* Recent reports are available on the BJS website. Older reports do not seem to be available online but may be available in libraries with Federal documents collections.

Department of Homeland Security

The Department of Homeland Security (DHS), https://www.dhs.gov/, is separate from the Department of Justice, but with a mission that is related to "secure the nation from the many threats we face" (U.S. Department of Homeland Security 2022). It is composed of different agencies that work together to carry out this mission, including the Federal Emergency Management Agency (FEMA), https://www.fema.gov/, and the Office of Immigration Statistics, https://www.dhs.gov/office-immigration-statistics.

Types of data provided by DHS vary by agency; each agency has its own data on its website, and there is no way to search data from all agencies under the department at the same time. However, there is a lot of useful information to be found and little, if any, duplication between agencies. For example, the Office of Immigration Statistics publishes reports about immigration, border security, and refugees while the Customs and Border Protection office maintains a database of intellectual property rights violations.

The DHS also operates the Department of Homeland Security Digital Library, https://www.hsdl.org/c/. This site is "the nation's collection of documents and resources related to homeland security policy, strategy, and organizational management." The information is divided into three collections, https://www.hsdl.org/c/about/. The first is freely available to the public. The second is open to government officials at the local, state, tribal, territorial, or federal levels as well as the U.S. military. It is also available to eligible research and educational institutions. The third collection—the Restricted Collection—"is a repository of sensitive materials collected from national, state, and local fusion centers, threat analysis centers, and law enforcement organizations. It is available only to U.S. government officials or active members of the U.S. military." Data and statistics in the DHS Digital Library are primarily links to those datasets and reports on other government websites, which makes sense. The library collects and provides access to reports and documents from many different places rather than creating its own content. For example, searching for information about active shooters will return documents from the FBI and the Department of Defense, but also reports and analyses from city and state police and fire departments, emergency response protocols and drills from organizations like the National Retail Federation, and academic theses written by students at the U.S. Army Command and General Staff College and the Naval Post Graduate School. The DHS's structure and types of data collected are noted in Figure 2.

Some of the most useful data available through DHS agencies include the *Yearbook of Immigration Statistics* and the Federal Emergency Management Agency's (FEMA) open data. The *Yearbook of Immigration Statistics*, https://www.dhs.gov/immigration-statistics/yearbook, includes data on how many foreign nationals DHS granted permanent or temporary residency in the United States each year, how many applied for asylum or refugee status, and how many became naturalized citizens. The *Yearbook* also compiles data about actions taken to enforce immigration laws each year. Currently, the years available are 1996–2019.

The OpenFEMA Data Sets website, https://www.fema.gov/about/openfema/data-sets, includes information about disasters and disaster assistance, the FEMA flood insurance program, hazard mitigation programs, and other data related to the mission of FEMA. Datasets include

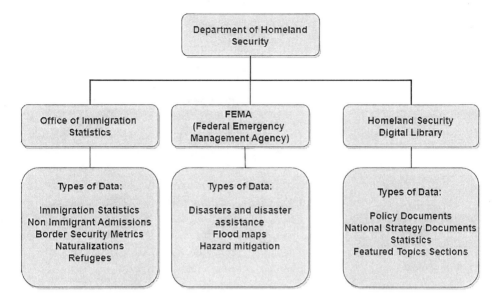

Figure 2: Flowchart showing the different agencies under the Department of Homeland Security and the different types of crime and justice data available from each.

disaster declarations areas, housing assistance program data for both renters and homeowners, and hazard mitigation projects.

Because the data is presented in datasets rather than charts, graphs, or tables, it can be difficult to navigate, especially for those not familiar with using Excel or other common data management programs. FEMA even cautions that several of its datasets exceed the capabilities of commonly used spreadsheet applications. This will require more advanced techniques to work with the data and some are recommended on the website.

Conclusion

While looking for data related to crime and justice can be challenging, a good first step is being able to figure out which government agency would collect data related to the topic that is of interest to you. It is important to consider the topic first, rather than the specific question, since data is often reported differently than might be assumed. While it may not be possible to answer the exact question you have, you should be able to find information related to your topic that may help.

Because the way agencies collect data can change over time and might affect the data itself, it is also good to take a look at this when you are using data from agency websites. One recent example is the changes to the FBI's National Incident-Based Reporting System, https://www.fbi.gov/services/cjis/ucr/nibrs. The agency website notes that getting all reporting agencies to switch over to the new data reporting system takes time, and that because the system is changing, care must be taken when trying to compare older data to newer data.

Finally, whenever there might be overlap in where data on a topic is being collected, it is worth looking at all of those places. While the exact data probably will not repeat itself, you may be able to uncover a more nuanced look at your original questions. For example, if you are looking for data about crime, you might check both the FBI's Crime Data Explorer, https://cde.ucr.cjis.gov/LATEST/webapp/#/pages/home, and the *National Criminal Victimization Survey*. These sources look at similar issues, but from different angles, and taken together can provide a broader view. Searching for government data is a challenge, but it can be a fun one if you know where to look and if you understand the ways data can be manipulated and reported.

References

Reitz, Joan M. 2014. "Deep Web." *Online Dictionary for Library and Information Science.* Accessed March 24, 2022. https://products.abc-clio.com/ODLIS/odlis_d.
University at Albany. n.d. *Sourcebook of Criminal Justice Statistics.* "About Sourcebook." Accessed March 24, 2022. https://www.albany.edu/sourcebook/about.html.
U.S. Bureau of Justice Statistics. 2009. "National Crime Victimization Survey." Accessed March 28, 2022. https://bjs.ojp.gov/data-collection/ncvs.
U.S. Department of Homeland Security. 2022. "About DHS." Last updated April 5, 2022. https://www.dhs.gov/about-dhs.

What's in a Policy?

Government Information Resources to Help Inform Policy Analysis and Research

Amanda McLeod

Introduction

On its face, policy analysis and research may not seem to lend itself to practical applications, as much of policymaking takes place outside of the daily lives of individuals. However, this fails to capture the ways in which the effects of policies can reverberate through communities. Friedman (2017) defines policy analysis as "the science and art of using knowledge to assist policymakers so that better choices will be made" (3) and further suggests that the "purpose of public policy analysis is to advise decision makers" (6). Given Friedman's definitions, it may appear that policy work is in the sphere of political figures and academics, rather than the typical library user. However, these users are one of the decision makers Friedman references.

For example, an individual seeking information to make informed decisions in an election can be seen as a critical decision maker (Friedman 2017, 5–6). In the same way, a community-based organization such as a food bank, perhaps affiliated with a larger entity like Feeding America, https://www.feedingamerica.org, could act as a decision maker that would benefit from access to policy research tools that enable the organization to better serve its community. Likewise, for some professions, familiarity with policy and research is critical. The field of social work, for example, has a strong emphasis on policy. The National Association of Social Workers (NASW) highlights the role of social workers to "develop and implement sound federal, state and local policy" (NASW 2021, 1). To be engaged in the process of policymaking, one must have knowledge of the current state of policy and the potential for upcoming changes. In addition to those actively working to develop policy, practicing social workers often need to stay informed about key social welfare policies that impact their work and the lives of their clients (NASW 2021). For example, a social worker in the child welfare field (an area designated as a key policy priority by the NASW) may need to locate reputable information about federal policies and foster care in order to better serve clients (NASW 2015). Any of these individuals or groups may need help locating information related to policies that impact their daily lives or work. With that view in mind, this essay will address the goals of policy research and analysis, identify freely available government information tools, and provide practical examples of when these tools might be useful.

Types of Policy Analysis/Research

For librarians, understanding that users may need to access information about various social and public policies is vital. Vidovich (2007) discusses "removing policy from its pedestal" and "dislodging policy from the exclusive domain of policy elites at the macro level and turning up the focus at the micro level" (295). This framing demonstrates the importance of demystifying the policy process and connecting with individuals. Library workers play a key role in helping facilitate access to tools for policy research, empowering users to be active participants in policy analysis and perhaps even in policymaking. There are times when these questions may arise more frequently. For example, in the lead-up to a major election, patrons may seek information about the candidates and their positions on key issues. Because library workers need to remain nonpartisan and provide unbiased assistance, having a firm grounding in public government information resources can be helpful. This is true both for library workers who staff information or service desks as well as anyone who provides reference or research services.

This section of the essay will detail several key government resources that are available electronically and are freely accessible to any member of the public. Given the scope of this essay, only U.S. federal government information resources will be considered. There are government information resources available to support policy research at the state and local levels. The resources in this essay will cover primarily Congress and legislative branch agencies.

Congressional Resources

Because many policies that have a direct impact on an individual's life originate in Congress (through legislation and law-making), resources created by Congress and through the work of legislative branch agencies can be a fertile ground for research, from tracking a bill through Congress to in-depth research reports produced by government agencies. This section will cover key resources and provide use cases for when these tools might be best used. When using these resources, both library workers and members of the public need to be aware that it is not always possible to obtain assistance directly from the agencies themselves. For example, the Congressional Research Service (CRS) works exclusively for Congress, and it is unable to respond to any questions or inquiries unless they are related to employment or a specific job vacancy. The Government Accountability Office (GAO) suggests using the Library of Congress's Ask a Librarian service, https://ask.loc.gov/, if members of the public need additional assistance beyond the publicly available report. While many casual researchers might not seek that level of assistance, someone seeking more complex information or researching a more complicated policy might want additional support—that is also where local library workers can play a key role in helping locate resources. For example, someone researching healthcare policy in the United States might need to access information about the Patient Protection and Affordable Care Act of 2010 (Pub. L. 111–148), a.k.a. the Affordable Care Act, but given the wide-ranging impact of the law coupled with court decisions and later legislation like the American Rescue Plan Act of 2021 (Pub. L. 117–2), one could easily become overwhelmed and would likely benefit from the assistance of local library workers who have skilled knowledge about locating government information resources.

Congress.gov

Congress.gov is the online home for the U.S. Congress. As the official website for Congress, the "About" webpage, https://www.congress.gov/about, states that it provides "access to accurate, timely, and complete legislative information for Members of Congress, legislative agencies, and the public." Congress.gov allows researchers to identify members of Congress, locate voting records, search for legislation, and track legislative progress for bills. Currently, users can search all Congresses from the 93rd to the present day, with some historical Congresses also available. Historical congressional documents can also be accessed through the website A Century of Lawmaking for a New Nation: U.S. Congressional Documents and Debates, 1774–1875, https://memory.loc.gov/ammem/amlaw/ lawhome. html. When Congress is in session, users can view a livestream of House and Senate floors at Congress.gov. The website contains a tracker tool that allows users to easily see where a particular piece of legislation is in the process of moving through Congress. In essence, users can access important information about policies as they are being discussed and written. For the public, this can be important as the information may prompt them to contact their representatives to express their personal stand on a particular issue in hopes of persuading their representative to vote their way.

Identifying and tracking legislation can play a key role in policy research and analysis, both for professionals and lay users. When a researcher needs information on a particular policy, whether a single bill or a more wide-ranging policy issue, understanding what legislation has become law and what is pending is vital. The tools available through Congress.gov help facilitate that research. For example, an individual involved in healthcare advocacy through the Patients Action Network, https://patientsactionnetwork.com/, might need more information about pending legislation related to telemedicine. A basic search on Congress.gov for telehealth or telemedicine reveals multiple bills that have been introduced on this topic, including H.R.341, Ensuring Telehealth Expansion Act of 2021, which the online tracker shows has been introduced in the House and referred to committee. In addition to the tracker tool and basic search functions, there are advanced search options, so users can select the most appropriate scope for their search. Researchers can use the query builder to develop precise searches. Library workers need to become familiar with this helpful tool. Users can also browse site content, including items published in the *Congressional Record* and committee publications and reports.

Researchers can use Congress.gov to locate congressional reports on specific pieces of legislation. Committee reports are a type of congressional document and are typically one of four types: reports that accompany legislation, reports from investigative/oversight activities, conference committee reports, or committee activity reports. While these reports contain valuable information, policy research committee reports that accompany legislation can be a treasure trove. These reports are produced to document the need and rationale for the proposed law and provide necessary background information. For anyone examining a specific public or social policy (or indeed, any piece of legislation), it is worthwhile to determine if such a report exists because it can help situate the policy in a larger context. For example, Senate Report 117-65 (2022) accompanies S. 198 Data Mapping to Save Moms' Lives Act, a proposed law that related to maternal health outcomes in its mapping tools. The report provides context on issues of maternal mortality, particularly at the intersection of rural communities, telehealth, and broadband internet access.

Digging into these reports can offer vital information even for legislation that ultimately failed. Consider, for example, a community organization that does nondiscrimination advocacy. Understanding the legislative landscape would be critical to its work. The organization would benefit from using the resources located at Congress.gov to further its advocacy work. As one example, the 116th Congress proposed legislation that would have prohibited discrimination against natural hairstyles. House Report 116-525 (2020), Creating a Respectful and Open World for Natural Hair Act (shortened to CROWN Act), provided the background on the legislation. Highlights include a listing of prominent backers from community organizations, corporate entities, and civil rights organizations. It provides critical information about the state of hair discrimination and its impact on Black women. Even though the legislation failed to pass, a community activist could use the free resources on Congress.gov to identify key issues. For example, House Report 116-525 discusses state level developments in discrimination laws based on natural hairstyles or textures which could help provide a model for advocacy at state and local levels, as is the purpose of the CROWN Act Coalition, https://www.thecrownact.com/.

Other tools available through Congress.gov allow users to access profiles of their Members of Congress. These profiles include critical information about each Member, including legislation each has sponsored or co-sponsored, remarks recorded in the *Congressional Record*, and a link to roll call votes—e.g., how each Member voted on issues or legislation in the chamber served. This links to either the House or Senate website. This can come into play when an election is upcoming and potential voters want to learn more about the people who represent them and the policies they support. For potential voters investigating each Member's stance on issues that interest them, the filter option to narrow sponsored or co-sponsored information by subject-policy area is of particular interest. It provides a quick access point to see what types of legislation their elected representative is supporting. This can help the voter make a more informed decision in an election, supporting their role as a key decision maker (Friedman 2017).

Congressional Budget Office

The Congressional Budget Office (CBO), https://www.cbo.gov/, is a vital legislative branch agency. In its "10 Things to Know about CBO," https://www.cbo.gov/about/10-things-to-know, the CBO states that it "provides objective, nonpartisan information to support the budget process and to help the Congress make effective budget and economic policy." It produces a variety of products, including baseline budget and economic projections, cost estimates (for congressional bills), and long-term budget projections (2–6). Members of Congress can request reports, and nearly all bills introduced in Congress will receive a cost estimate analysis. This process is informally called "scoring," or a "CBO score," and is often reported using that language in the news reports. These reports estimate the impact of a bill or a law on the national budget over a particular time period, often five to ten years. Taken together, CBO reports can play a key role in understanding the economic impacts of U.S. government policies and can be a fertile ground for research.

Because the CBO score can make or break proposed legislation, it is important for anyone doing policy work to understand the cost estimates. CBO cost estimates are available on the CBO website, https://www.cbo.gov/about/products/ce-faq, and it "generally includes a description of the legislation, a statement about its estimated budgetary impact, and an explanation of the basis for that estimate." Cost estimates are generally ordered by a congressional committee. In addition to the main tables that show the estimated costs, there are other areas of interest within the report. For example, in the cost estimate for S.3590, the Drinking Water Infrastructure Act of 2020, the report includes highlights documenting the key points from the estimate, including what the legislation is proposing to do and key areas that are expected to impact the federal budget. In addition, it discusses areas of uncertainty that could impact the estimates provided. These appear in most cost estimates. In some cases, CBO also includes a section with comparisons to other cost estimates for similar legislation during the same Congress if those exist. In the cost estimate for S.3590, the Drinking Water Infrastructure Act of 2020, CBO refers to an estimate for a different Senate bill with similar features (S.1507) and likewise discusses a similar regulation put forth by the Environmental Protection Agency. The full report can be found at https://www.cbo.gov/publication/56690.

In addition to the cost estimates, the CBO website also has several user-friendly access points for users to discover publications and reports produced by the agency. The topics browse search, https://www.cbo.gov/topics, is particularly useful for public library workers and potential researchers. The topics pages collate varied CBO resources on key areas, including health care, taxes, education, and defense and national security. They are organized into several categories, including featured documents, Publications & Cost Estimates, Policy Options, and Recurring Publications. The topic pages sometimes offer quick estimates of government spending for key programs. For example, the health care topics page shows projections for Medicaid and Medicare in a sidebar while the taxes topics page has a side bar with projected revenue. CBO topic pages are likely to be useful to both users and public library workers who are assisting researchers, particularly if a user is researching a policy area without a specific law or bill in hand.

CBO also has interactive tools that allow users to gauge the impact of various budgetary processes. Featured interactive tools include an analysis of potential impacts of raising the minimum wage, https://www.cbo.gov/publication/55681. The tool allows users to adjust the statutory minimum wage for both regular workers and tipped workers, to explore options for longer implementation, and to see the estimated impacts on family income and employment. The interactive tools provide another access point for users to explore CBO data and discover potential impacts of policy changes.

These budgetary reports contain valuable information about the impact, direct or indirect, of some policies. It is, however, important to remember that CBO does not conduct policy research or analysis or make policy recommendations. Its purview is strictly nonpartisan, objective analysis of budget and economic issues. Therefore, it is ultimately up to the user to interpret how these products inform their own policy research.

Congressional Research Service

The Congressional Research Service (CRS) is a nonpartisan legislative branch agency. On its "About" website, https://crsreports.congress.gov/Home/About, the CRS states that it works for Congress "providing timely, objective, and authoritative research and analysis to committees and Members of both the House and Senate, regardless of political party affiliation." Prior to 2018, Congress did not require CRS written products to be shared publicly, though individuals could request documents from their Member of Congress. This changed with the Consolidated Appropriations Act, 2018 (Pub. L. 115–141), which required that reports be made available to the public. The CRS collection provides public access to the research products produced by CRS in accordance with the Act. The collection can be found at https://crsreports.congress.gov/, which launched on September 18, 2018.

CRS produces a variety of written products, including reports, In Focus segments, Infographics, Insights, Legal Sidebar, and Testimony. This section focuses on the following products: Reports, In Focus, Insights, and Legal Sidebar. Reports, typically indicated by an R, RS, or RL at the beginning of the report number, are more comprehensive documents that address issues before Congress. Reports focus on a wide range of policy topics of interest to both lawmakers and lay policy makers alike. For example, the report "Housing for Former Foster Youth: Federal

Support," available at https://crsreports.congress.gov/product/pdf/R/ R46734, provides an overview of federal housing support for young adults transitioning out of foster care that could be of interest to social workers, researchers, or community groups working with housing issues.

In Focus, Insights, and Legal Sidebar products are shorter, briefer documents. In Focus pieces, generally labeled with the IF prefix, provide a two-page overview of a topic as a quick synopsis. For example, the In Focus report "The Low-Income Housing Tax Credit: Policy Issues" discusses a federal tax program to incentivize the development of low-income rental housing, providing details of the program as well as some of the challenges. It is available at https://crsreports.congress.gov/product/pdf/ IF/IF11335. A community group addressing issues of affordable housing might find this type of report useful for informing their advocacy work and for understanding the landscape of affordable housing at the federal level. Insights, given the prefix IN, offer quick analyses of current topics for Congress, such as this document related to college financing, "Planning and Paying for College: Federal Government Resources." It is available at https://crsreports.congress.gov/product/pdf/IN/IN11563/. Finally, Legal Sidebar, labeled with the prefix LSB, are brief reports on recent developments related to the law such as the document "Supreme Court Decision Sheds Light on State Authority to Regulate Health Care Costs," which is available at https://crsreports.congress.gov/product/pdf/LSB/LSB10587.

When searching for documents in the CRS collection, it is important to be aware of several key areas that vary from typical search strategies. The default search is matched first against document titles and authors rather than searching full-text. To enable full-text searching, it is necessary to execute a search first, and then check the "include full text" box to expand the search. Searches are also set to match against all words in the query, so it is not necessary to use the Boolean operator AND, but Boolean operators OR and NOT can be utilized in the search. To ensure the search performs correctly, make certain to use all caps when typing in Boolean operators.

While the intended audience for the items released by CRS is Congress (and supporting its work), the products produced by CRS can also help support policy research and analysis for members of the public. To expand on a previous example, the child welfare social worker could use the publicly available CRS reports to expand his knowledge about policies related to foster care. While much of foster care work and administration occurs at the state level, there are federal policies like the Family First Prevention Services Act (Pub. L. 115–123) that have direct impacts. A search for related CRS reports reveals a number of publications that are directly to this vital federal law, including the report titled "Child Welfare: The

Family First Prevention Services Act of 2016," https://crsreports.congress. gov/product/pdf/R/R44538, from when the Act was first introduced. More general searches for foster care or child welfare can uncover additional federal policies relevant to social work practice if a practitioner is not seeking information about a specific policy or law. CRS reports are also useful for students enrolled in social work or political science and in related courses. Because CRS products help make situate policy in a legislative context, the products can also help researchers make sense of the legislation they have located using Congress.gov.

Government Accountability Office

The Government Accountability Office (GAO), https://www.gao.gov/, is another nonpartisan legislative branch agency. It is often described as the "watchdog" of Congress. On its "About" website, https://www.gao.gov/ about, the GAO states that it "examines how taxpayer dollars are spent and provides Congress and federal agencies with objective, non-partisan, fact-based information to help the government save money and work more efficiently." Like the other legislative branch agencies discussed previously, GAO supports the work of Congress, and the majority of its work is requested by Congress, although it also does research under the purview of the Comptroller General. It has some similarities to the CBO in that much of its work deals with financial aspects of federal policy, but the scope is different. CBO focuses on the economic and budgetary impact of policies and legislation, while GAO is tasked with ensuring the "accountability of the federal government for the benefit of the American people." This focus on accountability for the public sets it apart from the other agencies discussed in this essay.

Like the Congressional Research Service, GAO produces several different types of reports and publications. GAO supports Congress

> by auditing agency operations to determine whether federal funds are being spent efficiently and effectively; investigating allegations of illegal and improper activities; reporting on how well government programs and policies are meeting their objectives; performing policy analyses and outlining options for congressional consideration; and issuing legal decisions and opinions, such as bid protest rulings and reports on agency rules (GAO 2021).

On the GAO website, users can browse available products under the Reports & Testimonies menu. Reports are listed by release date, but researchers can use the menu filters to narrow by topic, date, and agency. Filtering for Agriculture and Food topic limits results to reports in those areas, including the 2022 report "Nutrition Assistance Programs: Federal Agencies Should Improve Oversight and Better Collaborate on Efforts to Support Veterans with Food Insecurity" discussing nutrition assistance programs for veterans experiencing food insecurity, available at https://www.gao.gov/products/gao-22-104740. While the browse search can be useful, the recommended strategy is to perform a search using the main website search bar. Searching in this way offers additional options for filtering results, particularly by content type. Available content types include reports, testimony, videos, and podcasts. Note that some reports produced by GAO have restricted access; these products contain classified or other information that cannot be publicly released (though many do have a publicly available version). Members of Congress or congressional staff can request access to these files. According to GAO's guidance for requesting restricted products, members of the public who wish to access restricted files should submit a Freedom of Information Act (FOIA) request following the instructions on GAO's website at https://www.gao.gov/foia-requests.

Other areas of interest include the agencies page which allows users to see GAO recommendations, reports, recommendations, and multimedia files for different federal agencies. The action tracker is another searchable feature. The tracker shows how the federal government and agencies are or are not addressing recommendations from GAO. This information can be of use to individuals or community organizers who are working to address problems impacting their communities. For example, a group organizing around safe housing using GAO resources to identify areas for advocacy could utilize the findings from the report "Rental Housing: As More Households Rent, the Poorest Face Affordability and Housing Quality Challenges." In this report, available at https://www.gao.gov/products/gao-20-427, GAO found that around 15 percent of rental units had quality issues and that lower-income and rent-burdened households were most likely renting properties with issues such as water leaks or rodents.

Conclusion

There is a wealth of freely accessible U.S. government information resources that can support policy research. While the typical library user seeking out information on federal policy is not likely to be actively engaging in the creation of policy, the implementation and impact of those policies have an impact on their lives. Having access to tools that help individuals and groups identify areas of policy that concern their lives is key to helping those same individuals advocate for themselves and their community. From social workers, both in micro and macro settings, to citizens seeking to make a more informed decision about voting, to college students, and community organizations, many different groups of people can benefit from understanding ways in which policies are developed and implemented. For library workers, having a strong working knowledge of U.S. government information resources allows them to connect their users with free, authoritative content that helps policy researchers further their goals.

REFERENCES

Friedman, Lee. 2017. "Public Policy Making and Public Policy Analysis." In *Does Policy Analysis Matter? Exploring Its Effectiveness in Theory and Practice*, edited by Lee Friedman Berkeley, 1–43. Oakland: University of California Press.

Government Accountability Office. 2021. "GAO at a Glance." Revised August 2021. https://www.gao.gov/assets/2021-08/gao_at_a_glance_english.pdf.

National Association of Social Workers. 2015. "Child Welfare: Strengthen Child Welfare Service Delivery to Enhance Child and Family Well-Being." Accessed May 17, 2022. https://www.socialworkers.org/Advocacy/Policy-Issues/Child-Welfare.

National Association of Social Workers. 2021. "2021 Blueprint of Federal Social Policy Priorities: Recommendations to the Biden-Harris Administration and Congress." Accessed May 17, 2022. https://www.socialworkers.org/Advocacy/Policy-Issues/2021-Blueprint-of-Federal-Social-Policy-Priorities.

Vidovich, Lesley. 2007. "Removing Policy from Its Pedestal: Some Theoretical Framings and Practical Possibilities." *Educational Review* 59, no. 3: 285–98. https://doi.org/10.1080/00131910701427231.

Finding and Contextualizing Government Images

JENNIFER CASTLE

"The photograph is literally an emanation of the referent. From a real body, which was there, proceed radiations which ultimately touch me, who am here; the duration of the transmission is insignificant; the photograph of the missing being, as Sontag says, will touch me like the delayed rays of a star."

—Roland Barthes (2010, 80–81)

"Photography is simultaneously and instantaneously the recognition of a fact and the rigorous organization of visually perceived forms that express and signify that fact."

—Henri Cartier-Bresson (2015)

Introduction

While "government images" might bring to mind such things as topographical maps, aerial photos of farmland, or snapshots of staid legislative buildings, there is far more to them. Did you know academics, artists, writers, filmmakers, scrapbookers, musicians, and app and web developers use government images every day for many reasons including educational, promotional, and informational purposes? This essay aims to organize image galleries/libraries in a way that is easily accessible. Furthermore, the essay will help to contextualize government images. For the average person, locating and legally using images can be fraught with complications. Discerning what various copyrights mean or even how to cite them properly can be daunting. How do you navigate such a complicated landscape? Two words: public domain.

What Is Public Domain?

This section should not be considered a definitive source on the public domain. Laws vary between mediums. This essay and the author are not providing legal advice. If you have questions, consult an attorney.

Merriam-Webster Dictionary defines public domain as "the realm embracing property rights that belong to the community at large, are unprotected by copyright or patent, and are subject to appropriate by anyone" (Merriam-Webster Dictionary 2022a). Creative materials considered public domain are not subject to intellectual property laws such as copyright, patent, or trademark (Stim 2014). Public domain encompasses all works that are not restricted by copyright and do not require a license or a fee to be used. The only caveat is that individual works belong to the public; collections (or collective works) may be copyrighted (Stim 2014). Works fall into the public domain for three reasons:

1. The work is not considered copyrightable by law.
2. The works have been given to public domain by the author, known as "dedication."
3. The copyright of the work has expired (Whitten 2015).

For example, the works of Jane Austen are in the public domain and can be made into screenplays, adapted for the stage, or recorded as audiobooks, and the physical book scan be used in mixed media art. The oeuvres of Barbara Strozzi, Kate Chopin, and Mabel Normand are there either by virtue of having been created before the advent of copyright or their copyright terms have expired.

Where to Begin

In general, government images are considered in the public domain. While there are familiar sources for government images (e.g., the Library of Congress and the National Archives and Records Administration), others may not be as apparent or as readily found. An easy, broad place to start is the ubiquitous Google Images, https://www.google.com/imghp, and include site:gov in the keyword search. Please note Google Images does not provide information if an image is in the public domain. Another government source is USA.gov, https://www.usa.gov/explore/, an engine that searches hundreds of government agencies, departments, and programs in English and Spanish. For specific topics, the following comprehensive, though certainly not exhaustive, list (government websites change regularly) will assist researchers to locate images.

Restrictions may apply to images. Review the policies of individual sites for this information.

Animals, Places, and Plants

The U.S. government has many agencies and departments that create and collect images of flora, fauna, and their locations. They range from the Department of Agriculture to the Department of Fish and Wildlife to the National Parks Service. Photographs found on these sites are taken by government workers such as National Park rangers and biologists, university researchers, trained "citizen scientists," and captured by remote wildlife viewing cameras (National Park Service 2021). The images serve as records for research, conservation, and posterity, but can sometimes be stunning captures of nature or surprising glimpses of rare species.

- United States Antarctic Program (USAP), https://photolibrary. usap.gov/#1-1—This site includes historical images, people, scenery, science, stations and research vessels, transportation, and wildlife in Antarctica. Images are free for non-commercial use; the photographer and National Science Foundation must be credited. The USAP states, "No one may reproduce the photos for personal or commercial profit, use the photos on products for sale (e.g., t-shirts, coffee mugs, etc.) or use images for advertisement without express permission from the photographer." Any questions should be sent to the USAP photo librarian at photolibrarian@usap.gov. When downloading an image, the usage agreement will appear. The usage statement is available at https://photolibrary.usap.gov/ information.aspx.
- USDA Agricultural Research Service (ARS) Image Gallery, https://www.ars.usda.gov/oc/images/image-gallery/—A source of 6,500 high-quality digital photographs such as animals, crops, field research, and insects are available from the ARS Office of Communications. Photos in the Image Gallery are available free of charge and are copyright-free, in the public domain unless otherwise indicated. The Agricultural Research Service asks the photos not be used to infer or imply ARS endorsement of any product, company, or position. The copyright statement is available at https://www.ars.usda.gov/oc/images/copyright/.
- U.S. Fish & Wildlife Service (USFWS) National Digital Library, https://digitalmedia.fws.gov/digital/—Search images, video, documents, audio, and maps for materials concerning fish,

wildlife, plants, and their habitats. By selecting "Browse All," results can be limited by media type. Look for "Rights" in the item description. Most images are in the public domain. Images are also searchable through the USFWS's Flickr accounts by region (e.g., Southeast), https://www.flickr.com/photos/usfwshq/. Images found on Flickr often have an attributive license, which can be located under the upload date on each image.

- National Agriculture Library's Special Collections, https://www. nal.usda.gov/—Special Collections houses rare books, manuscript collections, nursery and seed trade catalogs, photographs, and posters from the 1500s to the present. Materials cover a variety of agricultural subjects including horticulture, entomology, poultry sciences, and natural history, and are not limited to domestic publications. Most information presented on the website is in the public domain and may be freely distributed or copied, but the use of appropriate byline/photo/image credits is requested. Some materials on the U.S. Department of Agriculture (USDA) website are protected by copyright, trademark, or patent, and/or are provided for personal use only. Such materials are used by USDA with permission, and the USDA has attempted to identify and label them. The copyright statement is available at https://www.nal. usda.gov/web-policies-and-important-links.
- National Park Service (NPS) Historic Photo Collection, https:// www.nps.gov/subjects/hfc/nps-history-collection.htm—This is a "collection of 400,000 images of America's special places, the people that care for them, and the visitors that love them." The NPS appreciates a citation or acknowledgment as the source. However, when such information is published or republished commercially, in part or in full, the copyright notice must include a reference to the original U.S. government work (17 U.S.C. 403), such as: "No protection is claimed in original U.S. Government works" or "No claim to original U.S. Government works," https://www.nps.gov/ aboutus/disclaimer.htm.
- National Park Service (NPS) Photo Gallery Multimedia Search, https://www.nps.gov/media/multimedia-search.htm#sort=Date_ Last_Modified%20desc—Multimedia credited to NPS without any copyright symbol are in the public domain. For copyright and usage information, multimedia credited with a copyright symbol (indicating that the creator may maintain rights to the work) or credited to any entity other than NPS must not be presumed to be in the public domain; contact the host park or program to determine ownership.

Art and Architecture

The U.S. government has a long and rich history when it comes to art and architecture. Much of federal architecture includes Georgian and neoclassical elements. However, in 1962, Daniel Patrick Moynihan's "Guiding Principles for Federal Architecture" outlined three directives:

1. Federal buildings should "reflect the dignity, enterprise, vigor, and stability of the American National Government," and incorporate local architectural traditions while using economical construction practices that have proven dependable and maintainable, and accessible to the disabled;
2. An "official style" must be avoided, and the government should pay more to avoid uniformity; and
3. Consideration for the location and development of the building "in cooperation with local agencies" is the first step (U.S. General Services Administration 2019).

Sixty years later, it continues to inform architectural decisions for innovative government buildings. During the Great Depression, the Roosevelt administration began the Works Progress Administration, and the National Endowment of the Arts was created for the "Great Society" during Lyndon B. Johnson's tenure (Bauerlein and Grantham 2009, 13). These and other agencies have funded the creation of public art throughout the nation.

- Architect of the Capitol (AOC) Art Collection, https://www.aoc. gov/explore-capitol-campus/art—AOC employees are responsible for the care and preservation of more than 300 works of art, architectural elements, and landscape features. Images are in the public domain and, unless otherwise noted, may be used without permission for educational, scholarly, or personal (i.e., nonpromotional, nonadvertising) purposes. Some images may not be suitable due to size. The image terms of use statement are available at https://www.aoc.gov/image-terms.
- Art in the Senate, https://www.senate.gov/reference/Index/Art_ in_the_Senate.htm—Images of the artwork found in the Senate wing of the U.S. Capitol and the Senate office buildings. Please use appropriate byline/photo/image credits for any images used. Offices under the jurisdiction of the Secretary of the Senate cannot grant literary or reproduction rights to materials in its collection. Those who wish to publish or reproduce published or unpublished materials must secure permission from the legal copyright

claimant under U.S. copyright law. The copyright information statement is available at https://www.senate.gov/artandhistory/history/common/generic/Photo_Collection_of_the_Senate_Historical_Office.htm.

- General Services Administration (GSA) Fine Arts Collection, https://www.gsa.gov/fine-arts—Most material on the site is free of copyright and may be copied and distributed without permission for personal, educational, non-commercial use only. Citing the GSA site and a link to the website is much appreciated. Some photos and graphics licensed are restricted. Please check for copyright or photo credit. Some GSA and GSA-affiliated seals, logos, and insignia are the property of the federal government and *may not be used without permission*. Other images, text, terms, phrases, slogans, and/or designs appearing on GSA websites also may be the trademarked property of others, used by GSA under a license. Prior to using such a trademark, it is the user's responsibility to acquire any necessary permission from the owner(s) of the trademark. The media usage guidelines are available at https://www.gsa.gov/gsagov/media-usage-guidelines.

- National Gallery of Art (NGA), https://www.nga.gov/open-access-images.html—The NGA has an open access policy for images of works of art in the permanent collection that the NGA believes to be in the public domain. Images of these works are available for download free of charge for any use, commercial or non-commercial. Image downloads are now available directly from the object pages on this website. More than 50,000 images are available for download, and additional images will be added for free access as more works are photographed and as works of art enter the public domain. Certain images found on the NGA's site are unavailable (i.e., still under copyright or copyright unclear, privacy or publicity issues exist, work is not fully owned by the NGA). The open access policy is available at https://www.nga.gov/notices/open-access-policy.html.

- Objects of Art: The National Library of Medicine (NLM), https://www.nlm.nih.gov/exhibition/tour/tableofcontents.html—Images on this site are not suitable for printing due to size. Find portraits such as NLM directors and images of sculptures housed within the library. The copyright statement is available at https://www.nlm.nih.gov/web_policies.html.

Astronomy

When it comes to astrophotography, one need look no further than the National Aeronautics and Space Administration (NASA). Breathtaking (and painstaking) achievements capturing images of the cosmos, from planets light years away, to solar sun flares, and the surface of the moon can all be found on NASA sites. Satellites also record geophysical data of Earth, helping us learn about the ever-changing landscape. These images are invaluable documentation of the universe and aid in our understanding of how expansive it is.

- Gateway to Astronaut Photography of Earth, https://eol.jsc.nasa. gov/—Images created by astronauts on subjects such as natural hazards and disasters, glaciers, and capital cities.
- NASA Image and Video Library, https://images.nasa.gov/—Consolidates imagery and videos in one searchable location. Users can download content in multiple sizes and resolutions and see the metadata associated with images, including EXIF/camera data on many images.
- NASA Image Galleries, https://www.nasa.gov/multimedia/ imagegallery/index.html—Organizes images by topics such as events and missions.
- NASA History Images Archives, https://www.nasa.gov/content/ nasa-history-images-archive—Credit to the contributor is provided for each image.
- NASA Space Science Data Coordinated (NSSDC) Archive Image Resources, https://nssdc.gsfc.nasa.gov/image/—NASA's archive for space science mission data. General and specialized image services and other NASA data archive/service centers like the Jet Propulsion Laboratory (JPL) and the Space Telescope Science Institute can be found on this site. Acknowledgment to NASA and NSSDC as the source of the image is required. The media usage guidelines are available at https://www.nasa.gov/multimedia/ guidelines/index.html.
- Photojournal, https://photojournal.jpl.nasa.gov/—NASA's astronomy photos. JPL's image use policy is available at https:// www.jpl.nasa.gov/jpl-image-use-policy.
- Visible Earth, https://visibleearth.nasa.gov/—A catalog of NASA images and animations of the planet. Most images published on the site are freely available for re-publication or re-use, including commercial purposes, except for where copyright is indicated. NASA asks a credit statement be attached with each image or else

credit Visible Earth; the only mandatory credit is NASA. Visible Earth's brief image use policy statement is available at https://visibleearth.nasa.gov/image-use-policy.

Climate and Weather

The U.S. government has been collecting climate and weather information since its inception, but the advent of telegraphs allowed a network of weather observatories to be connected to observe, relay, and eventually forecast data. Around the turn of the twentieth century, the Weather Bureau began experimenting with kites, then airplane stations in the 1930s (National Weather Service 2020). Since then, there have been significant advances in technology through radar and satellites, but this is not limited to data. The National Oceanic and Atmospheric Administration (NOAA) is a guiding force for astonishing photographs of climate and weather events whose photo library organizes roughly 80,000 images.

Images credited to NOAA are in the public domain and may be freely distributed and copied, but NOAA should be given appropriate acknowledgment of any subsequent uses of a work. Educational use is encouraged as the primary goal of the library. *This general permission does not extend to the use of the NOAA emblem/logo.* The policy statement is available at https://repository.library.noaa.gov/Content%20and%20Copyright.

- NOAA Photo Library https://www.photolib.noaa.gov/—A portion of the collection is also offered through the library's Flickr account, https://www.flickr.com/photos/noaaphotolib/.
- National Ocean Service Imagery, https://oceanservice.noaa.gov/gallery/—Links to galleries and collections such as marine sanctuaries, coastal management, response and restoration, and historical maps and charts.
- National Severe Storms Laboratory (NSSL), https://www.flickr.com/photos/noaanssl/—NSSL's research spans weather radar, tornadoes, flash floods, lightning, damaging winds, hail, and winter weather. Most images are public domain, but some are under copyright (refer to the NOAA policy statement).

Geography and Maps

When it comes to geography and maps, many government agencies have images available. Two of the largest contributors are the Central

Intelligence Agency (CIA) and the U.S. Geological Survey (USGS). The *CIA World Factbook* is a comprehensive almanac of official country data and statistics, including images, and the USGS library is recognized as one of the world's largest Earth and natural science libraries, providing services, collections, and expertise essential to the USGS mission.

- *CIA World Factbook*, https://www.cia.gov/the-world-factbook/— Search for flags and maps of countries. The *Factbook* is in the public domain. Accordingly, it may be copied freely without the permission of the CIA. The official seal of the CIA, however, may *not* be copied without permission as required by the CIA Act of 1949 (50 U.S.C. 403m). The copyright and contributors' statement are available at https://www.cia.gov/the-world-factbook/about/copyright-and-contributors/.
- U.S. Geological Survey Library, https://www.usgs.gov/programs/usgs-library—Advanced search of the catalog provides an option for Library Photographic Collection. Rights can be found on the Display Resource of an image. The U.S. Geological Survey requires an acknowledgment of its information in this format: "(Product or data name) courtesy of the U.S. Geological Survey; (Product or data name) produced by USGS; (Data name) data compiled by USGS, or similar." Visit Acknowledging or Crediting USGS at https://www.usgs.gov/information-policies-and-instructions/acknowledging-or-crediting-usgs. The copyrights and credits statement is available at https://www.usgs.gov/information-policies-and-instructions/copyrights-and-credits.
- USGS Multimedia Gallery: Images, https://www.usgs.gov/products/multimedia-gallery/images—Photographs dating back to "when the USGS was surveying the country by horse and buggy," documenting climate change. Click on the image to confirm if it is in the public domain; for some images, permission may need to be obtained from the creator.

History and Government

The National Archives and Records Administration (NARA) and the Library of Congress (LOC) are the preeminent United States institutions recording the nation's history of the federal government. The NARA catalog houses architectural and engineering drawings, maps and charts, photographs, and other graphic materials. The collections of the LOC Prints & Photographs Division include photographs, fine and popular prints and drawings, posters, and architectural and engineering drawings.

- Library of Congress: Prints and Photographs Online Catalog (PPOC), http://www.loc.gov/pictures/—The LOC attempts to indicate whether an image is in the public domain or has no known restrictions. However, it also suggests users conduct their own rights evaluation and outlines the steps on its Copyright and Other Restrictions That Apply to Publication/Distribution of Images: Assessing the Risk of Using a P&P Image page, https://www.loc.gov/rr/print/195_copr.html. The rights and restrictions web page is available at http://www.loc.gov/rr/print/res/rights.html.
- NARA Catalog, https://www.archives.gov/research/catalog—Most images are in the public domain, but some may be under copyright. NARA has a great number of images with certain individuals depicted who may claim rights in their likenesses. Users must contact the individuals depicted or their representatives. To learn more, visit the NARA privacy and use policy page, https://www.archives.gov/global-pages/privacy.html#copyright. Check the "Access Restrictions" field of each record for more information.
- Presidential Libraries, https://www.archives.gov/presidential-libraries/about—The Presidential Library system is composed of fifteen libraries. These facilities are overseen by the Office of Presidential Libraries in the National Archives and Records Administration. Most materials in the libraries are in the public domain. Copyright law (17 U.S.C. 108) allows copies for private study, scholarship, or research. The copyright status of some materials is unknown or under copyright protection. These materials require the permission of the copyright holder before publication. Please check individual library sites for further details.
- Senate Historical Office (SHO) Photo Collection, https://www.senate.gov/artandhistory/history/common/generic/Photo_Collection_of_the_Senate_Historical_Office.htm—The SHO maintains approximately 35,000 still pictures, slides, and negatives. The collection includes photographs and illustrations of former senators, news photographs, editorial cartoons, photographs of committees in session, and other images documenting the institutional history of the Senate and the careers of senators. The images are available for use by the media, congressional offices, academic researchers, and the public. The copyright information statement is available at https://www.senate.gov/artandhistory/history/common/generic/Photo_Collection_of_the_Senate_Historical_Office.htm.

Medicine and Science

Medical photography can help identify patient issues and confirm diagnoses, and images wildly vary from observable ailments to bacteria and viruses. The most common government sites to find medical photographs are the National Library of Medicine (NLM) and the branches of the Department of Health and Human Services such as the Centers for Disease Control and the National Cancer Institute. Science photography also ranges from the visible to the macro. The National Science Foundation (NSF) and Science.gov are excellent resources to locate scientific images, including those taken using spectrophotometry, ultraviolet, and x-rays.

- Health and Human Services (HHS) Image Galleries, https://www.hhs.gov/web/services-and-resources/image-galleries/index.html—Links to the galleries of more than twenty agencies. Many HHS agencies maintain galleries of images that are in the public domain. Visit the galleries at the links listed on the page or the directory of the HHS Flickr accounts for more information on how images should be used and credited, if necessary.
- National Library of Medicine (NLM): Digital Collections, https://collections.nlm.nih.gov/—The NLM's free online repository of biomedical resources, including still images. A search can be refined to search for public domain images. All content in Digital Collections is in the public domain unless otherwise noted. The NLM requests users source information by including the phrase "Courtesy of the U.S. National Library of Medicine" or "Source: U.S. National Library of Medicine." For further details, see the copyright section of the NLM Web Policies page at https://www.nlm.nih.gov/web_policies.html. The digital collection policy is available at https://collections.nlm.nih.gov/about.
- National Science Foundation (NSF) Multimedia Gallery, https://www.nsf.gov/news/mmg/index.jsp—Image subjects range from Arctic and Antarctica to physics and are intended for private, educational, and/or nonprofit/non-commercial use. Check each photo for special restrictions. The NSF logo cannot be used in a manner that falsely implies employment by or affiliation with NSF and cannot be used to imply or endorse a product or service. Further, permission to use NSF visual media (graphics, photos, and illustrations) is granted on a case-by-case basis. Since resources are in the public domain, created by NSF contractors, or used by NSF with specific permission granted by the owner, visual

media found on the site should not be reused without consent. The multimedia gallery policy is available at https://www.nsf.gov/news/ mmg/conditions.jsp?med_id=188036&from=.

- Science.gov, https://www.science.gov/—An engine that searches more than sixty databases and 2,200 scientific websites to provide users with access to more than 200 million pages of authoritative federal science information. Select the Multimedia tab to view image results.

Military

Images created by military personnel are part of their official duties and are not eligible for copyright. Most military photographs are taken by armed forces photographers, foreign militaries, and private commercial sources with subjects such as "personnel, combat operations, training, facilities, equipment, land vehicles, aircraft, and ships" (National Archives and Records Administration 2021). Department of Defense (DoD) photo collections are military-related, but they also include more general pictures of events, people, and locations. Collections related to the U.S. Navy have specific emphasis on ships, aviation, places, wars/events, activities, and significant individuals associated with naval history.

All images created by DoD photographers receive a Visual Information Record Identification Number (VIRIN), which uniquely identifies every piece of visual information. To learn about the components, visit How to Create at VIRIN at https://www.dimoc.mil/Submit-DoD-VI/Digital-VI-Toolkit-read-first/Create-a-VIRIN/. The DoD Public Use Notice of Limitations, https://www.dimoc.mil/resources/limitations/, outlines how some images on available on respective military departments may be owned by non–DoD entities, regardless of whether the material is marked with a copyright notice or other indication of non–DoD ownership or interests. Separate policies on using images containing military persons, places, and things for "commercial advertisement, marketing, promotion, solicitation, or fundraising purposes" is found on the DoD Visual Information instructions page, https://www.dimoc.mil/References/DoD-VI-References/DoD-Instructions/.

Military department and other DoD component names, insignia, seals, symbols, and similar marks may be protected as trademarks or service marks and may not be used in commerce without prior written permission. The U.S. Air Force Photos policy is available at https://www.af.mil/News/Photos/. Although these collections are military-related, they also include more general pictures of events, people, and locations.

The Defense Imagery Management Operations Center "Public Use Notice of Limitations" is available at https://www.dimoc.mil/resources/limitations/.

- Defense Visual Information Distribution Service, https://www.dvidshub.net/—Users must register to download images. Copyright falls under DoD's Principles of Information, https://www.defense.gov/Resources/Principles-of-Information/.
- U.S. Department of Defense Photos, https://www.defense.gov/Multimedia/Photos/—Search by keyword or image collections. The DoD requires attribution for images. No alterations to an image in a way that will misrepresent the original (such as cropping, and resizing is acceptable), and ensure the photo has been released. Photo credits will include the photographer's name. The DoD's imagery policy is the same as the U.S. Air Force's photo policy.
- History and Heritage Command, https://www.history.navy.mil/our-collections.html—Most images found in the collection are in the public domain and may be downloaded and used without permissions or special requirements. Those which are not will be noted in the copyright section of the image description.

Law Enforcement

Photos available from the Department of Justice (DOJ) and the Drug Enforcement Agency (DEA) are generally limited to public affairs and drug identification, respectively. Though there are some images in the DOJ archives of events and national and international landmarks and locations, the images found on the archive site only date back to the 2010s. For older photographs, search NARA and the LOC. The images found here may not be suitable for all viewers.

- U.S. DOJ, https://www.justice.gov/archives/photo-gallery-archive—Unless otherwise indicated, information on DOJ sites is in the public domain and may be copied and distributed without permission. Citing the DOJ as a source is appreciated. Use of any DOJ seals is protected and requires advance authorization. The copyright status and citation policy website is available at https://www.justice.gov/legalpolicies.
- DEA: Drug Images, https://www.dea.gov/media-gallery/drug-images—DEA falls under DOJ copyright status and citation policy.

Citing and Contextualizing

After locating the images, now what? For academic integrity, it is imperative to cite who or what organization created them, but there is additional information that needs to be documented:

- Title of work
- Date of work
- Date image was access
- Medium, size/ dimensions (if available)
- Institution where image/work is located
- Name of website or database image is located
- Rights information

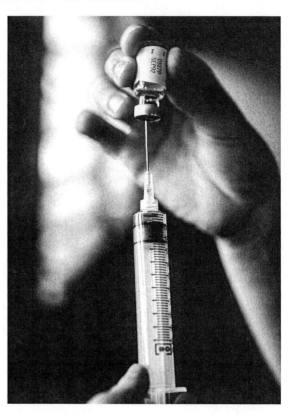

Why is this important? For a few reasons: to give the creator credit for their work; to allow others to find and reuse the image; and to participate in the scholarly conversation. Imagine participating in a significant historical event and photographing a key moment that is used by scholars and artists a century from now. You would probably want to be remembered as the person who took the photograph. Furthermore, you would not want the image taken out of context. Con-

Image 1: Without context and investigation, this image could represent anything from vaccinations to opioid addiction. The photograph was taken during Gabon Medflag in 1988 when U.S. military personnel were immunizing Gabonese from many diseases, years before the opioid crisis and the Covid-19 pandemic (National Archives, https://catalog.archives.gov/id/6438779).

text is defined as "1: the words that are used with a certain word or phrase and that help to explain its meaning; 2: the situation in which something happens: the group of conditions that exist where and when something happens" (Merriam-Webster Dictionary 2022b). To illustrate, imagine a microscopic photo of a disease taken by the National Institute of Allergy and Infectious Disease being used on a county health department's website, then imagine the image being used on a white supremacy message board. The same image can be interpreted a multitude of ways.

The photo in Image 1 is a good example. The Covid-19 pandemic has widened the debate regarding vaccinations. Without providing the necessary information for context, viewers might interpret the image as taken since the 2019 outbreak, or the syringe contains the vaccine. The title, in fact, provides a significant amount of information: "A syringe is prepared for giving immunizations during Gabon Medflag '88, in which U.S. military personnel provide medical assistance and training to the Gabonese. Villagers are being immunized against mumps, polio, measles, rubella, yellow fever and typhoid" (Department of Defense 1988).

Conclusion

The websites assembled in this essay offer a wealth of images but using them effectively means adhering to standards and relating certain information associated with each photo. Government images in the public domain are the simplest to use, but copyrighted photos are still worth consideration. Be sure to tell the story of the image with proper background and credit. Not providing the context for a picture can change its perception, while failing to credit the photographer does a disservice to the person who captured the image. The federal government is an amazing resource for locating images in the public domain and copyrighted images.

REFERENCES

Barthes, Roland. 2010. *Camera Lucida: Reflections on Photography*. New York: Hill & Wang.
Bauerlein, Mark, and Ellen Grantham, eds. 2009. *National Endowment for the Arts: A History, 1965–2008*. Washington, D.C.: National Endowment for the Arts. https://www.arts.gov/sites/default/files/nea-history-1965-2008.pdf.
Cartier-Bresson, Henri. 2015. *The Decisive Moment*. Göttingen: Steidl.
Department of Defense. Armed Forces Information Service. Defense Visual Information Center. 1988. *A syringe is prepared for giving immunizations during Gabon Medflag '88, in which U.S. military personnel provide medical assistance and training to the Gabonese. Villagers are being immunized against mumps, polio, measles, rubella, yellow fever and typhoid*. Accessed February 3, 2022. https://catalog.archives.gov/id/6438779.
Merriam-Webster Dictionary. 2022a. *Public Domain*. Accessed December 18, 2021. https://www.merriam-webster.com/dictionary/public%20domain.

Merriam-Webster Dictionary. 2022b. *Context.* Accessed February 3, 2022. https://www.merriam-webster.com/dictionary/context.

National Archives and Records Administration. 2021. "Still Pictures: Military Images and Posters." September 27. Accessed June 6, 2022. https://www.archives.gov/research/still-pictures/military.

National Park Service. 2021. "Wildlife Monitoring and Wildlife Viewing Camera Systems: Frequently Asked Questions." November 4. Accessed June 6, 2022. https://www.nps.gov/pore/learn/nature/wildlife_monitoring.htm.

National Weather Service. 2020. "The National Weather Service at 150: A Brief History." Accessed June 6, 2022. https://vlab.noaa.gov/web/nws-heritage/-/the-national-weather-service-at-150-a-brief-history.

Stim, Rich. 2014. "Welcome to the Public Domain." Stanford Libraries. Copyright & Fair Use. Accessed January 12, 2022. https://fairuse.stanford.edu/overview/public- domain/welcome/.

U.S. General Services Administration. 2019. "Guiding Principles for Federal Architecture." *U.S. General Services Administration.* February 26. Accessed June 6, 2022. https://www.gsa.gov/real-estate/design-and-construction/design-excellence/design-excellence-program/guiding-principles-for-federal-architecture.

Whitten, Sarah. 2015. "CNBC Explains: How Copyrights Become Public Domain." Accessed January 12, 2022. https://www.cnbc.com/2015/09/25/cnbc-explains-how-copyrights-become-public-domain.html.

PART II

Education

A Guide to the U.S. Census for History Teachers

NICOLE WOOD

Introduction

The United States census "tells us who we are and where we are going as a nation," determining everything from apportionment in the U.S. House of Representatives to funding for schools, hospitals, and roads (U.S. Census Bureau 2021a). With a mission to "serve as the nation's leading provider of quality data about its people and economy" (U.S. Census Bureau 2021b), the U.S. Census Bureau collects, organizes, interprets, and distributes data that is used by government agencies, businesses, universities, community groups, and other researchers to inform future decisions and resource distribution. This data is preserved and, over time, transformed into primary source material that can detail the demographic, economic, and cultural history of the United States.

In addition to telling us "who we are" and "where we are going," the census paints a rich history of who we were and where we have been. The questions asked offer as much information as the answers given. How are questions on race, ethnicity, and immigration informed by an ever-evolving understanding of what it means to be an American? How were these questions impacted by sentiments on slavery, colonization, or the belief in Manifest Destiny? Why did the first post–Civil War census introduce questions about voting rights? The answers to these questions provide data on tangible demographic trends over time, but the questions themselves reveal shifting values and interests.

This essay will provide an overview of freely available, web-based resources that high school teachers and university instructors can use to make census data approachable and easy to understand. It will draw from information available on government websites, such as the U.S. Census

Bureau's *Statistical Abstract* and Decennial Census by Decades. It will also include instructions for using data aggregators, such as the U.S. census data tables, which can be found on the IPUMS National Historical Geographic Information Systems (NHGIS) website, https://www.nhgis.org/. The essay will conclude by providing tips for interpreting and extracting narratives from the raw data through practical examples from instruction sessions at Austin Peay State University's Woodward Library.

U.S. Census Bureau Information

The U.S. Census Bureau has preserved over 232 years of statistical data. Questions asked in the Decennial Census are not standardized and have been altered and expanded to accommodate the information needs of the federal government. The first national census was conducted in 1790 to apportion seats in the House of Representatives and determine each state's share of debt incurred during the American Revolution. This tethered a state's representation to its taxation, a lack of which was a primary cause for seeking independence from Great Britain (Whitby 2020, 72–78). The Census of 1790 only recorded four variables: the number of white males above or below the age of sixteen, the number of free white females, the number of other free persons, and the number of enslaved persons. Today, the U.S. Census Bureau collects, organizes, and disseminates data through the *Decennial Census of Population and Housing, American Community Survey* (ACS), the *Census of Governments*, the *Economic Census*, and over 130 surveys and programs, such as the *Census of Jails* and the *Small Business Pulse Survey*. The modern Census Bureau can provide information on everything from fertility rates to the percentage of the population without an internet subscription.

The evolving scope of the information measured can pose challenges when conducting research using census data, particularly when analyzing changes over time. Researchers must ensure that the same factors are evaluated from one year to the next. Additionally, the data gathered by enumerators do not always match the descriptions provided on official documents. According to the 1860 census form, a person could be described as White, Black, or Mulatto. However, in the instructions provided to enumerators, possible categories included White, Black, Mulatto, or Indian, and in the actual collected data, almost 35,000 people were described as "Asiatic" (National Archives and Records Administration, n.d.; Census Office 1860, 15; Manson et al., 2021). In 1870, the authorized list expanded to include Chinese and American Indians (U.S. Census Bureau, n.d.a.). By the mid-twentieth century, enumerators could select

White, Negro, American Indian, Japanese, Chinese, Filipino, and Other (U.S. Census Bureau 1961, cxiii). Categories have continued to grow and now include more nuanced options for persons of Asian, Pacific Islander, and Hispanic/Latinx heritage (U.S. Census Bureau, n.d.b.).

Considering the complicated history of race, immigration, and colonization in the United States, it is no surprise that the federal government does not use the same terminology as it did in 1790; however, researchers should also take note of other inconsistencies such as one-off questions and changing data collection practices. For example, the 1890 census included an inquiry to determine the number of women who were widowed after the Civil War, which was used for pension legislation (Blake 1996), and the 1930 census introduced a question regarding home radio ownership, which helped the U.S. Department of Commerce regulate radio frequencies (Schor 2017, 331). As data collection practices became more objective and measurable, the Census Bureau changed its practices as well. Before 1940, enumerators used tests to determine if an individual was illiterate. In 1940, this evolved into the less biased quantification of educational attainment (Anderson and Ryan 2012, 32). While census data can appear complicated and overwhelming, several online resources can make analysis approachable regardless of one's research background.

Online Resources

The U.S. Census Bureau has published several online resources to help users summarize and interpret data:

- **Data Explorer,** https://data.census.gov/. The U.S. Census Bureau's dissemination platform for demographic and economic data. As of this publication, tables and maps are available from 2000 to the present.
- **Decennial Census of Population and Housing by the Decades**, https://www.census.gov/programs-surveys/decennial-census/decade.html. This report provides an overview of each U.S. Decennial Census, including authorizing legislation and intercensal activity, relevant historical facts and cultural context, official publications, and enumerator instructions and questionnaires. Recent decades include photos, infographics, and data tables.
- **History Worksheets**, https://www.census.gov/programs-surveys/sis/activities/history.html. Interactive educational assignments created by the U.S. Census Bureau and targeted toward students

in K–5 through 12th grade. Corresponding teachers' guides are included in the materials.

- **Infographics and Visualizations**, https://www.census.gov/library/visualizations.html. Utilizes the full range of data collected by the U.S. Census Bureau to visualize patterns and trends through graphics, charts, tables, and maps.
- **Statistical Abstract of the United States, 1878–2012**, https://www.census.gov/library/publications/time-series/statistical_abstracts.html. An annual summary of statistics from the U.S. Census Bureau, Bureau of Labor Statistics, Bureau of Economic Analysis, and other federal agencies published by the U.S. government. Supplemental series include the *State and Metropolitan Area Data* and *County* and *City Data* books. Available for download in PDF and Excel formats.
- **U.S. Census Through the Decades**, https://www.census.gov/history/www/through_the_decades/. This webpage "follows the evolution of the decennial census by detailing the events surrounding each of them." Examples include internal and external crises, shifts in cultural interests, and generational "defining moments" (U.S. Census Bureau, n.d.b.). Fast facts, overviews of enumeration and census-related technological advancements, the index of questions, questionnaires, and census instructions are organized for easy access.

In addition to the U.S. Census Bureau's online resources, there are other web resources that can enhance census instruction including:

- **Library of Congress—U.S. Census Connections: A Resource Guide**, https://guides.loc.gov/census-connections/introduction. A resource guide that consolidates census finding aids, reference publications for the U.S. Decennial Census, Economic Census, Census of Agriculture, and Census of Governments, and links to related resources in the Library of Congress' print and online collections.
- **National Archives and Records Administration's Census Records**, https://www.archives.gov/research/census. This information hub links users to individual census records, answers to frequently asked questions, information on the process of developing census forms, instructions for enumerators, and explanations for symbols and abbreviations.
- **National Historical Geographic Information System (NHGIS)**, https://www.nhgis.org/. Houses and disseminates summary tables and time series of demographic, agriculture, and economic data.

Users can download compatible geography boundary files to assist with mapping. Files are available from 1790 to the present.

Tutorials

The resources above provide access to data that has already been interpreted, but it is sometimes necessary to look at the raw data to create instructional materials on specific subjects. This section includes two practical examples from instruction sessions at Austin Peay State University's Woodward Library. The first tutorial is beginner-friendly and uses Social Explorer to determine trends in high school graduation rates between 1940 and 2000. The second tutorial is targeted at individuals with prior data analysis experience. It offers instructions for downloading, cleaning, and mapping census data from IPUMS' NHGIS in QGIS, a free, open-sourced software available at https://qgis.org.

Tutorial 1—Beginner

This tutorial utilizes Social Explorer, https://www.socialexplorer.com, allowing users to browse and create thematic maps from census data. After creating a free, basic account, users can map a limited number of census tables at no cost. Examples include population density from 1790 to the present and more detailed demographic data from 1940 to the present. A paid plan is required to access all Social Explorer data and features; however, non-paying users can view maps designed for educators and students to "inspire creativity, encourage hands-on learning, and equip [students] with desired skills" (Social Explorer, n.d.). This tutorial provides instructions for creating a web map comparing high school completion rates by U.S. county in 1940 and 2000 and can be performed with the data and tools included in the basic plan. The final product can supplement instruction on changing child labor laws, school segregation, urbanization, and compulsory education. Additional guides and video tutorials can be found at https://www.socialexplorer.com/help/guides-videos.

The tutorial can be summarized in the following steps:

1. Create a new map.
2. Identify and select appropriate data.
3. Build a comparative display to show high school attendance rates across different years.
4. Visualize the data for interpretation.

STEP 1: CREATE A NEW MAP

From the Social Explorer home page, create a new base map by select-ing the "Create new" button in the upper left-hand corner of the screen, then select "United States" as the map of interest. A title may be added for clarity. The default display for the new base map shows a five-year estimate of population density per square mile as recorded in the American Com-munity Survey.

STEP 2: IDENTIFY AND SELECT APPROPRIATE DATA

This tutorial focuses on educational attainment. To find the corre-sponding datasets, click on "Change data." The default display for avail-able information is organized by category. In the upper menu, change the display to "All data (by source)." The relevant datasets can be found by selecting the variables displayed in Table 1.

Table 1: Social Explorer Selection
Criteria for Tutorial 1 Data

	1940	*2000*
Data organized by	All data (by source)	All data (by source)
Source	Census 1940 Census Tract, County, State and U.S.	Census 2000
Table	T43—Educational Attainment for Population 25 Years and Over	T43—Highest Educational Attainment for Population 25 Years and Over
Variable	High School 4 Years	High School Graduate or more

STEP 3: CREATE A COMPARATIVE DISPLAY TO SHOW HIGH
     SCHOOL ATTENDANCE RATES ACROSS DIFFERENT YEARS

To add a second map, return to the main display and change the view to side-by-side or swipe by selecting "Compare" and choosing the desired view. The screen will be divided into halves. Side-by-side displays a complete, linked view of both maps. Swipe overlays the maps, allow-ing users to toggle between views by dragging the curser. Once the sec-ond map has been created, the displayed data can be changed by repeating Step 2. These two views are displayed in Image 1a, Image 1b, and Image 2. The map in Image 2 is for "Population 25 Years and Over: High School." The left side is from the 1940 Census; the right side is from the 2000 Census.

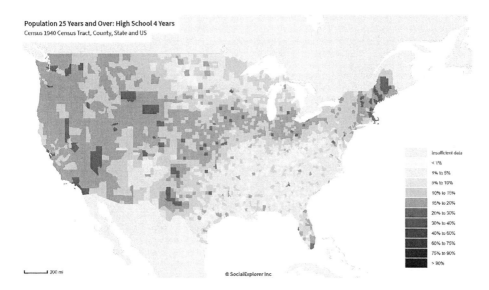

Image 1a: High school graduates as a percentage of the total population 25 years and older in 1940. At Least Some High School (1 to 4 Years): High School 4 Years, 1940 (Social Explorer based on data digitally transcribed by Inter-university Consortium for Political and Social Research. Edited, verified by Michael Haines. Compiled, edited, and verified by Social Explorer. Accessed July 19, 2022).

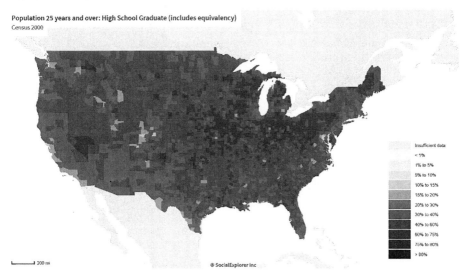

Image 1b: High school graduates as a percentage of the total population 25 years and older in 2000 High School Graduate or more (includes equivalency), 2000 (Social Explorer based on data from U.S. Census Bureau. Accessed July 19, 2022).

Image 2: High school graduation rates displayed in a swipe view. High School Graduate or more (includes equivalency), 2000 (Social Explorer based on data from U.S. Census Bureau. Accessed July 19, 2022).

Step 4: Visualize the Data for Interpretation

Social Explorer offers a variety of options for visualizing data. Variables can be displayed by state, county, or census tract (if available) in graduated shades that use darker or lighter colors to denote higher or lower percentages, bubbles that use size to display values, or dot density. Users can add annotations, images, labels, and point markers. Image 1a, Image 1b, and Image 2 show the percentage of the population over the age of 25 with four or more years of high school education by county as shaded areas.

These maps can be used to spark a conversation in the classroom. Why was educational attainment so much lower in 1940? What were the most popular jobs, and what amount of education would likely have been required for employment? Were there industries that benefited from child labor? Looking at a numerical table can provide the same information, but visual data is easier to digest and allows students to identify patterns quickly.

Tutorial 2—Intermediate

This tutorial demonstrates methods for calculating changes in literacy rates at the state level for the population of the United States between 1880 and 1930, which can be used to visualize the long-lasting effects of anti-literacy laws that were in place before and during the Civil War. Tools used in the tutorial include IPUMS' NHGIS, Excel, and QGIS. The tutorial can be summarized in the following steps:

1. Download source tables and GIS files from IPUMS' NHGIS.
2. Consolidate and perform data cleanup in Excel.
3. Load and join source tables and GIS files in QGIS.
4. Symbolize the data to create a visual narrative.

Step 1: Download Source Tables and GIS Files from IPUMS' NHGIS

IPUMS' NHGIS, https://www.nhgis.org/, provides summary tables of census data, other nationwide surveys, and corresponding Geographic Information Systems (GIS) boundary files from 1790 to the present. The NHGIS Data Finder, https://data2.nhgis.org/, allows users to filter, sort, select, and download tables and boundary files for different years and geographic levels, including census tracts, counties, and states. The website does not provide tools for data analysis, but it supplies file formats that support use in spreadsheets, statistical software, and GIS applications.

When downloading census data, it is essential to consider discrepancies resulting from evolving data collection practices and the changing cartographic boundaries of a growing nation. For example, census tracts were not implemented until the census of 1910, and they were not defined nationwide until the year 2000 (U.S. Census Bureau, n.d.c.). For this tutorial, it is necessary to note that several territories were converted to states between 1880 and 1930, resulting in 1930 data that have no counterpart in the census of 1880.

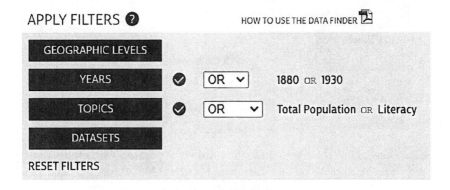

Image 3: Filters and Boolean operators for tutorial 2 data (NHGIS Data Finder database, *https://data2.nhgis.org*).

IPUMS NHGIS data are available at no charge; however, researchers must create an account and agree to a usage license before accessing the data. This registration form includes a required field for the researcher's institution or employer. New users can select from an existing list of institutions or suggest a new institution. The existing list focuses heavily on higher education and non-profit organizations, but IPUMS NHGIS will approve suggestions for K–12 schools and public libraries.

As displayed in Image 3, data utilized in this tutorial can be downloaded through the NHGIS Data Finder by filtering results to include the decennial years 1880 OR 1930 and the topics of Total Population OR Literacy.

After applying the filters, corresponding data will appear under tabs grouped by source tables, times series tables, and GIS files. The source tables and GIS files required to complete this tutorial are listed in Table 2.

Table 2: IPUMS NHGIS Source Tables and GIS Files for Tutorial 2

Source Tables

Table Name	Universe	Year—Dataset
NT1. Total Population	Persons	1880_cPAX
NT1. Total Population	Persons	1930_cPAE
NT15. Number of Persons 10 Years of Age and Over Who Are Unable to Read	Persons 10 Years and Over Who Cannot Read	1880_sPHX
N20. Illiterate Population 10 Years of Age and Over by Race/Nativity	Illiterate Persons 10 Years and Over	1930_cPAE

GIS Files

Year	Geographic Level	Basis
1880	State	2000 TIGER/Line+
1930	State	2000 TIGER/Line+

Source tables for literacy include the number of persons who are unable to read or write divided by age, race, and sex. To calculate the percentage of the population that falls into each category, it is necessary to also download the source tables for the total population. GIS files include the geographic census boundaries needed to organize and visualize data from the summary tables. To download the needed files, click on the green button next to the corresponding entries under the source table and GIS files tabs. As files are selected, a data cart will appear in the upper right-hand corner of the page. Use the "Continue" button in the data cart to review and finalize data selections.

When GIS files are included in a download, it is necessary to determine a geographic level for the source tables. On the data options page, match the geographic level of the source tables to the GIS files. They will be joined by clicking "Select Geographic Levels." In this tutorial, the geographic level of "State" should be selected for all files. Once the geographic levels have been determined, click "Continue" in the data cart. Source tables can be downloaded as comma-separated values (CSV), which is best for mapping, or as fixed width, which is best for statistical packages.

Step 2: Consolidate and Perform Data Cleanup in Excel

Download and unzip the CSV files. The folder will include a text-based codebook, which houses a code dictionary. This codebook is indispensable for interpreting the downloaded data, as column headings in the CSV files are not explicit. If needed, the codes in the column headings can be altered in Excel to match the corresponding definition. For example, in the CSV file for the total population in 1880, column AOT001 holds the total population of each state.

Open the CSV file using Excel. To find the percentage of the population that was illiterate in 1880 and 1930, combine the statistics for 1880 total population and 1880 literacy in one worksheet and the statistics for 1930 total population and 1930 literacy in another worksheet. To calculate the percentage of the population that was illiterate, create a formula that divides the illiterate population by the total population and multiply by 100. For example, =A2/B2*100. Copy the formula for each state. The total percentage of the population that is literate can be determined by subtracting the illiterate percentage from 100. Clean up any discrepancies between the two datasets; Alaska, Hawaii, and Oklahoma were enumerated in 1930 but not 1880, and North and South Dakota were established from the Dakota Territory. Save the 1880 results and the 1930 results as separate CSV files.

Step 3: Load and Join Source Tables and GIS Files in QGIS

Create a new project in QGIS and add the shape and CSV files. Using the layer dropdown menu, upload the shapefiles for 1880 and 1930 as vector layers, which can be identified by the .SHP file type. If asked to select a Coordinate Reference System, take care to choose the same option for each added layer. The CSV files should be uploaded as delimited text layers with "no geometry" selected under the geometry definition options. The shapefiles will appear as maps, while the CSV files are uploaded as tables with no visual component. To display literacy rates on the map, it is necessary to join the CSV and shapefiles. Right-click on the layer titles in the left-hand menu and open the attribute tables for the shape and CSV files. Identify a unique column heading that appears in both. For NHGIS downloads, this is the GISJOIN header.

Right-click on a shapefile and open the properties. Select the joins tab in the left-hand menu and click on the green plus to create a new table join. Use the corresponding table as the join layer, i.e., the 1930 literacy table should be joined to the 1930 shapefile. Select GISJOIN as both the join field and target field. Once the layers have been joined, close the properties dialogue box and right-click on the shapefiles to open the attribute tables. New fields for the total population, literate population, and the calculated percentage fields should appear as new columns.

STEP 4: SYMBOLIZE THE DATA TO CREATE A VISUAL NARRATIVE

To display literacy data, it is necessary to symbolize the newly joined shapefiles. Right-click on the shapefiles and open the properties dialogue box. Select the symbology tab in the left-hand menu and click on the green plus to add a new rule. The default display is a single symbol. This can be changed using the drop-down menu at the top of the dialogue box. Other options include categorized, graduated, and rule-based. A categorized render helps display distinct categories, such as the significant political affiliation of each state. A graduated render shows quantitative differences using a range of colors. For example, a graduated render of literacy rates would display states with low literacy in light colors and states with higher literacy in progressively darker colors. A rule-based render allows users to create defined rules and expressions using SQL-based queries.

Numerical data is best symbolized using the graduated symbology. After changing the display to graduated, use the dropdown menu to select the value to display. For this tutorial, choose the column that contains the calculated percentage of the population that is literate. Use the color ramp to select a preferred color scheme. Click on the "classify" button to create the symbology, and click on "apply" to display the new values on the map. The examples below show literacy rates in 1880 and 1930, from highest (dark) to lowest (white), organized into five classes. This is shown in Image 4 and Image 5.

The numerical ranges for each class may not be the same for the 1880 and 1930 maps. This can be seen in the legends for each shape layer.

The literacy rate increased between 1880 and 1930, resulting in different data ranges. In 1880, the literacy rate ranged from 56 to 98 percent; in

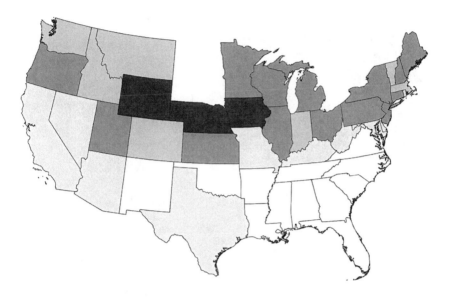

Image 4: Literate individuals as a percentage of the total population 10 years and older in 1880, from highest (dark) to lowest (white) (NHGIS Data Finder database, *https://data2.nhgis.org*).

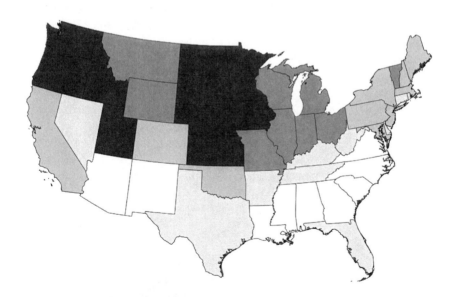

Image 5: Literate individuals as a percentage of the total population 10 years and older in 1930, from highest (dark) to lowest (white) (NHGIS Data Finder database, *https://data2.nhgis.org*).

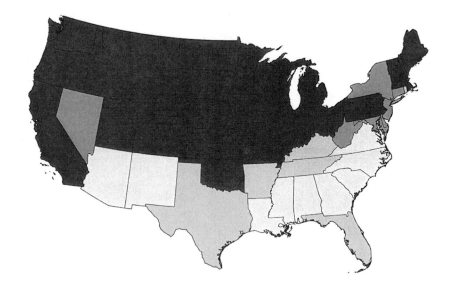

Image 6: Literate population in 1930 displayed with a rule-based render (NHGIS Data Finder database, *https://data2.nhgis.org*).

1930, the range was 84 to 99 percent. Using the QGIS autogenerated classifications, one might look at the maps and assume that some southern states saw no increase in literacy over time and that Arizona experienced a decrease in overall literacy. This could be fixed through data normalization or by altering the rules for symbolization. Image 6 shows the 1930 literacy rate by state using a rule-based render to create classes that match the 1880 values.

According to the National Center for Education Statistics, changes in literacy rates between 1880 and 1930 were largely driven by post-civil war educational opportunities for the African American population (1993). A more in-depth project could calculate percentage change by race, which would show a narrowing gap as more people gained the right to primary education.

Conclusion

The U.S. Census Bureau is the federal government's largest statistical agency. It is the "leading source of information on the nation's people, places, and economy," yielding counts of "population size and growth as well as detailed portraits of the changing characteristics of our communities" (U.S. Census Bureau 2021). This essay provides a small sample of the online resources available to help educators present this immense amount of data in easy-to-digest summaries and visualizations. Additional tutorials based on instruction sessions at Austin Peay State University's Woodward Library demonstrate methods for creating original maps as supplemental materials for specific historical topics. Incorporating census data in the classroom can establish history as a cross-curricular subject, blending it with statistics, geography, and sociology. It can also serve as an introduction to primary source and data-driven research.

REFERENCES

Anderson, Mark, and Marianne Ryan. 2012. "One Hundred and Eighty Years of Great Statistical Collections from the U.S. Census Bureau: A Retrospective." *Reference and User Services Quarterly* 52, no. 1: 30–32. https://journals.ala.org/index.php/rusq/article/view/3796/4149.

At Least Some High School (1 to 4 Years): High School 4 Years. 1940. Social Explorer based on data Digitally transcribed by Inter-university Consortium for Political and Social Research. Edited, verified by Michael Haines. Compiled, edited, and verified by Social Explorer. Accessed July 19, 2022.

Blake, Kellee. 1996. "'First in the Path of the Firemen': The Fate of the 1890 Population Census, Part 2." *Prologue Magazine* 28, no. 1 (Spring). https://www.archives.gov/publications/prologue/1996/spring/1890-census-2.html.

Census Office. 1860. *Instructions to U.S. Marshalls. Instructions to Assistants.* Washington, D.C.: George W. Bowman, Public Printer. https://www.census.gov/history/pdf/1860instructions.pdf.

High School Graduate or more (includes equivalency). 2000. Social Explorer (based on data from U.S. Census Bureau). Accessed July 19, 2022, at 16:27:07 GMT-5.

Manson, Steven, Jonathan Schroeder, David Van Riper, Tracy Kugler, and Steven Ruggles. 2021. IPUMS National Historical Geographic Information System: Version 16.0 [dataset]. Minneapolis: IPUMS. http://doi.org/10.18128/D050.V16.0.

National Archives and Records Administration. n.d. "1860 Federal Census." Archives.gov. National Archives and Records Administration. Accessed June 15, 2022. https://www.archives.gov/files/research/genealogy/charts-forms/1860-census.pdf.

National Center for Education Statistics. 1993. "Literacy from 1870 to 1979." National Center for Education Statistics. https://nces.ed.gov/naal/lit_history.asp.

Schor, Paul. 2017. *Counting Americans: How the US Census Classified the Nation.* New York: Oxford University Press.

Social Explorer. n.d. "Resources for Educators and Students." Accessed June 15, 2022. https://www.socialexplorer.com/teach-and-learn/data-snacks?category=.

U.S. Census Bureau. n.d.a. "History: 1790." Accessed June 15, 2022. https://www.census.gov/history/www/through_the_decades/index_of_questions/1790_1.html.

U.S. Census Bureau. n.d.b. "History: 2020." Accessed June 15, 2022. https://www.census.gov/history/www/through_the_decades/index_of_questions/2020.html.

U.S. Census Bureau. n.d.c. "History: Tracts and Block Numbering Areas." Accessed June 15, 2022. https://www.census.gov/history/www/programs/geography/tracts_and_block_numbering_areas.html.

U.S. Census Bureau. 1961. "Enumeration Schedules and Instructions." 1960 Census of Population: Volume 1. Characteristics of the Population. https://www2.census.gov/library/publications/decennial/1960/population-volume-1/vol-01-01-d.pdf.

U.S. Census Bureau. 2021. "Census Bureau 101 for Students." Last revised October 8, 2021. https://www.census.gov/programs-surveys/sis/about/students101.html.

U.S. Census Bureau. 2021a. "Our Censuses." https://www.census.gov/programs-surveys/censuses.html.

U.S. Census Bureau. 2021b. "What We Do." https://www.census.gov/about/what.html.

Whitby, Andrew. 2020. *The Sum of the People: How the Census Has Shaped Nations, from the Ancient World to the Modern Age*. New York: Basic Books.

Back to School

Education and Teaching Resources from the U.S. Government

Emily Rogers *and* Laurie Aycock

Introduction

One of the most plentiful areas of government information publication is the field of education. Tools for online learning include basic information sources, but many departments have created specific content for educational purposes. This content comes in the form of quizzes, games, and other activities and, in some cases, more complex online learning modules. While the U.S. Department of Education is an obvious choice for education information, almost any federal government department provides material that librarians can help current and future teachers consult for professional needs and adapt for classroom use. From science and health to civic and financial literacy to the arts and humanities, these resources cover a vast variety of subjects. Best of all, this information is free! This essay contains sections covering resources that librarians can recommend to educators. Spending time with these materials will give current and future teachers the information to increase their own knowledge about their teaching careers and to initiate creative lesson plans and classroom activities.

U.S. Department of Education

The most obvious federal website to begin the search for education and teaching resources is the U.S. Department of Education at https://www.ed.gov/. The homepage primarily serves as an entry point for further information on laws and regulations, grants, student loans, and data. Understanding the various offices that comprise the Department of Education can help visitors navigate this complex website. The list at https://www2.ed.gov/about/offices/list/index.html provides overviews and links to the home pages of offices such as the Office of Elementary & Secondary Education and the Office of English Language Acquisition, where the search bar is available to search for lesson plans, activities, and other resources. Librarians who provide homeschooling support may be especially interested in the Parents page at https://www2.ed.gov/parents/landing.jhtml?src=ln which includes sections of links for early childhood education, special education, reading resources, and "help your child learn" resources. Even more specific resources on education data are available at the National Center for Education Statistics (NCES) Kids' Zone website at https://nces.ed.gov/nceskids/about.asp. Games, quizzes, skill building drills, and facts and advice on education in general and college are available.

Another valuable NCES tool is the Common Core of Data "Search for Public Schools" database at https://nces.ed.gov/ccd/schoolsearch/. This search provides access to data on enrollment, student/teacher ratio, free and reduced-price lunch eligible numbers, and more about individual public schools and districts. A similar search is available for private schools at https://nces.ed.gov/surveys/pss/privateschoolsearch/. For the public school district search, information not only on enrollment but also on staffing and funding, including total revenue by state, local, or federal sources, is available. While there are some career development and job search resources available on the Ed.gov site, these school search resources can further assist future teachers in previewing schools and making career decisions.

More teaching and learning materials are available by moving beyond the ed.gov website to the many federal agencies that have developed resources that aim to support classroom teachers and provide additional learning opportunities for students. The remainder of this essay is divided into sections that focus on civic engagement and literacy; science, technology, engineering, and math (STEM); health and medical resources; data and financial literacy; and history, arts, and the humanities.

Civic Engagement and Literacy

Civics education is a part of state education standards throughout the United States. Many government agencies provide resources to aid educators in meeting those standards. The National Archives and Records

Administration (NARA) "Educator Resources" website at https://www. archives.gov/education has a multitude of resources for teaching civics literacy and engagement. For example, "We Rule: Civics for All of US" is an interactive distance learning program with several webinar modules for elementary school students. The "DocsTeach" online tool houses over 12,000 primary source documents—including letters, speeches, and videos—and nearly 2,000 engaging activities on topics from the American Revolution to contemporary times. With the "Working with Primary Sources" website, the document analysis worksheets are available to help students develop skills in understanding primary documents are available in two categories: one for younger students or those learning English, and the other for intermediate and secondary students. Educators can also access "Distance Learning" programs for their classes and "Professional Development Webinars."

NARA's DocsTeach "Elections and Voting" page at https://www. docsteach.org/topics/election provides teaching resources on topics such as the Electoral College and the expansion of voting rights. There are also suggested teaching activities on topics such as "Extending Suffrage to Women." USA.gov's "Voting and Elections" page at https://www.usa.gov/ voting offers links to frequent questions about voting and the presidential election process. The website is text-based and does not offer lesson plans or activities, but it could be navigated easily by older students. The U.S. Election Assistance Commission's "Voter's Guide to Federal Elections" website, https://www.eac.gov/voters/voters-guide-to-federal-elections, provides a downloadable voter's guide and a fact sheet about voting in multiple languages such as Chinese and Spanish. It also provides information on registering to vote and links to each state's election websites.

The U.S. Government Publishing Office's "Ben's Guide to the U.S. Government," https://bensguide.gpo.gov, instructs students about themes related to the U.S. government and about citizenship. Three modules of Learning Adventures, divided by age ranges, provide information on branches of U.S. governments, how laws are made, and on federally recognized tribes. A parents and educators page explains how the Learning Adventure modules are set up and provides links to other U.S. government websites for students and educators. The website is primarily text-based and will require students to read all the information or have it read to them. There are several interactive games that students can play, as well as printable crossword puzzles and word searches.

The Peace Corps' "Educators" webpage at https://www.peacecorps. gov/educators/ describes online education resources based on Peace Corps volunteers' experiences available through the Paul L. Coverdell World Wise Schools program. Nearly five hundred activities are available, searchable by type—such as lesson plans, recipes, and personal essays—or by topic, including international understanding, cuisine, or environment. Through the Global Connections program, educators can submit requests for a Peace Corps volunteer to interact with their classes through letter or email exchanges, webchats, or virtual or in-person presentations.

Science, Technology, Engineering, and Math

As the world grows increasingly complex, it is essential that students develop skills in Science, Technology, Engineering, and Math (STEM) literacy, problem solving, and critical thinking. It is also necessary to ensure that students have access to quality resources no matter where they live. Numerous federal agencies provide such resources for educators that are standards-based, developed by experts, and freely accessible.

The U.S. Department of Education's STEM webpage at https://www.ed.gov/stem is an excellent starting point. Teachers can sign up for the department's monthly STEM newsletter, which highlights funding opportunities, resources such as training programs and webinars, and STEM information from other government agencies. Archived newsletters are also available for viewing. STEM Education Briefings are live-streamed videos on a variety of topics including early math, summertime STEM, and environmental literacy. Educators can register for upcoming briefings as well as view archived recordings and presentation slides from previous briefings. The page provides links to other federal agency STEM websites with which the department collaborates in support of STEM initiatives. Links to grant application resources and to discretionary grant programs are provided for educators to apply for funding for STEM education projects.

The National Oceanic and Atmospheric Administration's (NOAA) "Education" portal at https://www.noaa.gov/education is an extensive "one stop shop" for all their resources for teachers and students. Under "Resource collections: Browse by topic," topics available include oceans, weather, climate, freshwater, and marine life. Resources for each topic include lessons and activities, background information, career information, multimedia resources, and data resources. There are also sections for "Data Resources for Educators" and "Education at Home." Under "Opportunities," there are links to educator opportunities, student opportunities, and grant information. Educator opportunities include links to information on science fairs and festivals, webinars, teacher workshops and training modules, and virtual school talks. Opportunities for students from K–12 through Postdoc include science camps and events, photo contests, internships, fellowships, and scholarships.

The National Weather Service's (NWS) "NWS Education" website at https://www.weather.gov/education/ provides numerous educator resources and student opportunities to learn about the weather and atmosphere. The Jetstream Online Weather Schools provide lesson plans on fifteen subjects such as the atmosphere, the ocean, satellites, and tsunamis. Data resources for the classroom, Citizen Science activities, videos on weather safety, and virtual visits from a meteorologist ("Connect with the NWS") are also included.

NOAA's "Teaching Climate," https://www.climate.gov/teaching, is a website for resources on climate literacy. It includes access to over 700 resources for teaching climate and energy. Clicking on the "See All Teaching Climate" link from the homepage, resources are searchable by grade level, from middle school to upper college, topic, or climate literacy principle. Some resources include Spanish versions. Materials include experiments, interactive tools, and multimedia resources.

The National Aeronautics and Space Administration's (NASA) "STEM Engagement" website at https://www.nasa.gov/stem provides almost 2,000 resources for educators and students from grades K–12 as well as higher education. The materials are searchable by grade level, subject, and/or type of material. Types of materials include educator guides and lesson plans, coloring sheets and games, art projects, and mobile apps. Teachers can sign up for the NASA Express email list, https://www.nasa.gov/stem/express, to receive weekly STEM updates. NASA also offers professional development opportunities for educators, such as webinars and virtual classroom workshops. Several of NASA's Space Flight Centers and other offices, such as Johnson Space Center and Kennedy Space Center, have their own web pages dedicated to teacher resources, such as leveled readers, math resources, educator professional development opportunities, career guidance, and lesson toolkits. These are listed in the Appendix. NASA's Kids' Club at https://www.nasa.gov/kidsclub/index.html provides games and activities for pre–K through 4th grade students. The "Kids' Club Picture Show" is a gallery of selected NASA pictures. Students can also view a slideshow of current and past astronaut crews on the International Space Station.

The U.S. Department of Agriculture's (USDA) Outreach and Education page at https://www.fsa.usda.gov/programs-and-services/outreach-and-education/index provides educator resources through its online National Agricultural Library (NAL) and through its various agency websites. The NAL has links to activities and curricula on agricultural literacy, as well as information on vocational education and job training. Within the USDA, the Forest Service "Conservation Education" Educator Toolbox at https://www.fs.usda.gov/main/conservationeducation is a page full of resources on forests and grasslands for students from early childhood through high school. Teachers can access background resources for lesson plans and links to professional development opportunities. Distance learning adventures, such as PollinatorLIVE, can be found in the Educator Toolbox under the grade levels. This includes webcasts, lesson plans, and videos. Educators can order materials for their students such as the *Natural Inquirer*, https://www.naturalinquirer.org/, an education journal produced for middle school science students, as well as educational materials featuring Smokey Bear and Woodsy Owl.

Natural Resources Conservation Service's (NRCS) "Resources" link at https://www.nrcs.usda.gov/about features resources on soil education, the water cycle, clean water activities, and backyard conservation lesson plans. S.K. Worm, the "official annelid" of the NRCS, guides students through activities about soil.

The U.S. Department of Energy's "DOE STEM" website, https://www.energy.gov/doe-stem/doe-stem, provides all the agency's STEM-related resources for students, teachers, and people in the workforce. Educators can access lesson plans, study guides, and classroom activities. Virtual and in-person events, such as online chats with STEM professionals, virtual tours, competitions, and videos, are searchable by grade level. College students, from undergraduates to Postdocs, can learn about internships, fellowships, contests, and competitions. Educators can receive monthly updates by subscribing to the STEM Rising Newsletter.

The United States Environmental Protection Agency's (EPA) "Learning and Teaching about the Environment" at https://www.epa.gov/students provides kindergarten through high school students with environmental education resources. Homework resources and activities include games, quizzes, activity books, and links to videos. Some of the topics covered are air, water, and recycling. In some cases, Spanish versions are available. Educator resources include environmental curriculum guides and lesson plans, links to professional development opportunities and grant information, and information on ordering free environmental publications for the classroom. Contact information for Regional Environmental Education Coordinators is provided so educators can find information on local resources, EPA programs, and EPA speakers.

The U.S. Department of the Interior Bureau of Land Management's "Teachers" website, https://www.blm.gov/educators, offers educational programs and activities on topics such as public lands management, habitats, and wildlife. Classroom investigations for secondary school teachers provide teaching guides, individual activities, and links to information on careers and service learning. Project Archeology and Hands on the Land are field classrooms for hands-on learning in natural and archeological settings. An "Educational Activities Database" provides comprehensive, standards-based activities searchable by subject, keywords, or grade level.

Health and Medical

Several U.S government agencies provide educator resources on health and medical topics including brain health, public health, early childhood development, and nutrition. The National Institutes of Health's (NIH) "STEM Teaching Resources" website, https://science.education.nih.gov, includes a comprehensive list of resources available from all the NIH offices, centers, and institutes. Resources for K–12 students include activities and coloring pages, apps, and games. Educator resources cover topics such as environmental health, healthy brains, preventing drug abuse, and eye and ear health.

The National Institute of General Medical Sciences' "Science Education" website, https://www.nigms.nih.gov/science-education, is a colorful page where educators can assess activities, multimedia resources, and STEM education projects for pre-kindergarten through high school students. Topics include Being a Scientist, Cells, Molecular Structures, and Chemistry. Scientists from the National Institute of Environmental Health Sciences' "Speakers Bureau," https://www.niehs.nih.gov/health/scied/speaker/index.cfm, are available to speak to classes on topics involving the environment and health, as well as on their job responsibilities and career experiences.

The Centers for Disease Control and Prevention's (CDC) "STEM at CDC," https://www.cdc.gov/stem/index.html, provides public health resources for kindergarten through high school students and educators as well as programs for college students. Student resources include comics, games, and apps such as the CDC Health IQ app and independent learning activities. Educator resources support teachers in providing real-world public health problems by focusing on skills such as critical thinking, problem solving, and collaboration. The CDC Science Ambassador Fellowship, https://www.cdc.gov/scienceambassador/, and regional training workshops are opportunities for STEM educators to network with CDC scientists, public health professionals, and other faculty to learn strategies for teaching public health concepts such as epidemiology and public health careers. Fellowships and internships are available for high school and college students interested in pursuing a career in public health.

For early childhood educators, the CDC's "Developmental Milestones Resources for Early Childhood Educators" webpage, https://www.cdc.gov/

ncbddd/actearly/Information-for-Early-Childhood-Educators.html,offers a free online training course. "Watch Me: Celebrating Milestones and Sharing Concerns" is a one-hour, four-module course on tools and best practices for monitoring development and communication with parents. The website offers free milestone checklists, children's books, and tip sheets for parents. These are free to download and print and are available in multiple languages.

Several agencies offer educator resources on nutrition, health, and food safety. The U.S. Food and Drug Administration's (FDA) "Nutrition Education Resources & Materials," https://www.fda.gov/food/food-labeling-nutrition/nutrition-education-resources-materials, provides hands-on games and activities about reading nutrition labels and "Science and Our Food Supply" teacher guides on topics such as food safety and dietary supplements for middle and high school students. The "Student & Teachers: Science Education" website, https://www.fda.gov/food/resources-you-food/students-teachers, offers links to the FDA's Professional Development Program in Food Science for middle and high school educators, the Food Safety A-Z Reference Guide, and the food safety education month activities.

The USDA offers a variety of resources on nutrition education. The Food and Nutrition Service's "Nutrition Education Materials" page, https://www.fns.usda.gov/tn/nutrition-education-materials, links to curriculum plans and teachers guides on MyPlate and standards-based nutrition education for elementary school students. MyPlate, https://www.myplate.gov/, is the USDA's nutrition guide, based on the Dietary Guidelines for Americans. It demonstrates the components of a healthy meal to enable Americans to make educated food choices. "Printable Materials and Handouts" from Nutrition.gov at https://www.nutrition.gov/topics/basic-nutrition/printable-materials-and-handouts covers topics such as recipes, reducing food waste, MyPlate print materials and activity sheets, and lesson plans on physical activity and food safety. The "For Parents, Caregivers, and Teachers" webpage provides links to resources on healthy eating and nutrition for pre-teens and teenagers at https://www.nutrition.gov/topics/nutrition-age/teens/parents-caregivers-and-teachers. For example, "Team Nutrition Cooks!" is a program that can be used in afterschool programs to teach elementary school students kid-friendly recipes that can spark an interest in healthy eating. Another example is "Fueling My Healthy Life," a project-based plan with multimedia resources, lesson activities, and assessment for teachers, and a Student Portal with interactive videos and quizzes for students.

Data and Financial Literacy

Building data and financial literacy is a primary concern for many educators as well as for those working in the financial and economic sectors. To address the need for learners to develop statistical skills, the U.S. Census Bureau launched the online "Statistics in Schools" program at https://www.census.gov/programs-surveys/sis.html. Created by teachers, subject area specialists, and educational standards experts, this extensive website provides teachers' guides and individual and classroom activities to help students apply real-life statistical data from the Census Bureau in subjects such as English language, history, math, geography, and sociology. Students learn that numbers can tell stories as they continue to explore monthly highlights, Constitution Day fun facts, congressional apportionment resources, and other materials connecting civic engagement with numerical data.

A variety of federal government agencies provide resources to help teachers lead instruction and help students develop financial literacy. The Federal Deposit Insurance Corporation's (FDIC) Money Smart Resources website at https://www.fdic.gov/resources/consumers/money-smart/ offers teaching and learning resources to assist educators and parents. The "Teach Money Smart" website offers accessible entry into five customized age-related resources: Money Smart sections for Young People, Young Adults, Adults, Older Adults, and Small Business.

One of the goals of Money Smart is to "help individuals build financial skills and confidence through knowledge and practice" (FDIC 2021). A recent addition to the Money Smart website is a series of financial games and related resources, "How Money Smart Are You?," listed under "Learn Money Smart," https://www.fdic.gov/resources/consumers/money-smart/ learn-money-smart/index.html. Viewers can play computer-assisted online games with or without an account on topics such as "Borrowing Basics," "Your Money Values and Influences," and "Making Housing Decisions." While the games are colorful and upbeat, the time commitments—10 to 25 minutes per game—and the subject matter make these games more suitable as learning tools for young adult to adult players than for children.

Not to be confused with the FDIC's Money Smart Resources, since 2002, the Federal Reserve Bank of Chicago offers an annual financial literacy week in April titled "Money Smart Week." While not an official federal agency, the Federal Reserve operates because of a federal Act of Congress and provides information for the public. Money Smart Week provides resources available online throughout the year at https://www. moneysmartweek.org/. Recordings of webinars from past years' observations include topics on saving, student loans, fraud, identity theft, and managing personal finances during the 2020 Covid pandemic. Information on community participation in the annual Money Smart Week is also available on the site; many programs take place in public and academic libraries. The American Library Association has co-sponsored Money Smart Week for several years, https://www.moneysmartweek. org/program-supporters/ala.

Of wider application is the Federal Reserve Board's website "Federal Reserve Education," https://www.federalreserveeducation.org/, with the goal of "equipping educators, educating students, and empowering consumers" (Federal Reserve Board, n.d.). Resources are available by audiences for grades K–4, 5–8, 9–12, college age, and adults. Several of the twelve Federal Reserve district banks also offer print (usually available in single copies) and downloadable financial literacy publications in English and some in Spanish for use in classrooms and with the public. For example, the Federal Reserve Bank of St. Louis (n.d.) provides a professional development opportunity on data literacy for librarians and is available at https://research.stlouisfed.org/info-services/ data-literacy-for-librarians/. For classroom use, the page "Resources for Teachers & Students in Economics and Personal Finance" at https://www. stlouisfed.org/education offers "Tools for Teaching with FRED," or Federal Reserve Economic Data, with lesson plans, classroom activities, tutorials, and instructional guides. This page also provides links to "Tools for Teaching with FRASER," or Federal Reserve Archival System for Economic Research, the archival source for Federal Reserve economic data, and to "Tools for Teaching with GEOFRED," which provides mapping resources for use with economic data. These sources are accessible under "For Teachers & Students." Finally, the St. Louis Fed website also provides the "Econ Lowdown Teacher Portal" located at https://econlowdown.org, which contains a resource gallery of economic materials, the capacity for K–12 and college instructors to create online classrooms and syllabi, and to monitor student progress through provided virtual educational materials.

Another source for financial literacy materials is the Internal Revenue Service, which for years produced the print series *Understanding Taxes* in various print and toolkit editions. Related resources came online in 2014 in the "Understanding Taxes" website/app at https://apps.irs.gov/ app/understandingTaxes/. This teachers' site, described as the "quick and simple way to understand your taxes," offers customizable and downloadable classroom resources as well as a student website with tutorials, activities, and simulations in which students can investigate twenty different taxpayers' tax issues. Because "Understanding Taxes" is based on 2014 tax law, the website directs users interested in current tax law to other resources. As an introduction to comprehending the principles of taxes for consumers, however, the "Understanding Taxes" website provides useful guidance and training for educators and students.

History, Arts, and the Humanities

Educators and librarians seeking resources for history, the arts, and the humanities can fruitfully begin their search with a tour of the Library of Congress (LOC) educator website at https://www.loc.gov/education/. "Today in History" offers a daily posting, including weekend days, of primary document material featuring images, historical facts, and additional resources. "America's Library," for elementary and middle school students, introduces biographical, music, geographic, games, activities, and reviews for U.S. historical periods. "Resources for Family Engagement" includes author programs, activity kits for various age groups, and printable images from the LOC's manuscript and print collections. Teachers can explore the "Teacher Resources" area to discover primary source sets, lesson plans, and professional development resources. "Read.gov" celebrates reading for all ages, including "Read Around the States" videos that feature members of Congress reading aloud their favorite books for children. Additional features include links to the LOC Literacy Awards, the "Celebrating Poems in Rural Communities" project, suggested reading lists, and Braille materials.

The Smithsonian Institution offers a wealth of materials for educators' and librarians' use in every field in which the organization has a museum. The Educator Resources page at https://www.si.edu/educators offers sections for teachers, including distance learning resources (under "Educator Resources"), professional development, and listed under each topic are additional pages for each Smithsonian Museum. "Fun Stuff for Kids and Teens" at https://www.si.edu/kids offers activities such as games, activities, and learning labs. These are divided into Art, History, and Culture; Science and Nature; and collection features. From reproductions of paintings to *Star Wars* to insects to robotic telescopes, educators, parents, and students can find activities and entertainment featuring the vast collections of the museums and other organizations parented by the Smithsonian.

Finally, the U.S. House of Representatives offers access to resources for educators, librarians, and students at https://history.house.gov/. The "History, Art & Archives" website offers virtual tours, resources for planning class visits, lesson plans, education fact sheets, primary source materials, a House History timeline, House trivia, and a glossary of terms frequently used by Congress.

Conclusion

This essay merely begins to name and describe the array of education resources available from the federal government for the assistance of librarians, educators, and families. Wherever a search for teaching support might start, ending up with these federal resources for educators and librarians will result in a rich collection of learning tools on a wide variety of topics. When in doubt, check individual agency websites for educational resources. In addition to the sites and other resources mentioned, the Appendix adds further online sites with valuable materials for this audience.

REFERENCES

Federal Deposit Insurance Corporation. 2021. "Money Smart Resources." https://www.fdic.gov/resources/consumers/money-smart/index.html.
Federal Reserve Board. n.d. "Federal Reserve Education.org." Accessed February 19, 2022. https://www.federalreserveeducation.org/.
Federal Reserve Bank of St. Louis. n.d. "Data Literacy for Librarians." Accessed February 19, 2022. https://research.stlouisfed.org/info-services/data-literacy-for-librarians/.

APPENDIX: ADDITIONAL U.S. GOVERNMENT EDUCATION AND TEACHING RESOURCES

Animal and Plant Health Inspection Service, https://www.aphis.usda.gov/aphis/resources/pests-diseases/hungry-pests/usda-efforts/educator-tools.
Bureau of Economic Analysis, https://www.bea.gov/resources/learning-center/bea-in-the-classroom.
National Air and Space Museum, https://airandspace.si.edu/learn.
National Institute of Food and Agriculture, https://nifa.usda.gov/agriculture-education-toolkit.
National Institute of Standards and Technology, https://www.nist.gov/education.
National Museum of African Art Student Gallery, https://africa.si.edu/education/student-gallery/.
National Museum of African American History and Culture, https://nmaahc.si.edu/learn/educators.
National Museum of American History, https://historyexplorer.si.edu/.
National Museum of Asian Art, https://asia.si.edu/learn/for-educators/.
National Museum of Natural History, https://naturalhistory.si.edu/education.
National Museum of the American Indian, https://americanindian.si.edu/nk360/lessons-resources/search-resources.
National Park Service, https://www.nps.gov/teachers/index.htm.
National Portrait Gallery, https://npg.si.edu/learn.
National Science Foundation, https://www.nsf.gov/news/classroom/.
National Zoo, https://nationalzoo.si.edu/education.
Smithsonian American Art Museum, https://americanart.si.edu/education.
Smithsonian Gardens, https://gardens.si.edu/learn/.
United States Botanic Garden, https://www.usbg.gov/educational-resources.
United States Patent and Trademark Office, https://www.uspto.gov/learning-and-resources/outreach-and-education.
Youth in Agriculture, https://www.usda.gov/youth.
Youth.gov Civic Engagement, https://youth.gov/youth-topics/civic-engagement-and-volunteering.

NASA Space Centers and Offices

Aeronautics Research Mission Directorate, https://www.nasa.gov/aeroresearch/resources/k-12.

Johnson Space Center STEM Engagement, https://www.nasa.gov/centers/johnson/stem/educators/index.html.

Kennedy Space Center Educator Resources, https://www.kennedyspacecenter.com/camps-and-education/educator-resources.

Langley Research Center STEM Engagement, https://www.nasa.gov/langley/education.

Marshall Space Flight Center STEM Engagement, https://www.nasa.gov/offices/stem/centers/marshall/home/index.html.

Financial Literacy 101

*Combating Misinformation and Debt with
Freely Available Government Resources*

CATERINA M. REED

Introduction

Navigating financial information and misinformation can be over-whelming for college students and recent college graduates. This can be due to the fact that most students are not familiar with financial literacy before entering college. Not all states require high school students to complete a financial literacy course in order to graduate. Although financial literacy legislation has increased in recent years (Morton 2021), high school education on this topic remains inadequate when compared to the international community. Data from a 2018 financial literacy survey illustrates that 15-year-olds from the U.S. have been surpassed by students of the same age in Canada, Estonia, and Finland (OECD 2020, 52). Therefore, it is critical that college students are equipped with financial literacy concepts before they graduate.

Financial literacy can help college students and recent graduates make informed decisions about their financial future. It is vital that students understand financial concepts for them to be confident in conversations relating to spending, saving, and investing money. Financial literacy is crucial for students. It allows them to recognize how to protect themselves from high interest loans, financial disasters, and complex and nefarious scams.

This essay will discuss the importance of freely available government information relating to financial literacy and money management. As trained searchers, librarians must be aware of the vast government resources available that can help guide college students through common financial literacy topics. However, government information can be difficult to navigate and parse; being able to find financial resources quickly and easily provides its own set of challenges. This essay will help librarians examine and consider government resources relating to budgeting and money management, credit scores and history, student loans, filing taxes, and consumer protection in the context of research guides, library programming, and reference consultations.

Searching for Financial Literacy Information

It is not easy to find reliable information on financial literacy and wellness. For example, Google search results for the term "financial literacy" display links from many .org and .com websites and even news articles. While these sources may have helpful information, it is best to consult government information that is specifically curated for consumer understanding and not for the purposes of generating profit. It should be noted that government websites do not make it to the first page of Google search results when one searches "financial literacy." Composing the search "government financial literacy" illustrates a drastic difference with all of the search results displaying .gov websites. A more specific way to filter Google results is to place the government website next to chosen search terms; for example, "environmental impact rocky flats site:epa.gov" (Brown 2020, 22) or, for this essay's purposes, "financial literacy site:usa.gov." Keep in mind that this more targeted way of searching only works if the government website or database is indexed by Google (Brown 2020, 19). Understanding how to search for government information is a step toward increasing financial literacy.

Government resources cover wide-ranging financial literacy issues; however, information can be found across various government websites. To clarify, Table 1 is constructed to illustrate where information surrounding certain financial topics can be found on the corresponding government websites.

Table 1. Non-Exhaustive List of Government Websites and Corresponding Topics

	Consumer. gov	Consumer Finance. gov	Federal Trade Commission (FTC.gov)	IRS. gov	Identity Theft.gov	StudentAid. gov	USA. gov
Budgeting	x						x
Credit cards, scores & history	x	x					x

	Consumer.gov	Consumer Finance.gov	Federal Trade Commission (FTC.gov)	IRS.gov	Identity Theft.gov	StudentAid.gov	USA.gov
Student loans		x				x	x
Filing taxes				x			x
Consumer protection	x	x	x		x		x

This essay is broken down by financial topic in the following order:
- Budgeting and money management
- Credit scores and history
- Student loans
- Filing taxes
- Consumer protection

In each section, the specific financial topic and pertinent government information will be explored.

Budgeting and Money Management

When assisting a student with financial literacy concepts, the first question you may want to ask is "what are your long-term financial goals?" Librarians can frame the daunting financial literacy conversation and help students have a healthy and open conversation about money. For many students, this may be the first time they are being asked this type of open-ended question. After identifying financial goals, students will be able to construct budgets with these goals in mind. The best place for a student to start their financial literacy journey is to create a personal budget. In the process of creating a budget, college students will have to collate their financial documents (e.g., pay stubs, student loan information, daily and recurring expenses). By creating a budget, college students will have a better understanding of where their money is coming from, where it is going, and how to reassess their spending habits if necessary.

Knowing how to budget money is a foundational financial literacy concept. A solid government resource to start with is the Federal Trade Commission's (FTC) Consumer.gov "Making a Budget" website, https://consumer.gov/managing-your-money/making-budget. Unlike many other government websites, Consumer.gov is not overwhelming and is easy to use, especially for users unfamiliar with financial literacy. This website helps to define key budget terms and provides a free, downloadable budget worksheet to complete. Consumer.gov is a valuable financial literacy resource, particularly for educators, and includes already developed lesson plans. Another useful budgeting webpage is Dantus' "Budgeting: How to create a budget and stick with it." This resource provides direct links to key downloadable Consumer Financial Protection Bureau tools such as the "Income Tracker," "Spending Tracker," "Bill Calendar," and "Budget Worksheet" (Dantus 2019). In using these tracking tools, students and recent graduates will have a grasp of budgeting in a comprehensive way.

For students who are already familiar with budgeting, librarians can introduce money management tools. Money management websites, such as MyMoney.gov, can be helpful in providing tips on saving and investing, protecting, spending, and borrowing money. MyMoney.gov provides various financial articles based on specific life events (e.g., paying for higher education). Other money management websites and toolkits have been gamified, such as "How Money Smart Are You?" (Federal Deposit Insurance Corporation, n.d.) and "Find Out Your Financial Well-being" (Consumer Financial Protection Bureau, n.d.). These two sources are available in Spanish. The Federal Deposit Insurance Corporation (FDIC) Money Smart program has been expanded to include fourteen different games. The FDIC launched a Spanish version of the program in early 2022 (Federal Deposit Insurance Corporation, n.d.). In addition to the "How Money Smart Are You?" program, FDIC's Learn Money Smart page also provides access to the Money Smart Podcast Network and curated Parent/Caregiver guides grouped by grade level. The Parent/Caregiver guides are excellent resources for college students who may have younger siblings at home or are parents themselves.

Credit Scores and History

According to Youth.gov, the rates of college student debt and credit card debt have increased dramatically (n.d.). College students may experience difficulty finding jobs, and if they are also incurring debt, it is crucial that they understand how to maintain financial health and wellness before getting into vicious cycles of relying on credit. Carrying a credit card balance does more than just affect credit score. It can be more difficult to pay back with variable high annual percentage rates (APR) and increasing inflation. Terms such as credit scores, specifically the phrase "FICO score," can be confusing to students. FICO, which stands for Fair Isaac Corporation, is a type of credit score, but how it is calculated can vary across different businesses and credit companies (Consumer Financial Protection Bureau 2020). Credit scores can vary from 300 to 850 (Consumer Financial

Protection Bureau 2020); scores above 700 are typically considered very good. The web pages "Credit, Loans and Debt," https://consumer.gov/section/credit-loans-debt, and "Credit and Debt," https://consumer.ftc.gov/credit-loans-and-debt/credit-and-debt, can be helpful starting points in explaining basic credit definitions, such as the difference between good and bad credit, and more advanced financial concepts including credit discrimination and payday loans.

One of the most empowering tools in understanding credit is a credit report. There is pressure on having a good credit score because it can have an impact on obtaining various loans, insurance, and even the chance of getting a job. For individuals who need to repair their credit, there may be additional pressure in "fixing" their credit by way of paying a debt consolidation agency. Before resorting to paying an organization—legitimate or fraudulent—students and graduates should be steered towards AnnualCreditReport.com. While AnnualCreditReport.com is not a government website itself, it is a recommended resource by the Consumer Financial Protection Bureau (2022). AnnualCreditReport.com is the only authorized website for individuals to receive a free copy of credit reports from one or more of the three credit bureaus: Equifax, Experian, and TransUnion. AnnualCreditReport.com can be intimidating for first-time users as it requires answers to detailed, seemingly tricky security questions which prevent unauthorized persons from accessing sensitive information. Once the questions have been answered, individuals are prompted to select which credit bureaus they would like to receive reports. It can be helpful to request a credit report from one of the three credit bureaus every six months in order to keep on top of any major credit changes or fraudulent charges. For example, a student can request their Equifax report in January and then request a report from Experian in July. By reviewing credit reports at least twice a year, students and graduates can be aware of any expected and unexpected financial changes. Examining a credit report can result in finding discrepancies. The webpage "Credit and Debt," https://consumer.ftc.gov/credit-loans-and-debt/credit-and-debt, has several articles on credit scores and why credit matters as well as sample letters on how to dispute errors relating to credit. Students and recent graduates must understand that it is possible to dispute credit errors and successfully remove errors from credit reports without having to pay an organization. Some students might not have credit cards or car loans yet but that does not mean that they should not be concerned about their credit reports and scores. Student loans, unpaid medical bills, and other bills sent to collection agencies are reported to credit bureaus. This will impact their credit scores. There is also the possibility of identity theft which will be addressed later in this essay.

Student Loans

Student loans are formidable debts that can take a lifetime to pay off. Student loans can have a positive impact on credit reports by establishing credit history before graduation. The longer the credit history, the better it is for credit scores. However, student loans can also have a negative impact on future purchases and loans. Large student loans can contribute to debt that exceeds the debt-to-income (DTI) ratio of 43 percent (Consumer Financial Protection Bureau 2019); debt in excess of the 43 percent DTI ratio can adversely affect the mortgage loan process. According to the Education Data Initiative's website, which gathers most of its statistics from government databases and research, "53% of millennials have not bought a home because [of] student loan debt" (Hanson 2022). It is important that currently enrolled college students receive in-depth financial aid counseling, or at the very least, review the Department of Education website, https://www.ed.gov, before committing to additional student loans. Students should be thoroughly educated on the different types of student loans and interest rates. They should also understand how to request loans only for necessary tuition and board costs. While this type of education is typically the responsibility of the financial aid office, librarians can be supportive of financial literacy in the area of student loans and forgiveness. Federal Student Aid, an office of the U.S. Department of Education, compiled a Financial Literacy Guidance that helps to explain loan borrowing needs and wants, private vs. federal loans, and repayment options (Federal Student Aid 2019). Librarians can have such government guidance readily available during consultations with students.

For current students, StudentAid.gov is essential in understanding the current and future impact of taking on student loans, particularly federal loans (Federal Student Aid, n.d.a). For recent college graduates, specifically those pursuing careers in the public sector, checking to see if they are eligible for the Public Service Loan Forgiveness (PSLF) program is a must. The PSLF program requires that graduates work full-time in a government or non-profit role. If graduates are working for an employer deemed "eligible," they must complete "120 qualifying payments" in order to meet the requirements for debt forgiveness (Federal Student Aid, n.d.b).

Filing Taxes

Filing taxes can be overwhelming even for the most experienced filers. The experience can be even more challenging for first-time filers, such as recent graduates, who are no longer claimed on their parent's tax returns. The most popular documents for working students and recent graduates are 1098-T (college tuition statement), 1098-E (student loan interest statement), and W-2s (employee wages) or 1099s (independent contractor wages). Before students decide to file taxes, they must first find out if their parent(s) plan to claim them as dependents when filing returns for the appropriate tax season. According to the Internal Revenue Service (IRS), to determine if a student is a dependent, the student must be under the age of 24. If the student is deemed independent, the student can file a tax return (2021).

The first step in helping independent filers is to guide them to IRS Free File (2020). It is possible, but unlikely, that college students and recent graduates are earning income above the threshold set by IRS Free File, which is currently $73,000 (2022a). Students filing taxes for the first time may have questions on how to use IRS Free File but might not know who to consult. The IRS created an extensive array of videos hosted on YouTube, one of which is "First Time Filing a Tax Return?" (2022b). Students, especially those who do not have a financial advisor or accountant at their disposal, may find the IRS video tutorials helpful.

Consumer Protection

Scammers and other nefarious parties can create additional challenges for those trying to maintain their financial health and wellness. While older adults most often tend to be the targets of financial fraud, scams (especially those that are Covid-19, cryptocurrency, or employment-related) can affect folks of all age groups. When presented with consumer protection resources, college students will be introduced to an aspect of financial literacy that can prevent them from being defrauded. Here is a listing of various government websites that provide extensive consumer protection information:

- *Consumer Financial Protection Bureau (CFPB)* | https://www.consumerfinance.gov/
  This is a comprehensive consumer protection and consumer education website. There are resources for college students as well as K–12 students, veterans, and older adults. There is a section of the website dedicated to librarians, which includes program ideas, virtual training, and outreach materials, https://www.consumerfinance.gov/consumer-tools/educator-tools/library-resources/. In addition to offering consumer education, CFPB allows for the submission of complaints about financial services. The section "Research & Reports," listed under "Data & Research," hosts free consumer financial reports and research

prepared and published by CFPB, which can be helpful for librarians and users.

- *Federal Trade Commission (FTC)* | https://www.ftc.gov/
This is where consumers can report various types of fraud and register for the national "Do Not Call" list. There are free resources regarding how to avoid scams in both English and Spanish that can be ordered in bulk, https://www.bulkorder.ftc.gov/. The FTC also has a library of media and videos relating to a variety of topics including loans, credit, and fraud, https://www.ftc.gov/news-events/topics.
- *IdentityTheft.gov* | https://www.identitytheft.gov
This is a government website, created by the FTC, specifically for consumers to report identity theft and fraud. Individuals can report instances of identity theft of various types such as medical, tax, or student loan-related, and also find sample dispute letters which can be sent to companies and credit bureaus.
- *United States Department of the Treasury* | https://home.treasury.gov/
This is a government meta-site that provides links to other government websites such as the IRS and Bureau of Engraving and Printing. The Department of the Treasury links to key webpages concerning taxation, fraud (particularly in relation to currency), purchasing bonds and securities, and submitting currency damage claims.
- *USA.gov* | https://www.usa.gov/
This website is a portal to U.S. government information and can be a helpful tool in wide-ranging topics such as employment, money and taxes, and how to go about finding unclaimed funds.

Financial Literacy Going Forward

With the basics covered, it is a good idea to check and see if your library created a financial literacy LibGuide; if not, creating a LibGuide would be a good next step. Several universities (e.g., University of Maryland, University of Illinois, Washington University in St. Louis, Florida State College at Jacksonville) created LibGuides specifically focused on financial literacy and provide links to financial aid resources. For example, the University of Oklahoma (OU) LibGuide, https://guides.ou.edu/financial_literacy/9things, highlights "9 Things Every College Student Should Know About Money," which is also a two-credit course available for OU students to take. Each major financial concept is broken down in a separate tab. Within each tab are helpful videos, books, websites, and additional resources.

Librarians can also consult with financial aid staff for university resources that can be included on a financial literacy LibGuide. In addition to creating a thorough LibGuide, one way to increase financial literacy is to embed some of these resources into an information literacy or government information instruction session. It may also be helpful to partner with your university financial aid office and host co-sponsored financial literacy events. For example, financial aid officers can be invited to speak at your library during Money Smart Week, https://www.moneysmartweek.org/, a national effort to increase financial literacy. Additionally, librarians can participate in pre-established campus-wide financial literacy events, such as the "Game of Life." As they enter the "Game of Life" event space, students are given a salary and must visit different tables where they learn how to budget with their pretend salary and see how spending habits and day-to-day costs add up. This event has been successful at institutions such as Stony Brook University (2018) and Champlain College (Champlain Media 2019).

Conclusion

Financial literacy is an essential skill for college students and recent graduates as they enter an oftentimes precarious job market and an even more precarious economy. Yet, trustworthy financial information can be hard to find and in this day and age, most people click on the first link they find in their search. Librarians can work to include government information, specifically regarding financial aid and literacy, to ensure that college students have a baseline of information to reference before making financial decisions. It is impossible to cover all of the topics discussed in this essay in one reference interaction; however, having educational resources easily accessible, creating and maintaining a financial literacy LibGuide, and hosting financial literacy events can have a lifetime effect on college students and recent graduates.

REFERENCES

Brown, Christopher C. 2020. *Mastering United States Government Information: Sources and Services*. Santa Barbara, CA: ABC-CLIO.
Champlain Media. 2019. "Game of Life Teaches Students About Budgeting and Everyday Expenses After Graduation." *The View*. October 23. https://view.champlain.edu/2019/10/23/game-of-life-teaches-students-about-budgeting-and-everyday-expenses-after-graduation/.
Consumer Financial Protection Bureau. n.d. "Find Out Your Financial Well-being." Accessed January 11, 2022. https://www.consumerfinance.gov/consumer-tools/financial-well-being/.

Consumer Financial Protection Bureau. 2019. "What Is a Debt-To-Income Ratio? Why Is the 43% Debt-To-Income Ratio Important?" Last reviewed November 15, 2019. https://www.consumerfinance.gov/ask-cfpb/what-is-a-debt-to-income-ratio-why-is-the-43-debt-to-income-ratio-important-en-1791/.

Consumer Financial Protection Bureau. 2020. "What Is a FICO score?" Last reviewed September 4, 2020. https://www.consumerfinance.gov/ask-cfpb/what-is-a-fico-score-en- 1883/.

Consumer Financial Protection Bureau. 2022. "How Do I Get a Copy of My Credit Reports?" Last reviewed January 1, 2022. https://www.consumerfinance.gov/ask-cfpb/how-do-i-get-a-copy-of-my-credit-reports-en-5/.

Dantus, Courtney-Rose. 2019. "Budgeting: How to Create a Budget and Stick with It." June 5. https://www.consumerfinance.gov/about-us/blog/budgeting-how-to-create-a-budget-and-stick-with-it/.

Federal Deposit Insurance Corporation. n.d. "How Money Smart Are You." Accessed January 11, 2022. https://www.fdic.gov/resources/consumers/money-smart/learn-money-smart/index.html.

Federal Student Aid. n.d.a. "Federal Student Loans for College or Career School are an Investment in Your Future." Accessed February 9, 2022. https://studentaid.gov/under stand-aid/types/loans.

Federal Student Aid. n.d.b. "Public Service Loan Forgiveness (PSLF)." Accessed February 9, 2022. https://studentaid.gov/manage-loans/forgiveness-cancellation/public-service.

Federal Student Aid. 2019. "Financial Literacy Guidance from Financial Student Aid." Accessed January 12, 2022. https://financialaidtoolkit.ed.gov/resources/fin-lit-guidance.pdf.

Hanson, Melanie. 2022. "Student Loan Debt Statistics." Last updated April 10, 2022. https://educationdata.org/student-loan-debt-statistics.

Internal Revenue Service. 2020. "IRS Free File: Ideal for Young and First-Time Filers." Accessed January 31, 2022. https://www.irs.gov/newsroom/irs-free-file-ideal-for-young-and-first-time-filers.

Internal Revenue Service. 2021. "Dependents." Accessed January 31, 2022. https://www.irs.gov/faqs/filing-requirements-status-dependents/dependents.

Internal Revenue Service. 2022a. "IRS Free File: Do Your Taxes for Free." Accessed February 3, 2022. https://www.irs.gov/filing/free-file-do-your-federal-taxes-for-free.

Internal Revenue Service. 2022b. "Videos." Accessed February 9, 2022. https://www.irs.gov/newsroom/videos.

Morton, Heather. 2021. "Financial Literacy 2021 Legislation." Accessed December 20, 2021. https://www.ncsl.org/financial-services/financial-literacy-2021-legislation.

OECD. 2020. *PISA 2018 Results (Volume IV): Are Students Smart about Money?* PISA. Paris: OECD Publishing. https://doi.org/10.1787/48ebd1ba-en.

Stony Brook University. 2018. "Top 12 Things a Graduate Should Know About 'The Game of Life.'" *Stony Brook University News*, May. https://news.stonybrook.edu/student-spotlight/top-12-things-a-graduate-should-know-about-the-game-of-life/.

Youth.gov. n.d. "Facts About Youth Financial Knowledge & Capability." Accessed December 28, 2021. https://youth.gov/youth-topics/financial-capability-literacy/facts.

Appendix

Financial Literacy LibGuides
Florida State College at Jacksonville. n.d. "Financial Literacy Libguide." Accessed February 2, 2022. https://guides.fscj.edu/financial_literacy.
University of Illinois. n.d. "Financial Literacy Libguide." Accessed February 2, 2022. https://guides.library.illinois.edu/c.php?g=348107&p=2346287.
University of Maryland. n.d. "Financial Literacy Libguide." Accessed February 2, 2022. https://lib.guides.umd.edu/financialliteracy.

University of Oklahoma. n.d. "Financial Literacy Libguide." Accessed February 2, 2022. https://guides.ou.edu/financial_literacy/9things.
Washington University in St. Louis. n.d. "Financial Literacy WashU Libguide." Accessed February 2, 2022. https://libguides.wustl.edu/financial-literacy-college-students.

PART III

Genealogy

Using Federal Government Documents for Genealogy Research

Jennifer Crowder Daugherty
and Andrew Grace

Introduction

Federal documents contain a goldmine of information about people and places for genealogists to explore. The complex nature of these types of documents can sometimes discourage casual researchers from using them. This essay will act as a guide to enable anyone to identify which sources might be helpful to their genealogical search and how they can be accessed. It is not meant to be exhaustive but instead serves as a starting point. Land records, immigration records, military records, and congressional records all aid in documenting the lives of individuals. They may tell the story of a family member's movements between states, service in the military, or dealings with the government. Most of this information goes beyond vital data like birthdates and birthplaces. Instead, it helps tell a richer story of one's ancestors and how they lived in the world.

Each section of this essay includes the record type, a brief explanation, and how the records can be located. Some include how to locate additional resources on the topic. Where available, information for free access is listed. For some, sources accessed are only available through pay sites. Due to the nature of online resources, some of the sites indicated might change, but understanding what the records are and how they are identified will make it easier to find them in other places.

U.S. Census Records

When government documents are mentioned in connection with genealogy, the U.S. federal census is usually the first thing that comes to mind for researchers. Article I, Section II of the U.S. Constitution mandates that a census, or count of the people, take place every ten years to help determine representation in Congress. The first census occurred in 1790; to date, twenty-three censuses have been administered. The census allows genealogists the ability to research deep into family trees and find information spanning centuries. It is often the only record available indicating an individual's age or relationship to others in a household (U.S. Census Bureau, n.d.).

The release of the Census Population Schedules operates on a seventy-two-year embargo, meaning personally identifiable data is withheld from public release for seventy-two years. The restriction is meant to protect an individual's privacy and for safety reasons. While basic data is released in datasets and publications issued by the Census Bureau, it is more demographically focused or based on aggregates of information (NARA 2021b).

Available census records may not provide researchers with all their answers, as some of the questions asked on the schedules changed every ten years, with some being sparser than others on what it contained. The census questions usually reflected events affecting the U.S in the previous decade. For example, after the depression, the 1940 census asked questions about employment and how long an individual had been employed during the last year. From 1790 to 1840, the census named only the head of the household, while the 1850 census listed all household members, including their marriage dates and original birthplace. A fire mostly destroyed the 1890 census, but surviving remnants include a Veteran's Schedule to count soldiers who had fought for the Union and were still alive, or their widows. Although supposedly only Union Veterans would be counted, many enumerators also included Confederate Veterans (U.S. Census Bureau, n.d.).

The Census Bureau issued schedules covering topics such as Agriculture and "Slave" (enslaved person) in addition to the Veteran's Schedule. Agriculture Schedules list details regarding the size of farms and the type of work being performed. The "Slave" (enslaved person) Schedules only listed "owner" (slaveholder), age, and sex. Researching census records prior to 1870 can be very difficult for Black Americans, because the records only counted, and not enumerated by name, enslaved people. The census pre–1870 listed free people of color by name.

The 1880 Special Census of Indians enumerated Native Americans living on reservations. The Bureau of Indian Affairs compiled other census rolls of Native Americans separately from the Decennial Census. The various rolls and the history of enumerating Native Americans is a complex topic out of the scope of this essay, but detailed information can be found in the National Archives and Records Administration (NARA) information guide, *Indian Census Rolls, 1885–1940*, available online at https://www. archives.gov/research/census/native-americans/1885-1940.html.

There can be inaccuracies about an individual due to the way the Census Bureau collected and recorded the information. An enumerator would go house to house, ask questions, and handwrite the responses. It is important to note that sometimes the information recorded came from someone besides a family member, such as a neighbor, who may have unintentionally given the wrong information. Name spelling and birth-date information is commonly incorrect. Up until 1960, the enumerator decided the race of individuals, with so many of them incorrectly labeling the individuals, compared to how each person would self-identify. Racial categories and ethnic identification on the census have had a long, fraught history. More on the subject can be read on the "Measuring Race and Ethnicity Across the Decades: 1790–2010," U.S. Bureau of Census site at https://www.census.gov/data-tools/demo/race/MREAD_1790_2010.html.

The freely available website FamilySearch.org provides a search-able index to most available census images. The index corresponds to the digitized images of the NARA microfilmed census pages. In most cases, the original census records were destroyed after they were micro-filmed. Other commercially available subscription sites including Ances-try.com®, MyHeritage.com™, ProQuest's HeritageQuest Online (usually only available through an institutional library), and Fold3.com® also have the indexed images. Copies of the microfilm up to 1930 are available in the NARA reading room, in most public libraries, or for purchase. Start-ing with the 1940 census, NARA released the digitized images online and Familysearch.org later indexed the images through crowdsourcing. NARA released the 1950 census images on April 1, 2022, at https://1950census. archives.gov/. Artificial Intelligence/Optical Character Recognition soft-ware for handwriting was used to create a rudimentary index which will be corrected through crowdsourcing (NARA 2021b).

An additional tool for searching the census is the Soundex Indexing System, created during the Roosevelt Administration as a Works Prog-ress Administration Project. A history of the development of the project is available at https://www.archives.gov/publications/prologue/2002/spring/ soundex-projects.html. It created a sound-based indexing code to names listed on the 1880, 1900, 1910, 1920, and 1930 censuses for twelve states. With an alphanumeric code, it allowed like-sounding names to be found, no matter the spelling. Its original purpose focused on aiding the Cen-sus Bureau in locating individuals for verification of vital information, but it has greatly benefited genealogists trying to locate like-sounding names spelled differently (NARA 2021b).

For more information on the U.S. census, including descriptions of the materials available in each census, along with example forms and other helpful information, see the NARA Census Guide at https://www.archives.gov/research/census/online-resources.

Bureau of Refugees, Freedmen, and Abandoned Lands

In March of 1865, Congress formed the Bureau of Refugees, Freedmen, and Abandoned Lands, or Freedmen's Bureau. Congress tasked the agency with supervising and managing issues as they arose regarding refugees, freedmen, and land that had been seized or confiscated during the Civil War. Responsibilities of the Bureau included handing out rations, assisting with pensions, and reviewing requests for land or property to be returned. The assumption is often made that Freedmen's Bureau records are only relevant to those researching the formerly enslaved, but it also contained individual identifying information on those in the South who were left indigent after the Civil War and applied for assistance, white or black children orphaned because of the War, former slaveholders who refused to release their formerly enslaved peoples or their children, those who engaged in work contracts with the formerly enslaved, and those who had to apply for their land to be returned after the war or who had other issues that fell under the purview of the Bureau. There are even separate censuses completed in specific communities documenting the formerly enslaved included in the records (NARA 2021a).

When starting a search for Freedmen's Bureau materials, begin with accessing the guide on the NARA site at https://www.archives.gov/research/african-americans/freedmens-bureau. All the records are microfilmed and some are digitized. Filter your search to digital materials on the site by using the limiters for file type or email NARA directly for assistance at Archives1reference@nara.gov. FamilySearch.org and Ancestry.com® both have digitized images from the microfilm and each makes available a corresponding searchable name index. The Smithsonian's National Museum of African American History and Culture and NARA are hosting a crowdsourcing transcription project to fully transcribe the documents. Once completed, this will open the materials for additional keyword searching and add to their usability. More information can be found at https://nmaahc.si.edu/explore/initiatives/freedmens-bureau-records.

Immigration and Naturalization Records

In the U.S., knowing where to look for immigration and naturalization records depends on the time period. The laws changed several times and affected whether the records would be kept at the county, state, or federal level. Prior to the passing of the U.S. Naturalization Law in 1906 (Public Law 59-338, chapter 3592; 34 Stat. 596), which created a Federal Naturalization Service, any court could grant citizenship status, including those at the local and state level (USCIS 2020). NARA microfilmed select records from these lower courts and a guide to their availability can be located at https://www.archives.gov/research/immigration/naturalization/micro film.

From 1906 until 1991, the naturalization judicial process moved to the federal courts. These federal court records are available for request through NARA. After 1991, the Immigration and Naturalization Service handled the naturalization process, and the U.S. Citizenship and Immigration Services (USCIS) handled the records. USCIS does maintain copies of all naturalization files from 1906 to 1956. Records and index searches by USCIS are performed through a Freedom of Information Act (FOIA) Request submitted at https://www.uscis.gov/records/request-records-through-the-freedom-of-information-act-or-privacy-act. An individual's own naturalization file can be requested, or another's file can be requested if the other person grants permission. There is a fee for the service (USCIS 2020).

Immigration and the process for it has changed over time and affected where the records are held. Before 1924, individuals entering through the ports of New York came through Castle Garden or Ellis Island. Opened from 1830 to 1892, Castle Garden served as the nation's first immigration center and welcomed over eight million individuals; the State and City of New York operated the facility (NARA 2021c). Passenger lists from ships that came into Castle Garden are available via a free searchable database at https://www.familysearch.org/search/collection/1849782. The federal government operated Ellis Island from 1892 to 1924 and over twelve million immigrants came through the center. Passenger lists from ships that came into Ellis Island are freely searchable at https://www.statueofliberty.org/. Ancestry.com® digitized these and other passenger lists for ship manifests. Some are also available on FamilySearch.org.

Additionally, records of individuals entering the country before and after the Immigration Act of 1924 (Public Law 68-139; 43 Stat. 153), which limited the number of immigrants allowed into the U.S. through a national origin quota, are also available. NARA and USCIS both hold copies of the Registry files, or records for individuals who entered the United States prior to July 1 of 1924 (there is no other record); and Visa files, or the original arrival records for individuals after the Immigration Act of 1924 (USCIS 2020). There is a seventy-five year embargo on the release of these records.

Two government resources have passenger lists and ship manifests available. Microfilm is available at NARA, https://www.archives.gov/ nyc/finding-aids/passenger-lists.html, and requires physically accessing the information. However, the Access to Archival Databases, http://aad. archives.gov/aad/, allows for searching Russian, Irish, German, and Italian immigrants in certain time periods via its website.

Passport application records dating from 1795 to 1925 are another possible resource for individuals to use. Indexes to the applications are available at Familysearch.org and Ancestry.com®. These sites digitized most of the applications, but copies of applications can be purchased through the NARA, https://www.archives.gov/research/genealogy/ passports, if the requestor has the appropriate Microform Publication Number which can be found by consulting the appropriate indexes at https://www.archives.gov/research/passport/applications-microfilm. html#m1371. Applications usually included the applicant's name, birthdate, birthplace, current address, and a physical description. Later applications included a photograph.

The War of the Rebellion: A Compilation of the Official Records of the Union and Confederate Armies

A Compilation of the Official Records of the Union and Confederate Armies is a 128-volume set containing Civil War records gathered by the War Records Office and submitted to Congress. Congress originally published the records between 1880 and 1901 as part of the Congressional Serial Set. The records date between 1861 and 1865 and are organized into four series. Series I contains fifty-three volumes and covers reports, orders, returns (responses), and correspondence on the succession of the states and southern seizure of United States Property; and on military operations and campaigns, in chronological order. Series II contains eight volumes and covers correspondence, orders, reports, and returns (responses) regarding Prisoners of War and state or political prisoners. Series III contains five volumes and covers miscellaneous orders, reports, returns (responses), and correspondence for the Union authorities, and between the Confederacy, that does not fit topically into the other two series. Series IV contains three volumes that cover the miscellaneous orders, reports, returns (responses), and correspondence for the Confederate authorities, excluding the correspondence already published in Series III. Volume IV of Series IV contains a general index to the entire series. This collection is of interest to anyone researching their family that may have served in the Civil War.

As these materials were gathered from numerous sources, some documents may contain inaccurate information. They were also set to type directly from the manuscripts, leaving more room for errors to be made. Some sections may have missing reports or other documents that should have been included. A printed, detailed index is part of the original set for finding names of individuals, company names, as well as places and names of battles. Using the general index with the print set of the *Official Records* may be cumbersome due to the size and nature of the collection.

Many of the volumes are digitized and freely available on HathiTrust. org. Using the index with the digitized images will allow researchers to focus their search, though the entire set is keyword searchable. Some university websites also have the collection available online, including The Ohio State University at https://ehistory.osu.edu/books/official-records. An index is available from the Library of Congress at https://www.loc.gov/item/03003452/.

Compiled and printed later, the *Official Records of the Union and Confederate Navies* is a much smaller set with two series and only thirty volumes. Series I contains twenty-seven volumes covering correspondence, reports, and orders for Union and Confederate naval operations including the blockades. Series II contains three volumes covering miscellaneous Confederate Naval records, except for the statistical data of the Union ships in volume one, including correspondence between the Confederate Navy and agents abroad and Confederate State Department and diplomatic agents abroad, muster rolls of Confederate vessels, an investigation of the Naval Department, and letters of marque and reprisal. A general index is published separately.

Like the *Official Records of the Union and Confederate Armies*, the *Official Records of the Union and Confederate Navies* are digitized and freely available on HathiTrust.org. Additionally, they can be found on the Internet Archives at archive.org. The Portal to Texas History hosted by the University of North Texas Libraries, also contains a fully digitized and searchable set at https://texashistory.unt.edu/explore/titles/.

Other Military Records

Records that can be valuable sources of information of military service and family history information are the Official Military Personnel Files (OMPF), such as military registers, pay vouchers, muster rolls, draft records, and pension rolls. Fold3.com®, a database that focuses on military records, has digitized these types of documents from most major wars, including lesser-known ones such as the Mexican-American War and Spanish-American War. In addition, the website digitized all the compiled service records from the Confederate Army and selected ones from the Union, including the service records of the United States Colored Troops and pension indexes. FamilySearch.org and Ancestry.com® both have indexes and digitized images of select groups of these records (NARA 2016).

Veteran's OMPF records can be accessed publicly, sixty-two years from the service separation date. If the file is not older than sixty-two years, it must be requested through the National Personnel Records Center. More information about the process and the online request form can be found at https://www.archives.gov/personnel-records-center/ompf-access. The requestor must be the veteran or next-of-kin, as defined by the Center. A fire in 1973 destroyed many of the records dating from 1912 to 1960, so it is common for requests to result in no record found.

Bureau of Land Management Records

Founded in 1812, the federal government created the General Land Office (GLO) Records to manage the sale of public domain lands by the federal government to raise money for the U.S. Treasury. The GLO eventually became part of the Bureau of Land Management (BLM) in 1946. The BLM still manages the public land records of the public domain states which include Alabama, Alaska, Arizona, Arkansas, California, Colorado, Florida, Illinois, Indiana, Iowa, Kansas, Louisiana, Michigan, Minnesota, Missouri, Mississippi, Montana, Nebraska, Nevada, Ohio, Oklahoma, Oregon, New Mexico, North Dakota, Oregon, South Dakota, Utah, Washington, Wisconsin, and Wyoming. These records can assist in finding individuals who acquired land from the federal government dating back to 1788. They can also provide an overview of people living in a community during a certain time.

There are several types of land and related documents managed by the BLM. These include land patents, or land titles transferred from the federal government to individuals; survey plats, or survey records used to create and plot land; and field notes used to describe the surveyed lands. In addition, Land Status Records are used in the BLM Western State Offices, which manage the lands in the western part of the United States, to track the ongoing status of the land related to title, lease, and rights. Control Document Index Records include laws, proclamations, and withdrawals for restrictions or controls of public land and resources. Tract books are the basic indexes used by the BLM Eastern State Offices, which manage the public lands in the eastern part of the United States, that show when public lands changed hands in some of the public domain states.

There are over five million digitized records available on the BLM

site, https://glorecords.blm.gov/. If a record has not been digitized, a physical copy can be requested. Many of these documents have been microfilmed. The Land Catalog provides a comprehensive searchable index for
the digitized images (U.S. Dept. of the Interior, n.d.).

Official Register of the United States

The *Official Register of the United States* is a listing of all civilian, military, and naval employees (enlisted members are published in the military
registers), officers, and agents of the federal government. First published
in 1817, it continued being published biennially, along with each new
Congress, until it ceased in 1959. Members of Congress and various government agencies received copies; portions are included in the Congressional Serial Set for 1883–1893. The information contained in the *Official
Register* included names and dates of service, eventually expanding to
include other forms of compensation and aggregated salary information
for departments. The 1902 edition expanded the scope of the individuals
included, adding employees of the comptroller of currency (Deeben 2004).

Changes were often made to the *Official Register*, brought on by legislative order or driven by cost-cutting moves. For example, the postal section grew so large and difficult to compile that the government removed
Post Office personnel from the *Official Register* due to the 1913 Urgent
Deficiency Act (Public Law 63-32; 38 Stat. 208), which eliminated numerous nonessential government publications. In 1917, the *Official Register*
removed most military members, as the annual registers published by the
War and Navy department listed their names but continued to include
the names of military officers in administrative service in the District of
Columbia. Additionally, the 1917 cut included removing non-full-time and
contract employees (Deeben 2004).

The *Official Register of the United States* is searchable on https://www.
govinfo.gov/ by using the title of the document and searching for a specific
year. Keyword searching allows for a name search of an individual. Note
that their name may match other employees listed. HathiTrust.org also
has many volumes digitized and searchable on their website.

Social Security Administration Records

Social Security Applications

The U.S. Congress passed the Social Security Act in 1935 (Public Law
74-271; 49 Stat. 620) as part of the push for New Deal social programs and

paved the way for the creation of the Social Security Administration (SSA). The SSA tracked the earnings of employees and managing benefits under Social Security programs. The administration devised the Social Security number system to make tracking easier and more accurate. The SSA required an employed individual to apply for a Social Security Number using the SS-5 Form. The forms now serve as a valuable source of vital record information and are one of the few places where this information is captured centrally on a federal level. Historically, most other vital record data was captured at the state level. For more information on the geographical assignment of numbers, read the article The Story of the Social Security Number by Carolyn Puckett (2009).

The applicant completed the SS-5 Form and all information taken as given by the respondent with no proof of accuracy required until 1971. The form has varied on the information asked but usually included full name, date of birth, place of birth, employer, employer's address, father's name, mother's maiden name, and race. To request a copy of an application, you can do so under the Freedom of Information Act (FOIA) on the SSA website, https://www.ssa.gov/foia/request.html, and pay a fee.

There are some restrictions to requesting another person's application: (1) You must have written permission of the person or have proof of their death; (2) They must be over 100 years old, and you provide proof of their death; or (3) The person was born more than 120 years ago. These same requirements apply for parents listed on the form. To prevent the parents' names from being redacted on the form, one of the above criteria for them must be met. This causes problems for some researchers, as one of the common reasons to request the form is to find the names of the parents the applicant listed.

An index to some SS-5 applications can be searched on the NARA site, https://aad.archives.gov/aad/series-description.jsp?s=5057, through the Numerical Identification Files which are derived from the Numerical Identification System, or NUMIDENT. The NUMIDENT is the system the SSA uses to keep track of the records of individuals who have applied for a Social Security number. The files only contain information about deceased individuals from 1936 to 2007 or individuals who would have been 110 years old by December 31, 2007. Limited information from SS-5 applications, death claims, or any other changes to a person's record may be found here. Due to privacy concerns, there have been some retroactive edits made to the dataset.

Social Security Death Index

The Social Security Death Index (SSDI) is compiled from the SSA Death Master File. The Death Master File updates monthly from information received from various agencies and death claims made through the SSA. The Master File is not publicly available. After 2011, the SSDI became more limited. The SSDI removed information derived from state sources due to identity theft concerns. It now only contains the deaths reported through SSA claims. These same concerns have led to a three-year embargo being placed on the release of the dataset publicly. The most recent release was in 2016.

SSDI entries usually contain name, Social Security number, state that issued the number, date of birth, date of death, and location of last known residence on file with the SSA. (This is not the place of death.) Women were listed by their married name, if applicable.

There are many reasons someone might not be found in the index, including: most of the death records are from after 1962, when the system became computerized; data may have been entered incorrectly or in the wrong field; the incorrect information was submitted to the SSA, and the Death File is wrong; their death was never correctly reported to the SSA; or a final claim was never made.

Information obtained from the SSDI can be useful for requesting a copy of an SS-5 application. The SSDI is freely available on the FamilySearch.org site at https://www.familysearch.org/search/collection/1202535.

U.S. Congressional Serial Set

The U.S. Congressional Serial Set is over 17,000 volumes and holds the House and Senate Journals and the House and Senate Reports, beginning with the 15th Congress, 1st Session in 1817. The makeup of the Serial Set has changed over time and has included additional materials such as these at different points: The journals of the House and Senate, the *Statistical Abstract of the United States*, the congressional directories, and executive branch materials. The Library of Congress provides a guide to the Serial Set at https://www.loc.gov/collections/united-states-congressional-serial-set/about-this-collection/.

Accessing the information in the Serial Set can be cumbersome. Several indexes of the Serial Set have been compiled including, the most comprehensive version, the *CIS Congressional Serial Set Index*, 1789–1969, which included keywords, subjects, names, and organizations. The Index can usually be found in print at academic libraries, specialty libraries, large public libraries, and is available at the NARA Reading Room and Library of Congress. Specific records from the Serial Set have been pulled out and digitized on various sites. Thinking about what types of federal agencies or government businesses possibly involving your ancestor can help identify types of records to search for information about your ancestor.

Types of Records Contained in the Serial Set

Private Claims, Memorials, and Petitions: Citizens had the right, granted by the Constitution, to petition Congress for redress on any matter that involved injury by the government. Citizens used the memorials as an instrument to ask for a decision or action to be made by Congress. The House and Senate handled these claims and petitions through different instruments at various times. The House had a general claims committee in place from 1794 to 1946, in addition to varying committees on private land claims, and various war and pension claims. The Senate had a general claims committee from 1816 to 1946; but it also had a private land and a Revolutionary War claims committee. Other legislative committees handled claims that fell under their purview. Later, the judiciary committees of both bodies assumed the work of the House and Senate committees (Schamel 1995).

The Serial Set contains documentation of these committees and the various claims heard by them. Special indexes on claims list claimants' names, details of their cases, when introduced in what Congress and legislative session, what committee handled it, and resulting records produced including private relief bills enacted. These details help track additional information about the claim contained in the Serial Set and help point to the original files, now housed at NARA in the appropriate record set.

For military or war claims, affidavits of witnesses to events or service can often be found in the original files. The original files included marriage certificates, Bible records, and family trees to prove a relationship to a soldier. Some files even contained photographs submitted as evidence. These claims could be in reference to service in the Revolutionary War, War of 1812, Spanish-American War, Mexican-American War, Civil War, or World War I, including other skirmishes the U.S. may have participated. They also covered damages incurred because of the military (Hartley 2009).

Land claims focused often about disputes, including by those parties denied property they tried to obtain through the Homestead Act of 1862 (Public Law 37-64; 12 Stat. 392), and may contain patents, surveys, affidavits, maps, and information about other settlers in a particular area. Bounty land disputes or land given in exchange for military service would have been included and files might have documentation proving service or other evidence supporting their case. The files included claims against the Mexican government by U.S. citizens from before and after the Mexican-American War. The California Private Land Claims included claims by land holders trying to prove they had prior legal ownership under Mexico before the war, in order to maintain their land rights after California became a state.

Active from 1871 to 1880, the Southern Claims Commission reviewed claims made by southerners remaining loyal to the Union during the Civil War. The claims addressed losses of property taken, or given, to the Union Army during the war. The validity of the claim and the claimant's loyalty to the Union proved to be a rigorous process. Claimants sent in testimony from neighbors, letters, diaries, accounts of military service, wills, deeds, and other documentation as proof. The full case files are at NARA under the *Records of the Commissioners of Claims*, but claimants submitted the annual reports to Congress and are published in the Serial Set (NARA 1972). They contained basic information like the names of claimants, geographic location, and status of their claim. Later, the Serial Set included a consolidated index to the claims.

There have been other Serial Set indexes produced, along with select records that have been fully digitized. Some of these are available through FamilySearch.org, Ancestry.com®, and Fold3.com®. The St. Louis Public Library maintains a research guide to the Claims and has a geographic index listed by state, county, and claimant name. The research guide, https://www.slcl.org/content/researching-southern-claims-commission-records-resources, is "Researching Southern Claims Records-Resources." A guide to other locations of claim records and how to access them can be found on the National Archives site, https://www.archives.gov/research/military/civil-war/southern-claims-commission.

Registers and Directories: The Serial Set has changed over time and at times has included registers and directories for various government offices and agencies. The *Congressional Directory* listed detailed information about members of Congress, including biographies, terms of service, committee memberships, administrative assistants, and office locations. In addition, names of foreign diplomats, government department and office heads, members of judicial branches, and the government officials of the District of Columbia are all included. Before 1896, the Serial Set did not regularly include the Army and Navy (including Marine Corp) Registers and contained the list of all officers with their rank, pay, and allowances. The Air Force Register appeared under the Army Register in the 1940s and then, starting in 1951, the Serial Set listed them separately. Contractors for the military sometimes appeared in other published reports (Hartley 2009).

Reports, List, and Other Miscellanea: The federal government required many different governmental and other affiliated entities to submit regular reports, lists, and other documents to Congress. These materials have inadvertently proven to be a great source of information for genealogists. The Daughters of the American Revolution submitted regular reports to the Smithsonian. Part of that report listed the Revolutionary

War soldiers' graves along with biographical information for the deceased. The list was updated every year.

The Pensioner Rolls submitted to Congress included lists of individuals receiving a pension, including the roll of 1835 for Revolutionary War service and the 1883 roll for Civil War service. Other lists of names included those for lighthouse keepers and lighthouses, approved patents and patent holders, and passenger lists from the Collectors of Customs.

While there are some Native Americans, enslaved people, and Freedmen mentioned by name in the Serial Set, most references are in relation to actions taken by the government to a group. For example, the removal of the Cherokee from their land is detailed throughout congressional records, but most names of individuals are omitted. Indian Census Rolls were created but were not published in the Serial Set. Information can be found at https://www.archives.gov/research/census/native-americans/1885-1940.html. Individuals frequently included occurred in reference to petitions and disputes with the government, including appeals regarding decisions on land allotments and tribal status.

Finding references to specific groups can point to additional records that can assist in locating individuals by name. The University of Oklahoma, with a partnership with several other organizations, created a site that documents instances of Indigenous people mentioned in the Serial Set at https://digitalcommons.law.ou.edu/indianserialset/.

American State Papers

Published starting in 1831, the *American State Papers* contained the legislative and executive documents of Congress dating from 1789 to 1838. The *Papers* are arranged by series (subject) and then by order of Congressional session and date. Types of documents are similar to those found in the Serial Set, such as private claims and records pertaining to public lands. The Library of Congress digitized the complete collection. It can currently be accessed at https://memory.loc.gov/ammem/amlaw/lwsp.html, making it easy to find individuals mentioned. The digitized version and more information about the *Papers* can be found on the *Century of Lawmaking* site at the Library of Congress, https://memory.loc.gov/ammem/amlaw/.

Conclusion

There is a plethora of ways one's ancestors could have interacted with the federal government. Most interactions resulted in the creation of a record. Finding those records can be challenging, but this essay has hopefully offered enough of a guide to lead researchers on the right path. When approaching federal documents, thinking outside the box of what can be a genealogical source can result in greater success in exploring the lives of ancestors. NARA has additional resources and guides to help, including the "Genealogy Notes" in its *Prologue Magazine* found at https://www.archives.gov/publications/prologue, and its "Resources for Genealogists" page at https://www.archives.gov/research/genealogy. The federal government is a bountiful source to mine for genealogical information.

References

Deeben, John P. 2004. "The Official Register of the United States, 1816–1959." *Prologue* 36, no. 4 (Winter). https://www.archives.gov/publications/prologue/2004/winter/genealogy-official-register.html.

Hartley, Jeffrey. 2009. "Using the Congressional Serial Set for Genealogical Research." *Prologue* 41, no. 1 (Spring). https://www.archives.gov/publications/prologue/2009/spring/congressional-serial- set.html.

National Archives and Records Administration. 1972. "Records of the Commissioners of Claims (Southern Claims Commission), 1871–1880." https://www.archives.gov/files/dc-metro/washington/m87.pdf.

National Archives and Records Administration. 2016. "Access to Military Service and Pension Records." Research Our Records. Last reviewed August 15, 2016. https://www.archives.gov/research/order/order-vets-records.html.

National Archives and Records Administration. 2021a. "Freedmen's Bureau." African American Heritage. Last reviewed October 28, 2021. https://www.archives.gov/research/african-americans/freedmens-bureau.

National Archives and Records Administration. 2021b. "About Census Records." Research Our Records. Last reviewed September 13, 2021. https://www.archives.gov/research/census.

National Archives and Records Administration. 2021c. "Immigration Records." Research Our Records. Last reviewed November 8, 2021. https://www.archives.gov/research/immigration/naturalization.

Puckett, Carolyn. 2009. "The Story of the Social Security Number." *Social Security Bulletin* 69, no. 2. https://www.ssa.gov/policy/docs/ssb/v69n2/v69n2p55.html.

Schamel, Charles. 1995. "Untapped Resources: Private Claims and Private Legislation in the Records of the U.S. Congress." *Prologue* 27, no. 1 (Spring). https://www.archives.gov/publications/prologue/1995/spring/private-claims-1.html.

U.S. Census Bureau. n.d. "Overview." History. Accessed February 2, 2022. https://www.census.gov/history/.

U.S. Citizenship and Immigration Services. 2020. "Certificate Files, September 27th, 1906–March 31, 1956." Historical Record Series. Last reviewed January 1, 2020. Accessed February 2, 2022. https://www.uscis.gov/records/genealogy/historical-record-series/certificate-files-september-27-1906-march-31-1956.

U.S. Department of the Interior. Bureau of Land Management. n.d. "The Official Land Records Site." General Land Office Records. Accessed February 3, 2022. https://glorecords.blm.gov/.

Geography and Genealogy

Using Maps and Aerial Imagery from Government
Agencies for Genealogical Research

KELLY BILZ

Introduction

In genealogy, the question *who* is accompanied by *where* and *when*. Who are my ancestors? Where did they live? Where did they call home? Patrons conducting genealogical research often ask for historic maps of the towns and cities where their ancestors lived. Historic maps can bring neighborhoods to new light, spark the imagination about the day-to-day lives of our predecessors, and illustrate new connections. This essay will review some of the most useful tools for finding historic maps created by or made available by the federal government.

During my time as a local history associate in a public library and as a librarian-in-residence in the Geography and Map Division (GMD) at the Library of Congress, my work encountered many useful resources that can assist librarians and library patrons nationwide. It is my hope that, in this essay, the reader will become familiar with these different search tools and gain insight into the genealogical value and use of these materials. First, my review will go over how to find census district maps from the National Archives and Records Administration (NARA). Next is a description of two tools from the U.S. Geological Survey (USGS): Topo-View, for topographic maps, and EarthExplorer, for aerial imagery. Finally, my discussion will cover several of the resources available from the GMD.

National Archives and Records Administration

Finding Enumeration District Maps
for the Decennial Census

Census records are a common starting point for genealogical research, and many patrons want to find maps of the area covered by a particular census district. Genealogical databases, such as Ancestry.com® or FamilySearch.org, provide descriptions of these districts, but for maps of these areas, called enumeration district maps, we turn to the NARA maps, where the U.S. Census Bureau's historic materials are stored. Enumeration district maps show historic roads, town names, and division lines for magisterial districts, which can help pin down the location of an ancestor more precisely.

To find maps of a particular enumeration district, we will use some of the information found along the top of the original census sheet: the state, county, city (if applicable), and enumeration district number, which is in the upper-right corner, abbreviated E.D. No. (IPUMS USA, n.d.). The enumeration district number will help us locate a map in NARA's online catalog. For censuses of highly populated areas, there may also be a block number found in the upper-left corner of the census sheet, which will be useful once we have located the map. Note that coverage varies widely by location and year.

Example Search

Now, let us look up two maps, one for an urban area and one for a rural area. Each librarian has their own search style, and NARA's search interface will change over time, so my hope with these examples is that the user may identify the necessary keywords and develop the strategy that works best for them.

For our first example, we will use the first page of the 1940 census from Covington, Kentucky, https://catalog.archives.gov/id/127677782. Along the top of the sheet, we find that it covers magisterial district (township or other division of county) 1, ward 1, block 42, and enumeration district 59-1. The enumeration district, written on the original 1940 census sheet, is shown in Image 1.

Now we go to NARA's online catalog at https://catalog.archives.gov/. Search the phrase "census enumeration district map" with the year of the census, the state, the county name, and, if applicable, the city name. For this example, my search query is *census enumeration district map*

Image 1: Sheet 1A from the 1940 census of Covington, Kentucky, showing that the enumeration district covered is E.D. 59-1.

Kentucky Kenton County Covington 1940. The enumeration district number, e.g., "59-2" or "59-47," can also be included in the search, but note that it may not be part of the map title, since that will include the range of enumeration districts numbers covered, e.g., "ED 59-1–ED 59-57."

Once we click "Search," we find an item titled: "1940 Census Enumeration District Maps–Kentucky–Kenton County–Covington–ED 59-1–ED 59-57," https://catalog.archives.gov/id/5831961. This matches our enumeration district number from the census sheet, so we click on it to see the image. On the map itself, the enumeration district number will be handwritten over the area in question. In this case, ED 59-1 is on the banks of the Ohio River and Licking River, in the upper-right portion of the map, which is shown in Image 2.

The division lines drawn between enumeration districts may be faint, but we can use the block number, if available, to pin down the location more precisely. Our census sheet covered block number 42, which we can find labeled in one of the blocks closest to the Ohio River and bounded by streets labeled Greenup, Garrard, Riverside, and 2nd, located in the upper northeast portion of the map. For cities and heavily populated areas, enumeration district maps can be cross-referenced with the Sanborn Fire Insurance maps, which will be demonstrated in the section about the Library of Congress's Geography and Map Division (GMD).

Now we will look at an example from a more rural area in Mason County, Kentucky. In addition to towns like Maysville and Mays Lick—the birthplace of Buffalo Soldier and West Point graduate Charles Young (Kentucky Dept. of Tourism, n.d.)—the Mason County census has enumeration districts labeled only by number, not town name. We will look at this sheet from the 1940 census at https://catalog.archives.gov/id/127690138. Although less information is available—no incorporated place name, no ward number, no block number—we still see the enumeration district number, 81-10 in the upper right-hand corner. We enter our search in NARA's catalog: *census enumeration district map Kentucky mason county*

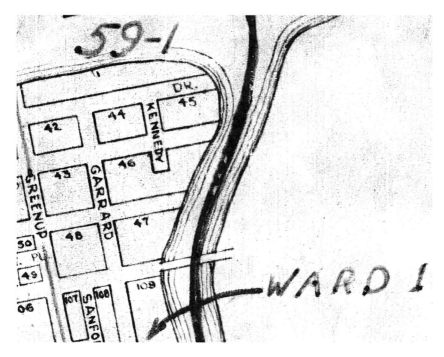

Image 2: Detail from the 1940 census enumeration district map for ED 59-1—
ED 59-57 in Kenton County, Kentucky, showing block 42.

1940 81-10. In our results, we find an item titled "1940 Census Enumeration District Maps–Kentucky–Mason County–ED 81-1–ED 81-19," https://catalog.archives.gov/id/5832017.

Once again, there is less detail than the map of Covington. Only state roads and highways are named, but towns and local landmarks like churches are listed. On this map, we find that 81-10, in the upper left portion of the map, is marked between Fernleaf and Germantown, which provides a clearer picture of the area than the census alone. Still, in cases like these, it would be a good idea to also look up the enumeration district description in the NARA catalog by omitting the word "map" from the original search or replacing it with "description."

If enumeration district maps from a given year or for a given location are unavailable, patrons may try reaching out to NARA or use other genealogical resources to locate their ancestors.

Additional Resources

For other cartographic collections at NARA that are useful for genealogy, see "Maps at NARA of Interest to Genealogists" at https://www.

archives.gov/research/genealogy/maps and the blog "The Unwritten Record" from NARA at https://unwritten-record.blogs.archives.gov/.

United States Geological Survey

Established in 1879, the United States Geological Survey (USGS) contains data, maps, and other publications, including two tools that are particularly relevant for historical research (U.S. Dept. of the Interior 2018). The first, TopoView, is a search interface for finding historic topographic maps, and the second, EarthExplorer, searches a variety of historic aerial photograph collections.

TopoView

On TopoView, https://ngmdb.usgs.gov/topoview/, users can search for topographic maps, organized into "quads," or quadrants, from 1880 to the present. TopoView covers all fifty U.S. states, American Samoa, the U.S. Virgin Islands, Northern Mariana Islands, and Puerto Rico. Topographic maps show the elevation and other natural features of a given location (USGS, n.d.). Though they may not be as useful for genealogy as, for instance, property maps, topographic maps can illustrate the growth of towns and subdivisions, locations of lakes and rivers, and mountains and valleys—the literal lay of the land. From TopoView's homepage, click the "View and Download maps now" icon in the right column or the "Get Maps" tab along the top. A screen with a base map of the United States appears, with the search bar in a column to the right or at the top of the screen on a mobile device.

There are two ways to search. First, because USGS's topographic maps are georeferenced, meaning they can be layered on a geographic information system map, the user can click and drag around the base map to a specific location. Then double-click that area (or tap the screen on a mobile device), and a blue pin will appear within a red square showing the coverage of the map/quadrant. Note that, depending on how the quads are arranged, the user may need to find multiple maps to get complete coverage of an area. A list of historic map results will appear in a gray column on the right or in the lower half of the screen on mobile. Results are arranged chronologically, with options to limit by scale.

The second option is to use the search bar to look up places by name. However, the location's name may not match map titles in the results. For example, if the user searches for "Hebron, KY," the maps in the results list are titled "Burlington, KY" (the county seat) and "Cincinnati, OH" (which is appropriate, since Hebron, Kentucky, is home to the Cincinnati airport, as displayed in Image 3). In this example search, the results are dated from 1914 to 2019, so more recent maps are included as well.

Clicking one of the results displays a set of options. First, there are four different file formats to download: JPEG, GeoTiff, KMZ, and GeoPDF. Clicking on the thumbnail image of the map will open the JPEG in a new window. As works by the federal government, these maps are in the public domain, so the user can download high-resolution files and use them at no additional cost.

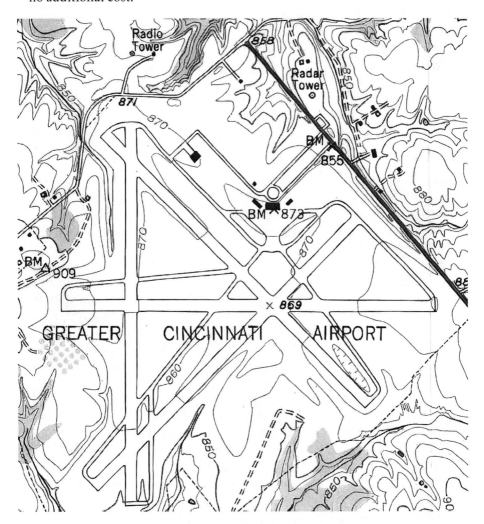

Image 3: Detail from USGS topographic map of the Burlington, Kentucky / West Cincinnati, Ohio, region, showing CVG airport and surrounding radio and radar towers.

Underneath the file formats, there is a map icon labeled "Show." Click on this to display the historic map overlaid on the base map and click the red x icon labeled "Hide" to remove it. The user can also adjust the map transparency to compare the modern-day base map with the historic view to see how roads have changed or if local landmarks have been built yet. For instance, in Hebron, Kentucky, maps from 1914 do not show an airstrip, as the maps from the 1950s do, but Interstate 275, built later, does not appear on either map.

With the "Share" icon on the left-hand side, the user can copy a URL to share it with a patron, e.g., in a follow-up email. This link will take patrons to the area of interest on the base map, but they must click the map to see the results.

EarthExplorer

Earth Explorer, https://earthexplorer.usgs.gov/, is a tool for finding aerial imagery from USGS's Earth Resources Observation and Science (EROS) Center. Like TopoView, EarthExplorer covers all U.S. states, Puerto Rico, American Samoa, the U.S. Virgin Islands, Guam, and the Northern Mariana Islands. Users may find EarthExplorer's search interface to be a bit tricky, so my method will be described step-by-step, but the user can also consult EarthExplorer's "Help" page for guidance.

On EarthExplorer's homepage, there is a column on the left arranged into four tabs: "Search Criteria," "Data Sets," "Additional Criteria," and "Results." Under the first tab, "Search Criteria," there are multiple ways to craft a search, but my preference involves the click-and-drag method to find my area of interest on the base map, just like we did using TopoView. For example, to find aerial photos of Hebron, Kentucky, the first thing to do is find it on the base map. Then, click the blue "Use Map" button (in the second "box" of the first tab). This selects the entire visible region of the base map as the search area and shades the whole area in red, similar to TopoView. From here, the user can zoom out on the base map to see blue pin icons outlining the search area. Click and drag those icons to adjust the search area. For finding U.S. territories in the Pacific Ocean, which may be difficult to locate on the base map, it is recommended to use "Feature Name" (in the first "box" of the tab) and then click on the "State" drop-down menu. Choose a territory, click the blue "Show" button, and then, in the table that appears, under "Placename," click the value to see imagery of that area.

Once the user has coverage of the area wanted, scroll down and click the blue "Data Sets" button to move on to the next tab. The Data Sets tab displays a list of different collections. Clicking the plus sign next to each collection name expands it to list its subcollections. For our search, we will click the plus sign next to "Aerial Imagery," the first list item. Subcollections, such as "Aerial Photo Single Frames," appear underneath. Clicking on the (i) icon next to the subcollection name will open a new tab with additional information about the dataset. My preference is to search broadly and check each aerial imagery collection in the list (even the Antarctic ones). However, if the user prefers to search more narrowly, the recommended datasets for successful searching are Aerial Photo Single Frames, DOQ, High Resolution Orthoimagery, NAIP, NHAP, and NAPP. After checking the desired datasets, click the "Results" button at the bottom of the tab. An example is displayed in Image 4, which shows a detail from an aerial image of Hebron, Kentucky, showing the CVG airport.

Image 4: Detail from an aerial photograph of the northern Kentucky area, showing the CVG airport.

Results are presented one dataset at a time, so do not be discouraged if a "No Results Found" message appears at first. Use the dropdown menu at the top to click through each dataset to see if any have images of the area of interest. Each of the results will have a thumbnail of the image (if digitized), metadata, and a row of options. Click on the foot icon to display the image's footprint on the base map, and then click the picture icon next to it to see the actual image overlaid on the base map. Note that the photo may not correctly align with the location on the base map. In each case, using local landmarks, roads, rivers, and coastlines can help orient the photograph. If there is no thumbnail image, a "Show Metadata" link may appear, which means that the image is unavailable, but the user can click on the foot icon to see the area it covers.

High-resolution scans are available to purchase with an EROS account, but the user can download a medium-resolution scan at no cost. Click the image thumbnail in the results list and in the popup window, click the image again to open the JPG file in a new window. Alternatively, in the initial popup window, click the "Open New Window" button for the image and its metadata to appear in its own tab, which has a Download button near the bottom of the screen. If the user wants to browse through multiple aerials before deciding which ones to download, this might be the best option for your research.

Additional Resources

NASA's Earth Observatory, https://earthobservatory.nasa.gov/, and Gateway to Astronaut Photography of Earth, https://eol.jsc.nasa.gov/SearchPhotos/, websites also have stunning images for scientific or general viewing. Additionally, the U.S. Department of Agriculture has collections of maps, https://www.usda.gov/topics/recreation/maps-and-brochures, including topographic maps and aerial photography, https://www.fsa.usda.gov/programs-and-services/aerial-photography/index. Not all of these are available online, but there are indexes that can be used to request individual sheets.

Library of Congress, Geography and Map Division

With over five million maps (Ehrenberg and Bilz 1996), the Library of Congress's Geography and Map Division (GMD) is the largest map library in the world, containing both government-made and privately-made maps in the public domain. This section describes public domain maps, such as Sanborn Fire Insurance maps, county atlases, gazetteers, and set maps, as well as government-made maps, like those by the Army Mapping Service. Ultimately, the entirety of GMD's digital collections, https://www.loc.gov/maps, is at your disposal. On the website, use the search box or click on "Collections with Maps" to browse.

Sanborn Map Collection

GMD contains multiple collections of fire insurance maps, also called cadastral maps (Stoner 2021), but Sanborn maps are perhaps the most well-known due to their wide coverage of American cities and level of detail. Use the general search box, select "Maps" from the dropdown menu next to it, and search for Sanborn maps; however, GMD provides a useful tool for accessing Sanborn maps, available through its Reading Room website: https://www.loc.gov/rr/geogmap/sanborn/. Use the dropdown menu to select a specific U.S. state, click "Search," and it will list the cities in that state with a Sanborn map. Note that, due to copyright reasons, not all available atlases are online; some are only accessible in print or through a subscription database.

Example Search (Cross-Referenced with Census Enumeration District Map)

For our example, we will look up a Sanborn map of Covington, Kentucky, from around 1940 to cross-reference with the enumeration district map we found earlier on the third page of this essay. Starting at GMD's Sanborn tool, select "Kentucky" from the dropdown menu and click on "Covington" in the list of cities that appear. Then, it will show a table listing Sanborn maps in GMD's collections. Fortunately, Covington has a lot of coverage, much of which is in the public domain and available online.

The closest map to 1940 is a 1949 atlas published in two volumes, listed as "1909–Jul 1949." The first year, 1909, indicates the base map's published year. The second year, 1949, is the year Sanborn added new map pieces with corrections and pasted them over the base map. These corrections include buildings built or demolished since the base map's publication year and the addition of new streets. Click the link for Volume 1, https://hdl.loc.gov/loc.gmd/g3954cm.g03152194901, and look at the graphic index map on the first page, which shows the areas covered by different sheets and volumes. The area of interest—the block bounded by Greenup, Garrard, Riverside, and 2nd Street—is in this volume and is in a yellow shaded block labeled 7 for Sheet 7.

Remember that the index map does not count as a sheet, so we must click through the pages until we reach the sheet labelled with the number 7 in one of the upper corners. In this case, Sheet 7 is image 8 out of 88. Note that the image and sheet numbers typically do not match if there is an index map or if the map contains multiple volumes. Looking for the Sanborn-assigned sheet number in the upper-left or upper-right corner is the most consistent and reliable way to find the area of interest. On Sheet 7, we find the streets that encompass the block labeled Block 42 in the 1940 ED map. On the Sanborn map, however, we can see the individual building footprints—in pink, indicating that they are brick, and labeled with the letter D, for "dwelling," as shown in Image 5—where an ancestor would have lived nine years earlier, as reported on the 1940 census. We can look at the buildings on the same sheet, which include city hall, a vocational school, laundries, and factories, to get a glimpse of everyday life for Covington residents in 1949: what buildings they walked past, what schools they attended, where they may have worked.

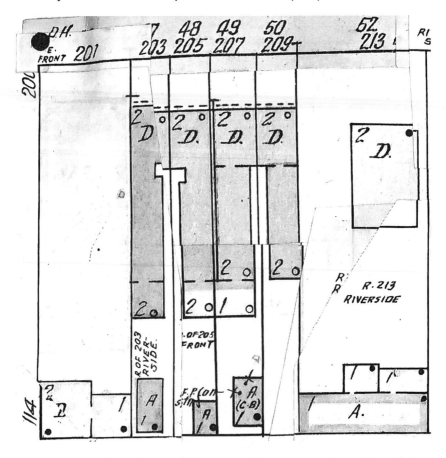

Image 5: Detail from Sheet 7 of the 1949 Sanborn Fire Insurance Map of Covington, Kentucky, Vol. 1, showing a row of dwellings (labelled *D.*). These are part of block 22 on the 1940 census enumeration district map.

Because of this level of detail, the Sanborn map collection is useful for a variety of historic research purposes. However, note that Sanborn maps reflect the societal conditions of their time of creation, which in 1940s Kentucky, included segregation. Be aware that some churches, schools, and gathering places may be labeled with outdated terms for racial and ethnic groups. For instance, on Sheet 20 of the Covington map, image 21 of 88, there is a segregated waiting room at a train station, and on Sheet 23, image 24 of 88, an African American Baptist church, both labeled as "colored." While this may spark interest in the histories of communities of color or promote dialogue about the impact of Jim Crow laws, these terms are harmful remnants of the times in which Sanborn produced maps and are a painful reminder of injustice.

Similarly, Sanborn maps label Asian and Pacific Islander spaces. Some businesses are labeled "Chin'e" for "Chinese" and can indicate the location of Chinatowns, as researchers have found in Sanborn maps such as Los Angeles, San Francisco, District of Columbia, Boston, New York City, and Seattle. For example, a row of buildings labeled "Chinese Tenem'ts [Tenements]" on Sheet 274, or image 26 of 114, in Volume 3 of the 1906 Sanborn map of Los Angeles is the location of the Chinese American Museum today, https://www.loc.gov/resource/g4364lm.g4364lm_g00656190603/?sp=26&r=0.67,0.375,0.656,0.326,0. In a 1916 Sanborn map of Butte, Montana, a shop labeled "Chine Drugs" [sic] shows the location of a Chinese pharmacy, today the site of the Mai Wah Society, https://www.loc.gov/resource/g4254bm.g4254bm_g049501916/?sp=2 4&r=0.641,0.895,0.233,0.11,0. Sanborn maps of Hawai'i especially show buildings that served vibrant communities, such as Chinese, Japanese, Filipino, and Native Hawaiian churches and language schools.

County Atlases

The Geographic and Map Division (GMD) also collects historic county atlases, published in the late 1800s to the early 1900s, showing the names of landowners and prominent landmarks. Like Sanborn maps, these are privately produced atlases but are widely accessible through GMD. These can be searched in the Library of Congress search box, https://loc.gov/, by selecting "Maps" in the dropdown box and searching "atlas" with the name of the state and county. Note that some atlases cover multiple counties and that county boundaries may have changed over time.

Military Maps

Maps made by the U.S. military cover the Revolutionary War and up to more recent conflicts. These maps, which are in the public domain,

are a valuable genealogical resource, especially for researching an ancestor's military service. Military maps also include those created by military
entities, such as the Army Corps of Engineers, outside of periods of conflict. GMD has several digital collections of military maps, such as Civil
War Maps, Military Battles and Campaigns, and World War II Military
Situation Maps, all of which can be found at https://www.loc.gov/maps/
collections/. The user may browse through these collections or search in
the general search box. It is recommended to search by the name of the
desired location first, since the names of mapping agencies may change, or
the cartographer may be credited to a specific general or regiment. From
there, the user may narrow their search by contributor and click on names
of military entities, such as "Defense Mapping Agency" or "Army Map
Service."

Set Maps

GMD also houses a large collection of set maps or maps that span
more than one sheet. Set maps over cover an entire country at a given
scale, e.g., 1:20,000. Due to the quantity of sheets in just one set, very few
are digitized. These maps can be accessed in person in GMD's Reading
Room, or feel free to use GMD's Ask a Librarian form, https://ask.loc.
gov/map-geography.

Set maps may be useful for genealogical researchers hoping to locate
communities outside of the United States where their ancestors may
have originated. The names of these towns might come from draft cards,
birth records, death certificates, or other documentation. In this case, the
researcher might use a gazetteer, or geographical dictionary, to learn more
about the town, including crucial information about its location. A gazetteer may help identify what province to find within a set map. GMD has
one gazetteer available online on its reading room page for place names
in Austria-Hungary prior to World War I: *Orts-und Verkehrs-Lexicon von
Oesterreich-Ungarn*, https://loc.gov/rr/geogmap/pdf/orts/orts.html.

Fortunately, many set maps also contain an index map. If the user
reaches out to GMD through Ask a Librarian, they will likely send an
index map to select the relevant sheet(s). It may be labeled with a number,
a number and direction (e.g., 44-SE), or other classification system. Note
that the collection may not contain every sheet. As always in research, be
resilient.

The user can also consult research guides by the Library of Congress,
https://guides.loc.gov/, to find resources for individual states, U.S. territories, and other research topics. An example of this is Native American

Spaces: Cartographic Resources at the Library of Congress, https://guides. loc.gov/native-american-spaces. Additionally, GMD's blog, "Worlds Revealed" at https://blogs.loc.gov/maps/, shares more information about items in the collections and can point toward useful search strategies. In a similar vein, GMD and the Library of Congress's social media accounts may also highlight useful materials and collections.

Conclusion

Maps are a vital tool for genealogy. More than a representation of geographic facts, maps document a place in time, and they allow researchers to pinpoint the location of their ancestors to better understand of their story. This essay has provided an overview of common tools for accessing historic maps proffered by three entities of the U.S. government: the National Archives and Records Administration, the U.S. Geological Survey (USGS), and the Geography and Map Division of the Library of Congress.

First, by using enumeration district maps from the National Archives and Sanborn maps held by the Library of Congress, researchers can pinpoint even the city blocks where their ancestors lived. Second, researchers can trace the growth of communities with topographic maps from TopoView by the U.S. Geological Survey, and they can browse aerial imagery on USGS's other tool, EarthExplorer, to add a more distinct sense of vividness to the place of interest. Finally, the Library of Congress—the library by, for, and of the people—offers a wide variety of collections, including the highly useful Sanborn maps, atlases, military maps, and set maps. As government resources, these resources are also all free to use.

These are just a few of the government resources that are most pertinent for librarians and patrons conducting genealogical research, and it is hoped that researchers find them as useful the author. However, the author is by no means an expert in the abundance of government information available, and so additional resources that delve deeper into these topics are noted in the Appendix. Happy researching!

REFERENCES

Ehrenberg, Ralph E., and Kelly Bilz. 1996. "Library of Congress Geography & Maps: An Illustrated Guide." Library of Congress Research Guides. Last modified April 30, 2021. Accessed March 2, 2022. https://guides.loc.gov/maps-illustrated-guide.
IPUMS USA. n.d. "1940 Census: Instructions to Enumerators." Accessed November 12, 2021. https://usa.ipums.org/usa/voliii/inst1940.shtml.

Kentucky Department of Tourism. n.d. "Charles Young Birthplace Cabin." Accessed November 12, 2021. https://www.kentuckytourism.com/mays-lick/history-heritage/african-american-heritage/charles-young-birthplace-cabin.

Stoner, Julie. 2021. "Fire Insurance Maps at the Library of Congress: A Resource Guide." Library of Congress Research Guides. Last modified April 20, 2021. Accessed March 2, 2022. https://guides.loc.gov/fire-insurance-maps.

U.S. Department of the Interior. 2018. "U.S. Geological Survey Marks 139 Years of Scientific Advancement." Accessed March 2, 2022. https://www.doi.gov/blog/us-geological-survey-marks-139-years-scientific-advancement.

U.S. Geological Survey. n.d. "What Is a Topographic Map?" Frequently Asked Questions. Accessed November 12, 2021. https://www.usgs.gov/faqs/what-a-topographic-map?qt-news_science_products=0#qt-news_science_products.

Appendix: Suggested Resources

Below are other relevant resources for finding and accessing historic and government maps.

- Congressional Serial Set via GovInfo, https://www.govinfo.gov/serialset/topic/M/Maps. Some documents and reports in the Congressional Serial Set have attached maps. As the serial set digitization project continues, some maps may only be accessible by a subscription database.
- Historical Map & Chart Collection from the National Oceanic and Atmospheric Administration, https://historicalcharts.noaa.gov/.
- HistoryHub, https://historyhub.history.gov/welcome. Researchers can connect with other genealogy researchers, many using government information, on this forum.
- National Parks Service, https://www.nps.gov/subjects/gisandmapping/index.htm.
- Other government publications. A researcher can use the Catalog of U.S. Government Publications, https://catalog.gpo.gov/F?RN=903659959, search in Google using "site:gov" to limit your results to government sources or browse government libraries. For example, the National Library of Medicine contains a book, *Final Report, Japanese Evacuation from the West Coast, 1942*, which has maps of evacuation centers and camps during the period of Japanese American internment during World War II, http://resource.nlm.nih.gov/01130040R.

PART IV

Health and Social Programs

Learning the Basics of Social Programs and Services Through Federal Government Sources

ANGELA L. BONNELL

Introduction

Understanding core U.S. social service programs and their current provisions is beneficial to individuals and communities. Knowing where to search for reliable, current, and understandable information for programs such as Head Start, Supplemental Nutrition Assistance Program (SNAP), Temporary Assistance for Needy Families (TANF), or Low-Income Home Energy Assistance Program (LIHEAP) can have a crucial effect on the well-being of individuals and families. By knowing key government sources, individuals can easily learn practical program information, as well as the historic, political, and economic factors that influence social services. Those in need, as well as professionals and students in fields such as social work, health care, and education can take advantage of sources that cover a breadth of material and accommodate different searching experiences. For those unfamiliar with government programs, locating practical and easy-to-understand information on social programs and services can begin at government search engines and portals such as USA.gov and benefits. gov. Users can then build from this basic information through relevant U.S. departments and agencies and their websites. Those needing more than basic information can explore government sources that introduce how social services are administered at the federal level. For those requiring an overview of the efficacy of programs, other sources provide independent, nonpartisan government analyses. Publications from the Census Bureau covering poverty and income statistical surveys can further add to users' understanding of social programs and need-based assistance in communities.

Literature Review

Libraries can play an important role and have a crucial effect on the well-being of individuals and families, as well as communities at large. This is documented in the library profession. Work from the American Library Association's Social Responsibilities Round Table (SSRT) in 1990 led to the adoption of ALA Policy 61, "Library Services for the Poor" (American Library Association 2007). Among its policy objectives is number 8, "Promoting increased public awareness—through programs, displays, bibliographies, and publicity—of the importance of poverty-related library resources and services in all segments of society." This work of SSRT led to the publication of *Poor People and Library Services* (Venturella 1998). Efforts in SSRT continue today, specifically with its Hunger, Homelessness & Poverty Task Force.

In reviewing library literature on this topic, San Francisco Public Library's hiring a full-time social worker and San Jose Public Library's creating the Social Workers in the Library program are frequently cited. Both took place in 2009. These proactive methods are exemplary, but many libraries lack the resources to mirror similar practices. It is worth underscoring that librarians are not social workers; the professional title of social worker is limited by licensure and education (National Association of Social Workers, n.d.). With this understanding in mind, in the 2019 publication, *Whole Person Librarianship: A Social Work Approach to Patron Services,* the authors share a variety of steps libraries can initiate. Zettervall and Nienow (2019, 43) establish that libraries are often a "first point of contact" for those experiencing homelessness, high mobility, food insecurity, and other need-based assistance. One of the more modest but important steps in helping users is obtaining contact information for programs that can meet their immediate needs. Findings from a 2022 study (Wahler et al. 2022, 61) reflect that an "increased number of patrons relied on library staff and resources to complete applications for unemployment and other social service benefits." According to an analysis of recently released data from the Census Bureau's "Survey of Income and Program Participation" (SIPP), prior to the Covid-19 pandemic, one in six older adults participated in a wide range of needs-based assistance programs. A majority of the nation's 54 million adults 65 years and over participate in Social Security (86 percent) and Medicare (93 percent) (U.S. Census Bureau, n.d.). Assisting members of the community is not limited to public libraries. Conditions of need are also prevalent among university student populations who face limited resources (Lederer et al. 2021, 15). Academic and public libraries have a role to play in assisting their primary clientele.

Making the Complicated Understandable

The saying "Well begun is half done" can be easier said than done when trying to find answers for complicated social programs administered across multiple governmental levels. The process is even more imperative and daunting in a world navigating a pandemic with its ensuing problems. For librarians assisting patrons unfamiliar with government processes, directing patrons to useful information can improve their wellbeing. A good beginning strategy is using a government search engine or portal such as USA.gov. Compared to searching from commercial search engines, limiting to a .gov (or .mil) site will produce smaller and more manageable results comprised of more relevant sources. Results typically refer to those federal agencies directly responsible for or tasked with administering needs-based programs. Agency pages are written in an easy-to-understand format and are less likely to overwhelm users with government jargon, acronyms, and series of government numbers or citations. Equally as important, the pages are authoritative and reflect up-to-date government practice. Many federal sites also offer additional features such as site assistance by telephone and chat, and include Spanish language searching and results. These websites are designed for patrons who might prefer to self-search or instead seek guided assistance. In either situation, they can browse from broad topic areas including benefits, grants and loans, or by more focused listings such as affordable housing, food assistance, and financial aid. They may also search by keyword and narrow results by including words such as "facts," "basic," or "about." Two particularly useful freely available government sites are USA.gov and Benefits.gov.

USA.gov

USA.gov is a freely available government search engine designed to search government services. Its mission, according to https://www.USA.gov/about, is to "create and organize timely, needed government information and services and make them accessible anytime, anywhere." It searches only publicly available federal, state, and local government websites with most ending in .gov or .mil. Users can browse by broad topic categories or perform keyword searches.

Results found in USA.gov typically lead to program and service information from those federal agencies authorized in the program's administration. For instance, one of the categories on USA.gov is "Food Assistance," listed under "Benefits, Grants, Loans." This page provides telephone numbers for hotlines to help those in immediate need. Many of the pages are structured to aid with specific needs of different populations such as women, infants, children, seniors, or those affected by natural disasters. Information is also divided into categories answering questions for different types of stakeholders such as program beneficiaries, local agencies, or collaborating organizations.

Federal agency sites include brief descriptions covering program goals, populations served, and frequently asked questions. For those needing to know where to turn, many federal agencies' sites include contact information for state, territorial, local, and tribal governments that distribute federal funding. If users require more in-depth background information, detailed statistics, policy briefs, and authorizing regulations are also found on federal sites. They provide important steppingstones especially helpful for those seeking federal funding or changes to programs over time.

Benefits.gov

As the official benefits website of the United States government, the mission of Benefits.gov, https://www.benefits.gov/about-us, is to increase "access to benefit information" and decrease the "difficulty of interacting with the government." As with USA.gov searching, users can browse or search by keyword and broad categories, but one of the site's core functions is to provide an eligibility prescreening questionnaire or "Benefit Finder." Users can answer a questionnaire that is used to compare against eligibility criteria from more than 1,000 federally funded assistance programs. Results lead to entries that answer questions such as "What is this program?"; "Who is eligible for this program?"; "How do I apply for this program?"; and "How can I contact someone?" From this site, users can contact state officers for individualized assistance and may also filter searches by state. Within a few clicks, a user can learn about a variety of programs and eligibility requirements.

Program Overview and Regulations

As an iterative process, searching can build from one search to another gradually. As users gain familiarity with and learn more about specific services, new search opportunities become available. For example, when browsing by category in Benefits.gov, interrelated services are highlighted such as LIHEAP, SNAP, and TANF. With these acronyms, users can perform known item searching in two federal government sources that cater to targeted searching. The sources, Assistance Listings and the

Code of Federal Regulations, are freely available and considered among the core list in a "basic collection" accessible for immediate use by the Government Publishing Office (GPO) and in designated Federal depository libraries.

Assistance Listings at SAM.gov

For those seeking information on social programs and services, Assistance Listings should be among the first sites consulted. This government site provides detailed public descriptions of federal programs that provide grants, loans, scholarships, insurance, and other types of assistance awards. Its primary purpose is to assist potential applicants in identifying programs that meet their specific objectives and to provide general information.

Some users may know this source by its previous iteration as the *Catalog of Federal Domestic Assistance* (CFDA). This resource originated in 1977 when Congress passed the Federal Program Information Act (Pub. L. 95-220). This Act established a comprehensive and centralized foundation for the annual publication *Catalog of Federal Domestic Assistance*. In 2018, the government consolidated the print and online CFDA with nine other federal systems to streamline the federal government awards processes. The General Services Administration (GSA) maintains the federal assistance information database through SAM.gov, but the GSA retired the title known as CFDA and made its data accessible as Assistance Listings. Each program is still identified with a unique five-digit "CFDA number."

Users can browse Assistance Listings across all government agencies to learn about potential funding sources or can limit to the search domain, "Assistance Listings," and search by program name. The site also allows for searching by the five-digit CFDA number, for instance, Head Start's five-digit CFDA number is 93.600. Each entry includes the program's popular name (for instance, "SNAP" for Supplemental Nutrition Assistance Program), an overview of program objectives, authorizations by statutory law (with citations to public laws and *United States Code*), financial information, criteria for applying, applying for assistance, compliance requirements with regulations cited in the *Code of Federal Regulations*, contact information, and a concise timeline history of the program, including name changes over time. A search example is displayed in Image 1.

Assistance Listings creates an opportunity for the user to delve further into understanding the program. For example, the Assistance Listing for "SNAP" cites its regulatory authority as "7 CFR 271–282." With this information in hand, the user can easily locate regulations for this

	Assistance Listing
Popular Name (SNAP)	
Sub-tier FOOD AND NUTRITION SERVICE	
Assistance Listing Number 10.551	
Related Federal Assistance 10.567 , 10.566	
View available opportunities on Grants.gov related to this Assistance Listing ↗	

Image 1: Example search result from Assistance Listings, https://SAM.gov, for Supplemental Nutrition Assistance Program (SNAP) showing the five-digit assistance listing numbers.

program by searching the *Code of Federal Regulations* online site. Regulations provide a quick and accurate mechanism to learn how a program is administered by the federal agencies. For instance, regulations typically define eligibility requirements, the application process, and program limitations.

Code of Federal Regulations

Its title might seem off-putting, composed of three administratively bureaucratic words: federal, regulations, and code. Nevertheless, this source is worth understanding. CFR, as it is typically referenced, codifies how federal agencies will implement laws. When Congress grants regulatory authority to a federal agency, it is taking advantage of that agency's expertise in an area. Whereas statutory laws passed by Congress are written broadly, administrative regulations are written to fill in the administrative details of the law. Regulatory law provides the mechanism for the law to adapt and change, since federal regulations can be updated more quickly than federal statutes.

The CFR is arranged into fifty broad subject areas and divided into chapters. It is further subdivided into specific regulatory areas. The fifty titles are revised annually on a quarterly and staggered basis. For those consulting the print volumes, each year is designated with a single unifying color on their front covers making it immediately identifiable from one year to the next. The CFR's breadth and organization can seem intimidating, but searching is made easier with a citation at hand. The CFR is available freely as the e-CFR (Electronic Code of Federal Regulations), https://www.ecfr.gov. Govinfo.gov also links directly to the e-CFR, https://www.govinfo.gov. It is produced by the Office of the Federal Register and the

GPO. It is not the official legal edition of the CFR but an unofficial editorial compilation that is updated daily.

The e-CFR site's most visible search box is designated for citation searching. To the new user, this may seem intimidating, but for those who have searched basic sites and understand administrative regulations, it can become more manageable. In using the example from the Assistance Listings, the program SNAP is regulated under "7 CFR 271–282." After typing this citation into the e-CFR search box, users are directly connected to Title 7, part 271 which provides SNAP's program information with purpose, scope, and definitions. At https://www.ecfr.gov/current/title-7/subtitle-B/chapter-II/subchapter-C/part-271, the user learns that SNAP is designed to "promote the general welfare and to safeguard the health and well-being of the Nation's population by raising the levels of nutrition among low-income households." Moving forward through the site, users can review the extraordinary depth and detail needed in implementing this program at the federal level. The pagination for the print edition of SNAP extends over 400 pages!

Independent, Nonpartisan Government Analyses

Up to this point, the federal government sources reviewed offer baseline information and the mechanics of assistance for social programs and services. Some users, including social workers, teachers, or local government officials, might require analyses of the efficacy of the programs or how they have changed over time. Several key federal government sources provide nonpartisan government analyses of the social programs.

Green Book

The House Ways and Means Committee report commonly referred to as the "Green Book," https://greenbook-waysandmeans.house.gov/, is officially titled *Background Material and Data on the Programs within the Jurisdiction of the Committee on Ways and Means.* As its title indicates, the volume provides background material and statistical data on selected major social programs covering health, welfare, retirement, disability programs, and other activities within the jurisdiction of the House Ways and Means Committee. Each chapter focuses on a broad service area and includes an introduction, overview, and legislative history. By typing the program into the site's search box, additional programmatic material such as tables, figures, and links to additional resources are also available. The Green Book's website features the current edition and includes an archive of previous online versions, dating back to 1994. Print volumes dating back to 1981 are available in many Federal depository libraries. The benefit of consulting earlier editions can be to trace changes in programs' scope and direction over the years. The Green Book is considered a standard reference work on American social policy in large measure because it is prepared by the nonpartisan Congressional Research Service (CRS) under the direction of Committee staff. Entries are written understandably and offer more than the program's description, mission, and legal authority. The descriptive report qualitatively provides context surrounding programs, making it valuable for those needing the program's legislative intent. Each entry also includes references to selected CRS Reports, also prepared by the CRS that are germane to the specific program.

Congressional Research Service Reports

In addition to preparing analyses for the Green Book, Congressional Research Service (CRS) staff also prepare CRS Reports, https://crsreports. congress.gov/. CRS is the public policy research arm of the Library of Congress. It provides high-quality research and analysis for committees and members of Congress. These reports, studies, and issue briefs are succinct and well researched and are updated regularly. Legislation passed in 2018 directed the CRS to make its reports available to the public. Until Congress passed this legislation, several organizations and universities actively collected and made publicly available older CRS reports. Another popular site is EveryCRSReport, https://www.everycrsreport.com/, which includes access to older and current CRS Reports. CRS Reports extend beyond the analyses of social services and programs, but searching by program name is an effective method to limit results. Recently published reports such as *USDA Nutrition Assistance Programs: Response to the COVID-19 Pandemic*, https://crsreports.congress.gov/product/pdf/R/R46681, and *Food Insecurity Among College Students: Background and Policy Options*, https://sgp.fas.org/crs/misc/R46817.pdf, address the impact of Covid-19 on programs, individuals, organizations, and communities at large.

Government Accountability Office Reports

For more than one hundred years, the U.S. Government Accountability Office (GAO), https://www.gao.gov/, has provided Congress and federal agencies with objective, non-partisan, fact-based information to help the government save money and work more efficiently. It is frequently referred to as the "congressional watchdog." Like other federal websites, the GAO site allows for keyword searching and browsing by date, agency, or topic. Broad categories such as Agriculture and Food, Education, Health Care, Housing, Veterans, and Worker and Family Assistance are directly relevant to social programs. From each category, the most recent reports are listed. Reports such as *Homelessness: HUD Should Help Communities Better Leverage Data to Estimate Homelessness*, https://www.gao.gov/assets/gao-22-104445.pdf, cover a specific research need and include a brief synopsis of the investigation and a lengthier report. Users can review GAO's Recommendations for the program and learn more under the "Why GAO Did This Study." GAO also includes podcasts for those interested in hearing the reports.

Legislative Information at Govinfo.gov

Some researchers may need to learn more about the political and economic factors of social programs as they were introduced, studied, debated, or evolved over time. Govinfo.gov helps in locating legislative background or legislative history for federal programs administered along multiple governmental levels. This online tool is the latest from among an impressive list developed by GPO since the 1990s that provides access to more than one million official authenticated full-text publications from all three branches of the federal government.

One area to check first is the featured collection, Popular Legislation, https://www.govinfo.gov/features/popular-legislation. This collection showcases frequently requested popular legislation, such as Social Security and its amendments, and provides links to a program's original statute, codification, related bill versions, bill history, congressional reports, presidential signing statements, and other related documents.

One of the fifty distinct collections in GovInfo, https://govinfo.gov, is the History of Bills. This content includes legislative actions on bills reported in the *Congressional Record*. In a print format, it is part of the *Congressional Record Index*, but electronically in govinfo.gov, it is a separate collection. By using the Advanced Search, researchers can select History of Bills under the Refine by Collection option and select from a variety of criteria such as keyword, bill number, and public or private law.

Another Advanced Search option includes selecting from the distinct collections in govinfo.gov and selecting metadata fields to perform targeted searching. Alternatively, users can perform a Basic search using a social program's name to yield comprehensive results on recent legislation. Those results can then be further redefined by facets such as collection, date, government author, organization, and person. Govinfo.gov is a robust search option for those wanting to expand their knowledge beyond the basics of a social program or service.

Data and Statistics

Another potentially intimidating element covering social services and programs includes locating relevant data and statistics. Fortunately, the Census Bureau provides a topic page covering "Income & Poverty," https://www.census.gov/topics/income-poverty.html, that highlights major household surveys and programs collecting income and poverty data. This site is arranged thematically into areas such as Income Inequality, Poverty, Program Income and Public Assistance, Small Area Income & Poverty Estimates and Well-Being. The information meets a variety of needs. Links to recent reports and statistics cover national, state, county, and metropolitan areas. Some data is available visually with charts, tables, maps, and other graphic elements. Specific reports such as *Benefits Received by Veterans and Their Survivors* and *Two Ways the U.S. Census Bureau Measures Poverty to Capture Clearer Picture of Poverty in America* are invaluable for those searching for program data not already discovered in previous searches.

Conclusion

Readily available and free U.S. government information sources are vital in understanding and evaluating social policy and programs. Knowing a selective list of sources provided in this essay is an efficient and effective mechanism to help users navigate social programs. From initial to advanced searching, federal government websites sites can serve as a springboard to more detailed information as it is needed by the user. Locating up-to-date and accessibly written social service program information can have a meaningful effect on the well-being of individuals and families.

References

American Library Association. 2007. "ALA Policy 61, Library Services for the Poor." Accessed January 13, 2022. https://www.ala.org/ala/ourassociation/governingdocs/policymanual/servicespoor.htm.

Lederer, Alyssa M., Mary T. Hoban, Sarah K. Lipson, Sasha Zhou, and Daniel Eisenberg. 2021. "More Than Inconvenienced: The Unique Needs of U.S. College Students During the COVID-19 Pandemic." *Health Education & Behavior* 48, no. 1: 14–19. https://doi.org/10.1177/1090198120969372.

National Association of Social Workers. n.d. "Credentials." Accessed February 7, 2022. https://www.socialworkers.org/Careers/Credentials.

U.S. Census Bureau. n.d. "Survey of Income and Program Participation (SIPP)." Accessed December 29, 2021. https://www.census.gov/programs-surveys/sipp.html.

Venturella, Karen, ed. 1998. *Poor People and Library Services.* Jefferson, NC: McFarland.
Wahler, Elizabeth A., Rebecca Spuller, Jacob Ressler, Kimberly Bolan, and Nathaniel Burnard. 2022. "Changing Public Library Staff and Patron Needs Due to the COVID-19 Pandemic." *Journal of Library Administration* 62, no. 1: 47–66. https://doi.org/10.1080/0 1930826.2021.2006985.
Zettervall, Sara K., and Mary C. Nienow. 2019. *Whole Person Librarianship: A Social Work Approach to Patron Services.* Santa Barbara, CA: Libraries Unlimited. https://doi.org/10 .1080/01930826.2021.2006985.

Appendix: Additional Readings

Hines, Samantha G. 2017. "Connecting Individuals with Social Services: The Academic Library's Role." *Collaborative Librarianship* 9, no. 2: 109–16. https://digitalcommons. du.edu/collaborativelibrarianship/vol9/iss2/.
Lloyd, Patrick. 2020. "The Public Library as a Protective Factor: An Introduction to Library Social Work." *Public Library Quarterly* 39, no. 1: 50–63. https://doi.org/10.1080/0161684 6.2019.1581872.

Public Resources for Public Health

Emily Alford

Introduction

This book demonstrates the diversity of areas government information covers. One specific area that touches everyone is public health. While many have specific conditions or concerns which apply to them personally, all people benefit from resources on nutrition, physical fitness, and preventative medicine. Like much government information, public health is constantly changing and evolving, and therefore resources with this information and guidance are often updated, along with new ones surfacing quite frequently.

The United States federal government provides a vast amount of information and resources related to public health. At times, this can be overwhelming for both researchers and the public in the beginning stages of searching for assistance. This essay provides an overview of key digital resources and tools provided by federal departments and agencies where librarians and library staff can direct their patrons. Lesser-known platforms, tips for successful outreach, and professional development resources for librarians will be discussed.

My Healthfinder

My Healthfinder, https://www.health.gov/myhealthfinder, is provided by the U.S. Department of Health and Human Services. The website is available in English and Spanish. It is a great place for anyone to begin browsing federal health resources. Users are able to enter basic information about themselves and their daily lives and receive a list of beneficial doctor visits, vaccinations, and tips on nutrition and physical activity. For instance, there are two separate lists of vaccinations appropriate for adults ages 19–49 and those 50 and older. Topics include heart health, obesity, sexual health, and pregnancy. Parents can find quality information on important topics such as the HPV (human papillomavirus) vaccine, current statistics on the virus demonstrating the importance of prevention, and when to ask a pediatrician about receiving it. Each topic such as this has dedicated pages of quality information and open sources for referral. When patrons with the broad goal of discovering what health resources are available to them inquire, My Healthfinder is a useful tool to begin the quest, especially when followed with a recommendation of one of the following two resources as appropriate.

HealthCare.gov

Much as My Healthfinder is a great place to start browsing public health resources, HealthCare.gov is a natural starting point for those patrons inquiring about health insurance information. This health insurance exchange website reaches those U.S. residents not having access to state exchanges by simplifying purchasing private insurance. Also found here are subsidies available to Americans with incomes from one to four times the poverty line, a marketplace for small business owners, and help for users qualified for Medicaid. Specific helpful tools include a quick start guide, plan and price comparisons, and a platform to find local assistance.

MyPlate

MyPlate, https://www.myplate.gov, is a resource created and operated by the Department of Agriculture, with a primary focus on educating Americans on how much they should eat from each food group. As shown in Image 1, users of the built-in widget, https://www.myplate.gov/myplate-plan, can enter their sex, age, typical amount of activity, height, and weight to create a custom MyPlate Plan demonstrating how to eat right for optimal nutritional health.

After considering the foods eaten on a daily basis, users are presented with specific ways they might improve their food habits based on variables such as life stage, ingredient availability, and budget. Additionally, MyPlate provides access to toolkits targeted at specific audiences and needs:

> ‣ Teachers and Educators, https://www.myplate.gov/professionals/ toolkits/communicators-and-educators—This is a separate toolkit

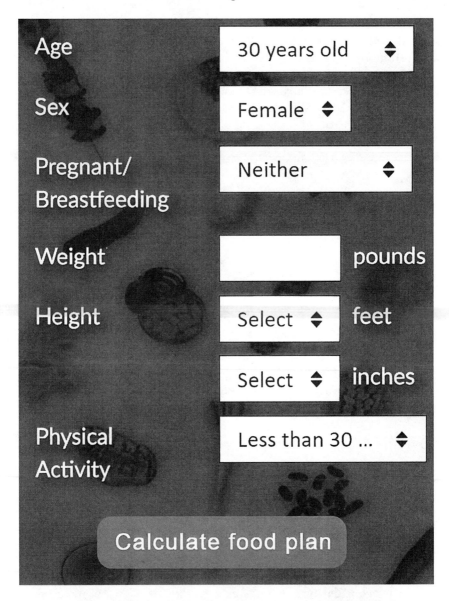

Image 1: MyPlate Plan built-in widget to allow for calculating food plan.

within MyPlate just for those working in the education field. The toolkit provides a wide collection of resources and lesson plans appropriate for various school levels.

> Food Supply Chain, https://www.myplate.gov/professionals/ toolkits/food-producers-and-retailers—Both retailers and food

producers can discover ways to incorporate MyPlate while working with customers.

- Community and Nutrition Professionals, https://www.myplate.gov/professionals/toolkits—Registered dieticians and other public health workers can find up-to-date information and resources to aid their work with patients and throughout the community.
- Household Meal Planners, https://www.myplate.gov/eat-healthy/healthy-eating-budget/make-plan—MyPlate provides free printable weekly calendars that grocery shoppers can use to create a shopping plan, along with ways to dine out with nutrition in mind, as seen in Image 2.
- Tech Savvy—Those who prefer using their smartphones and other technologies may choose to download the Start Simple with MyPlate application or the free Alexa application. These links are available from the homepage.

MyPlate offers some digital quizzes and other challenges to add some fun to their public education outreach, such as the "What's your Food Group IQ?" quiz.

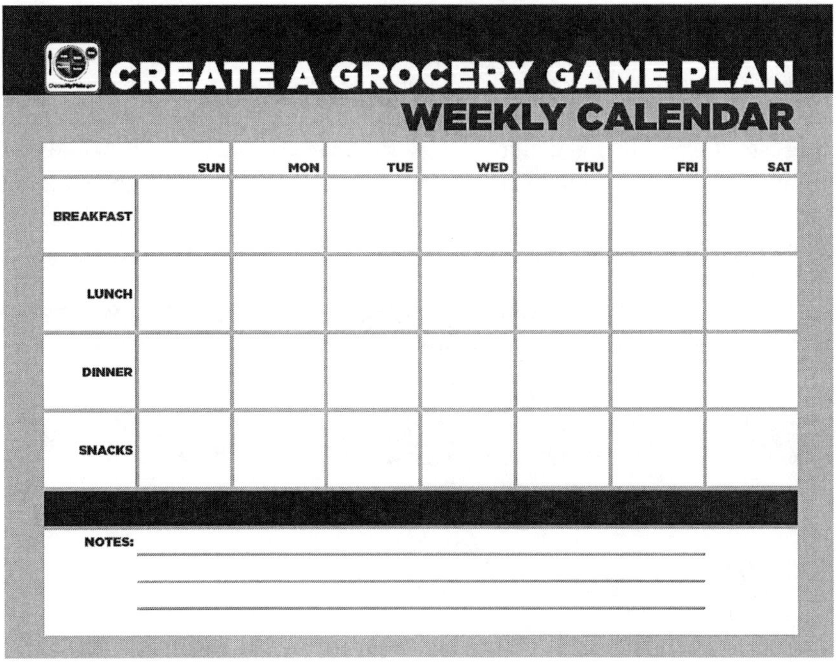

CREATE A GROCERY GAME PLAN
WEEKLY CALENDAR

	SUN	MON	TUE	WED	THU	FRI	SAT
BREAKFAST							
LUNCH							
DINNER							
SNACKS							

NOTES:

Image 2: Grocery game plan weekly calendar from MyPlate.

Resources from the Substance Abuse and Mental Health Services Administration

With a goal of lowering the effects of mental illness and substance abuse across the country, the Department of Health and Human Services oversees the Substance Abuse and Mental Health Services Administration (SAMHSA), https://www.samhsa.gov. Developed by Congress in 1992, SAMSHA's initial mission was to focus on creating more publicly available resources on these topics. Thirty years later, SAMHSA data can be downloaded by anyone and in a variety of formats.

There are a few specific interactive tools worth mentioning. The Quick Statistics tool, https://www.samhsa.gov/data/quick-statistics, can be used to obtain mental health services delivery system information from both public and private facilities, including residential treatment centers, outpatient locations, day treatment locations, and even Veteran Affairs centers. Users can see data gathered from a yearly census of treatment facilities which impacts policy analysis. This data consists of services, organization structure, and facility locations. The information primary helps local governments predict future needs. Image 3 depicts the type of data one can find by selecting a state and year to be provided with numbers on admissions or discharges.

SAMHSA also maintains an interactive National Survey on Drug Use and Health (NSDUH) tool, https://www.samhsa.gov/data/data-we-collect/ nsduh-national-survey-drug-use-and-health. Data can be found on both prescription and illegal drugs along with tobacco and alcohol. Evaluations of mental illness and substance abuse at an assortment of government

Ohio TEDS admissions aged 12 years and older, by primary substance use and gender, age at admission, race, and ethnicity: Percent, 2020

State: OH	All Substances	Alcohol Only	Alcohol with secondary drug	Heroin	Other opiates	Cocaine (smoked)	Cocaine (other route)
Total (Number)	17813	2090	2120	4496	1773	746	454
Total	100.0	11.7	11.9	25.2	10.0	4.2	2.5
Gender	**All Substances**	**Alcohol Only**	**Alcohol with secondary drug**	**Heroin**	**Other opiates**	**Cocaine (smoked)**	**Cocaine (other route)**
Male	58.5	66.2	67.0	56.4	50.0	47.9	56.6
Female	41.5	33.8	32.9	43.5	50.0	52.0	43.4
Unknown	0.0	0.0	0.0	0.0	0.0	0.1	0.0
Total	100.0	100.0	100.0	100.0	100.0	100.0	100.0

Image 3: Example of Quick Statistics tool provided by the Substance Abuse and Mental Health Services Administration (U.S. Department of Health and Human Services).

levels allow users to predict future needs and hone in on the scope of mental illness and substance usage across multiple years and within various subgroups. For instance, the map in Image 4 displays the percentage of young adults diagnosed with mental illness by state over the course of a selected year. The graph in Image 5 allows for the observation of trends over time.

Any Mental Illness in the Past Year among Adults Aged 18 to 25, by State: 2018-2019

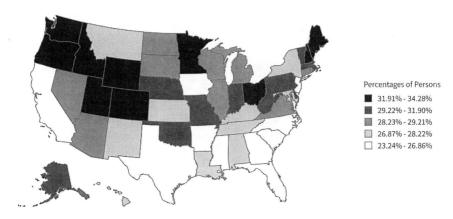

Image 4: Percentage of young adults diagnosed with mental illness by state over the course of a selected year (Department of Health and Human Services, Substance Abuse and Mental Health Services Administration).

Any Mental Illness in the Past Year among Adults Aged 18 to 25, by Geographic Area

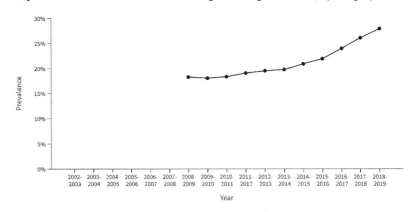

Image 5: Chart of any mental illness in the past year among adults aged 18 to 25, by geographic area (Department of Health and Human Services, Substance Abuse and Mental Health Services Administration).

Data from the Centers for Medicare and Medicaid Services

Within the Department of Health and Human Services is the Centers for Medicare and Medicaid Services (CMS), https://www.cms.gov. CMS operates https://data.cms.gov, a platform comprised of a variety of datasets and resources to utilize. Data is freely open to the public and downloadable in an assortment of formats. Developers utilizing the platform may tie the information to additional applications through an application programming interface.

The CMS data platform contains a multitude of interactive tools. Users are able to search for a Medicare Inpatient Prospective Payment System hospital and see which inpatient services are available there. There is a tool to search for physicians and their accompanying services, along with the ability to determine if a provider has elected not to accept Medicare. The platform even allows the public interested in prescription medications to search for Medicare Part D prescribers and see which medications they may offer.

Geographers and the public can find a variety of mapping tools within the CMS data platform under View Tools. Users can discover Medicare disparities in beneficiaries, such as by age or race, in addition to disparities in hospital quality and service costs at a variety of geographic levels. In Images 6 and 7, a user has utilized the Mapping Medicare Disparities tool, https://data.cms.gov/tools/mapping-medicare-disparities-by-hospital, to

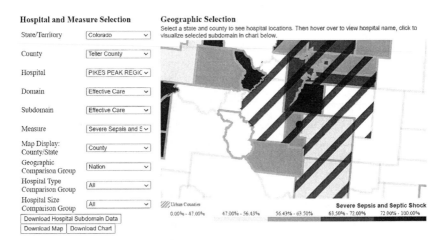

Image 6: An example of the Mapping Medicare Disparities tool provided by the Centers for Medicare and Medicaid Services.

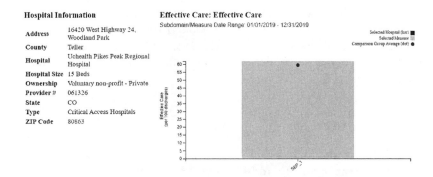

Image 7: Visualizing the determined level of effective care for data provided in Image 6 (Department of Health and Human Services, Centers for Medicare and Medicaid Services).

locate hospitals within a specific county in Colorado and then visualize the determined level of effective care for patients diagnosed with sepsis and septic shock.

Those interested in opioid prescribing levels at the county or state levels can use the mapping tools specifically on this topic. Market saturation and utilization mapping tools are also provided. Of special note is the Interactive Atlas of Chronic Conditions, which demonstrates the frequency of eighteen specific conditions, including cancer, diabetes, and stroke, among Medicare beneficiaries.

Finally, there are three groups of interactive dashboards CMS data users may want to consider using:

> ‣ Medicare Chronic Conditions Dashboards—These datasets consist of assessments of chronic conditions according to various geographies.
> ‣ Medicare Geographic Variation Dashboards—Depicted here are standardized per capita spending by location, specific services, and total standardized per capita spending.
> ‣ Drug Spending Dashboards—CMS data is used to show information on Medicaid program-funded medications, as well as Medicare Parts B and D medications.

Benefits.gov

Benefits.gov offers publicly accessible information on a host of benefits available. Previously named GovBenefits.gov, this resource simplifies the process of discovering federal benefit information by utilizing a federal agency partnership to maintain one platform for such searching. Potential beneficiaries are U.S. citizens, federal and state government entities, and businesses of all sizes. Useful categories to aid those looking for health-related benefits include family and children services, disaster relief, food and nutrition, and veterans' health.

Broader Resources

While the bulk of the resources mentioned in this essay stem from the Department of Health and Human Services, it is important to note that a wide amount of information and data is available from other federal departments. The Department of Labor, for example, maintains the Bureau of Labor Statistics (BLS), https://www.bls.gov. BLS contains data not only on worker characteristics and productivity costs but also vital data on state occupational injuries and illnesses. For example, one can refer to a map, https://www.bls.gov/iif/oshstate.htm, click on a specific state and find links to spreadsheets and Word documents on fatal and nonfatal work-related injuries for the past several years.

The Education Resources Information Center from the Department of Education, https://eric.ed.gov/, provides book sources, journal publications, and grey literature. The Department also includes a variety of peer-reviewed health data and research. The Department of Education operates the National Center for Education Statistics, https://www.nces.ed.gov, which provides tools such as *Digest of Education Statistics*, https://nces.ed.gov/programs/digest/, *DataLab*, https://nces.ed.gov/datalab/, and *Indicators of School Crime and Safety*, https://nces.ed.gov/programs/coe/. Included are numbers on mental health services available through public schools and data on illegal drug availability. The National Opioid Misuse Community Assessment Tool, https://www.opioidmisusetool.norc.org, a collaboration between the Department of Agriculture and the National Opinion Research Center at the Walsh Center for Rural Health Analysis at the University of Chicago, also focuses on the effects of drug use. Users of this tool can find overdose mortality rates by county and compare this data with social determinants. Selections like mental health facilities and injury-prone employment are demonstrated within the resource, and more niche determinants such as broadband access, household income, and educational attainment can be reviewed.

Finding Pertinent Information on Health Legislation

Academics, patients, and health product consumers are often interested in current legislation on public health measures and topics. It is important for librarians and library staff to be able to assist these patrons in finding the most recent actions of federal lawmakers. The Government Publishing Office (GPO) service's https://govinfo.gov provides free access to such information. GovInfo.gov uses high-quality searching technology and the creation of strong metadata on the mobile-friendly resource to provide the best accessibility possible. A certified digital repository guarantees the content, securely maintained by GPO, will continue to remain available. Users can browse by category, committee, author, or date, and are presented with a host of facets to simplify searches. In Image 8, a user researching legislation around obesity has located details on educational initiatives for corresponding health professionals.

There are several more specific resources for finding legislative information of which users will want to be aware. The following can be accessed through GovInfo.gov, or patrons can be referred directly to the sources themselves:

> ‣ Federal Register, https://www.federalregister.gov

The Office of the Federal Register releases daily regulations with general legal effect, proposed agency rules, executive orders, and other documents which are mandated by statute to be made available. Each year, the regulations in force are then collected in the *Code of Federal Regulations*. Patrons utilizing the *Federal Register* directly can even hover over a Sections tab at the top of the resource and find all the federal documents from the most recent year on broad topics such as Health Care Reform, https://www.

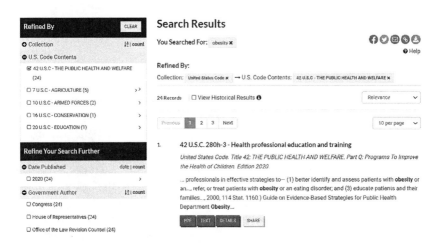

Image 8: An example of a search for legislation concerning obesity (U.S. Government Printing Office, GovInfo, United States Code, Section 42—The Public Health and Welfare. *https://www.govinfo.gov*).

federalregister.gov/health-care-reform. The *Federal Register* site has many reader aids, videos and tutorials, and users can create their own accounts to save information important to their needs.

> ➤ U.S. Code, https://uscode.house.gov

Relatedly, the U.S. Code, developed by the Office of the Law Revision Counsel of the House of Representatives, codifies the country's permanent laws by topic. Currently available online from 1994 to the present, a user may search by six-year increments. Utilizing the Advanced Search tool, https://uscode.house.gov/advancedsearch.xhtml, a patron might search a subject such as tobacco, select the current version, and be presented with a complete list of all relevant laws enacted and made effective in recent years. The site contains tips on best searching strategies, keyboard navigation, as well as Boolean and proximity connectors.

> ➤ Congressional Record, https://www.congress.gov/congressional-record

Last but far from least, the *Congressional Record* holds all congressional debates and proceedings. This publication goes as far back as 1873, and it is still released on a daily basis anytime Congress is in session. From the homepage, users can type in a term such as "water quality" and a list of full-text results including acts, resolutions, and statements will be generated. Also found in the *Congressional Record* is a glossary of legislative terms, citation referenced, and the ability to subscribe and to receive new alerts for optimal tracking of new activity.

Outreach

While professionals within the public health field may be aware of the federal resources discussed in this essay, library affiliates and the public may not. Librarians and library staff may need to perform outreach to ensure everyone is able to utilize such tools to their highest benefit. Pop-up exhibits can be especially useful for this. Great places to reach community members and professionals include public health fairs, farmers' markets, community parades and festivals, and other large gatherings which attract a flow of people interested in a certain topic. Libraries can create handouts with links and short descriptions of federal resources on a public health topic and have these ready to copy and distribute. Distribution itself can often be as easy as keeping a pile of MyPlate handouts (which are available to print from the site itself) next to a register at a farmers' market.

Libraries can host workshops on specific topics and demonstrate using these resources while at the same time promoting their own physical collections. Themed programs are a great way to catch the eye of interested attendees. Around Veterans Day, librarians might provide a workshop on government resources specifically for veterans, including those health tools from benefits.gov. Social media is a simple and free way to get out the word about such workshops, collections, or even simply a handy government online resource. Many federal departments and agencies have ready-to-use digital resources.

Professional Development

As public health resources and measures are constantly developing, it is imperative for librarians and library staff to stay abreast of current, quality resources and how to navigate them. Fortunately, there are a variety of ways to do this. The Federal Depository Library Program (FDLP) Academy Training Repository, https://www.fdlp.gov/training, contains recorded webinars and trainings provided by the GPO, depository librarians, and federal government employees. Recordings are sorted by subject and federal agency and include content such as "Stay Mentally Alert: Government Resources for Good Mental Health" and "Measles, Immunizations and Finding Accurate Health Information with MedlinePlus." The FDLP also hosts LibGuides, https://libguides.fdlp.gov/, which contain descriptions and links to resources on specific subjects of interest. These guides are sorted as subject guides, FDLP information, and hot topics.

There are many quality RSS (Really Simple Syndication) feeds available from the federal government, including those from the Substance Abuse and Mental Health Services Administration (SAMHSA) and the Centers for Medicare and Medicaid Services (CMS). CMS also has freely available informative podcasts, https://www.cms.gov/Outreach-and-Education/Outreach/OpenDoorForums/PodcastAndTranscripts. Also notable is that some state libraries host "Government Information Days." The Indiana State Library, https://feddocs.lib.in.us/gov-info-day/, is one example. These one-day conferences are typically free to attend in person. The recorded sessions can be found on the state library websites and are freely available for viewing.

Conclusion

In conclusion, educating patrons on these health resources from the federal government can be very rewarding. Often simply informing people these are available will fulfill an inquiry. Once librarians and library staff know where to go for what information, it is not as overwhelming as it may seem at first glance—both to the patron searching without guidance along with the professionals instructing on the resources. Creating tutorials to be used both internally and externally will make this process smoother and decrease repetition. Utilizing the discussed methods of professional development and where and how to successfully perform outreach, these tools can be used to the patron's highest advantage—and just maybe to the betterment of the patron's overall health and wellness.

Finding and Using Federal Information Relevant to People with Disabilities

Isabella Folmar *and* Blake Robinson

Introduction

As of 2019, approximately 13.2 percent of the U.S. population had a form of disability (Institute on Disability 2020, 3). There are many types of disabilities and impairments, including mobility-related, learning-related, communication-related, vision-related, and hearing-related. These disabilities may fall into the category of "visible" or "invisible" disabilities (Schomberg and Highby 2020). This ubiquity implies that most librarians in all types of libraries are serving patrons with disabilities every day, though they may not realize it.

People with disabilities often face enormous challenges across all aspects of life, and federal laws, regulations, and policies such as the Americans with Disabilities Act (ADA) often cut across all these aspects. Federal government information that pertains to persons with disabilities is often scattered across multiple agencies, presenting a challenge not only to patrons with disabilities themselves but also to librarians who may not be familiar with these resources. Consequently, the purpose of this essay is to familiarize librarians with key resources for people with disabilities in the domains of healthcare, employment, and education, along with a brief overview of significant legislation in this area.

Key Legislation

Any overview of disability rights information would be remiss without first examining the premier federal law mandating equal rights and opportunities for people with disabilities: the Americans with Disabilities Act of 1990 (Pub. L. 101-336, 104 Stat. 327). Originally enacted in 1990 and subsequently revised in 2008, the ADA prevents discrimination against people with disabilities in areas such as employment, public services, and public accommodations. The purpose of the ADA is to protect the rights of people with disabilities to participate in all areas of society, whether that may mean obtaining equal compensation from their employer as would a person without disabilities; receiving services from the government such as a public education; or obtaining services from commercial facilities, such as hotels and restaurants, without obstacles. However, while the ADA broadly protects the rights of people with disabilities to receive services from, and to be employed by, entities within the public and private sectors, Congress passed additional legislation to thwart discrimination in the areas of healthcare, education, and employment.

The Education of the Handicapped Act Amendments of 1990 (Pub. L. 101-476, 104 Stat. 1103) guarantees "a free appropriate public education" to children with disabilities, including special education services (104 Stat. 1112). This Act (104 Stat. 1141–42) renamed the Education for All Handicapped Children Act of 1975 (Pub. L. 94-142; 20 U.S.C. 1400) as the Individuals with Disabilities Act (IDEA). The 1990 amendments also provide for early childhood education intervention services for children and toddlers with disabilities. Finally, the Act allows for grants to state education departments, institutions of higher education, and related nonprofit organizations to support research for, and development of, special education services.

In 1973, Congress passed the Rehabilitation Act of 1973 (RHA) (Pub. L. 93-112, 87 Stat. 355) to establish affirmative action policies for organizations contracting with the federal government to employ individuals with disabilities. With major implications for the employment of people with disabilities, section 504 of the RHA expanded workplace protections for individuals with disabilities, particularly in instances of discrimination by employers in receipt of federal funds. The following year saw the passage of the Vietnam Era Veterans' Readjustment Assistance Act of 1974 (Pub. L. 93-508, 88 Stat. 1578), which the Department of Labor enforces to ensure equal employment opportunities for disabled veterans. Several decades later, the Workforce Innovation and Opportunity Act of 2014 (Pub. L. 113-128, 128 Stat. 1425) came about to engineer competitive integrated employment opportunities for individuals with disabilities.

The RHA offers protections for individuals with disabilities within the context of health care, as section 504 regulates all programs and services provided to individuals with disabilities through the use of federal funds, including those conducted by the U.S. Department of Health and Human Services (HHS). Similarly, section 508 of RHA mandates the accessibility of information technology used by programs in receipt of federal funding, including health care records created and maintained by HHS.

Beyond these pieces of legislation, the federal government implemented many other laws to protect individuals with disabilities. These areas include transportation, voting rights, telecommunications, architectural barriers, and the civil rights of "institutionalized" people. This includes individuals within government-operated mental health facilities, correctional facilities, pretrial detention centers, and juvenile detention centers. These legislative acts and associated public services and programs merit further analysis from the library community. Two good sources for this information include ADA.gov, administered by the Department of Justice, and the Library of Congress's research guide, "Disability Law in the United States: A Beginner's Guide," https://guides.loc.gov/disability-law.

ADA.gov offers information and technical assistance on the Americans with Disabilities Act of 1990, including the full-text of the regulations, the ADA's standards for accessible design, significant cases pertaining to the ADA, and technical documents concerning ADA requirements for small businesses and local governments. As of this writing, the newly available beta site, https://beta.ada.gov, offers a link on the home page for users to file an ADA complaint. This user-friendly beta version also offers a "topics" page, which includes in-depth sub-pages relating to service animals, accessible parking, mobility devices, and communication technologies for people with disabilities. As an additional helpful resource, the Library of Congress's "Disability Law in the United States: A Beginner's Guide," LibGuide features publications within the Library of Congress about disability law, links to federal law, links to regulatory agencies' websites, and federal publications about the use of service animals. This LibGuide also includes publications relevant to disabled veterans and legal reference materials relating to disability law.

Health Information

There are two key organizations that are essential for disability information in a health context: the National Library of Medicine (NLM), part of the National Institutes of Health (NIH), and the Centers for Disease Control and Prevention (CDC). The NLM and the CDC in turn are both part of HHS.

MedlinePlus, https://medlineplus.gov/, is the NLM's consumer health portal, useful in all libraries but especially in public libraries. MedlinePlus has a clean, accessible interface that showcases authoritative health information without problematic outside influences from, for example, pharmaceutical companies. Articles on MedlinePlus tend to follow a standard format. They summarize the topic in plain language and then link out to other, reliable sources for patrons to read.

For example, the article "Disabilities," https://medlineplus.gov/disabilities.html, contains a summary, a "Start Here" section that links to the CDC, scholarly sources such as clinical trials, journal articles, and resources for children. Articles vary in their ratio of scholarly- to non-scholarly content, but there are many parent-friendly, jargon-free sources related to diagnosing and assessing disabilities at an early age.

PubMed, https://pubmed.ncbi.nlm.nih.gov/, is the official NLM portal for citations and abstracts of medical literature, often with links to full-text from PubMed Central (PMC), https://www.ncbi.nlm.nih.gov/pmc/. It works similarly to many other library databases that librarians use but has some unique features. An advanced search lets the user "[a]dd terms to the query box," which can then be combined with Boolean operators. A useful feature of PubMed is that any NIH-funded research since April 7, 2008, must be made freely available in PubMed Central, NLM's full-text archive, twelve months after publication (National Institutes of Health 2021), with some copyright-related exceptions. This policy makes much recent medical scholarship freely available to all librarians and patrons which might otherwise be behind a paywall.

Using the advanced search, patrons can choose from a range of article types, such as clinical trials, randomized control trials, and systematic reviews. An even more effective way to search PubMed for information relevant to people with disabilities is by using the Medical Subject Headings (MeSH), an NLM-developed controlled vocabulary similar to the Library of Congress Subject Headings. This specialized system is helpful for mapping problematic terminology about disabilities to more current terminology.

Users can access the MeSH Database from the PubMed home page and then type in a search term. An initial search took the increasingly outdated term "Handicapped" and redirected it to the more current term "Disabled Persons." The PubMed Search Builder allows the user to construct a search using additional MeSH terms. For example, after searching for the phrase "Disabled Persons," the user checks the search result box for "Disabled Persons." On the right side of the screen, the user will locate "Add to search builder." The user has the option to select which Boolean operator to use; PubMed defaults to "AND." Selecting "AND" and clicking the button "Search PubMed" populates the "PubMed Search Builder" box with "Disabled Persons [Mesh]." Next, the user conducts a search for another MeSH term "Mental Health." The user can click on the heading "Mental Health" to explore its nuances or add the term to the Search Builder from the results list. This action results in the search "('Disabled Persons' [MeSH]) AND 'Mental Health' [MeSH]." After finalizing their selection, the user clicks "Search PubMed" to find relevant articles. Search results using MeSH are very similar to those from a keyword search, but they are more precise, especially given the wide range of terminology on the subject of disabilities.

As with the NLM's resources, the CDC's website, https://www.cdc.gov/, contains a mixture of material for both the expert (e.g., historical data on Lyme disease) and the layperson (e.g., a Covid-19 quarantine and isolation calculator), and its content is useful for all library types. When a user is searching for a disability or topic, the search bar is a good place to start. Users can find lots of valuable information, but it is not always easy to find the consumer-friendly landing page for a specific disability or topic this way. Consequently, the CDC has an A–Z list of many common disabilities under its "Diseases and Conditions" tab, including specific conditions such as ADHD (attention-deficit hyperactivity disorder) and autism, as well as broader categories like "Developmental Disabilities." These landing pages contain a wealth of information. For ADHD, the "Data and Statistics" page contains easy-to-parse statistics on the condition while providing librarians with links to the original surveys that collected the data. However, not all conditions or topics have their own CDC A–Z landing page. In these instances, using the search bar is the most effective strategy.

While it is possible to find information on some disabilities using the "Diseases and Conditions" menu on the CDC home page, a better option is to start with the A–Z entries "Disabilities and Health" or "Developmental Disabilities." Both provide information from the National Center on Birth Defects and Developmental Disabilities (NCBDDD), https://www.cdc.gov/ncbddd/index.html. Part of the NCBDDD's mission is to help children with developmental disabilities and adults with disabilities, so they have some pertinent information.

Clicking "Disabilities and Health" from the CDC index will display the NCBDDD's "Disability and Health Promotion" webpage. The "Disability & Health Overview" webpage discusses what disabilities are, how they affect people, and useful infographics on the topic. Their discussion of disability inclusion is a wonderful primer for people who may never have considered the topic before, and it explains how people with disabilities should be treated with dignity. The Data and Statistics page is great here as well, which includes state-by-state summaries and statistics.

The Developmental Disabilities landing page, https://www.cdc.gov/

ncbddd/developmentaldisabilities, contains a wide range of information for a variety of audiences. Parents can learn about typical developmental milestones for children up to age five. This information is crucial; whether children attain these milestones, experience delays, or do not reach them at all is the basis for accurate diagnosis of these disabilities. In addition, users can download fact sheets, infographics, posters, and multimedia content such as the "All Things ADHD" podcast at https://www.cdc.gov/ncbddd/adhd/materials-multimedia/index.html. The NCBDDD collects a range of disability-related content from across the CDC, but its annual report, https://www.cdc.gov/ncbddd/aboutus/report/, has some excellent summaries of what the Center is doing to help children with developmental disabilities. The report is written in plain language and contains links to reliable sources such as academic journal articles and advocacy groups such as the Tourette Association of America, making it excellent for students, researchers, and the public.

Finally, the NCBDDD's Disability and Health Data System allows users to find in-depth disability statistics by state. For example, clicking on Florida breaks down the state data by a wide range of indicators, such as demographics, barriers to care, and disability estimates. Users can see how many adults are out of work, unable to work, and employed. Data can be downloaded in PDF and CSV formats. The data at this time covers 2016–2019; more updates are expected in the future.

Education Information

Educational opportunities for students with disabilities have improved markedly since the 1960s when Congress began to pass a series of legislation to improve outcomes for this group (Center on Education Policy 2020b). Ensuring that children and college students with disabilities have access to quality education is a key concern for many parents. Fortunately, the U.S. Department of Education offers a wide range of resources for those who want to learn about this population and the issues they face.

Public education in the United States is composite in character, with federal, state, and local entities all playing a part in its operation (Center on Education Policy 2020a). Despite its democratic aspirations, public education excluded several groups, including students with disabilities (Center on Education Policy 2020b). Section 1414 of IDEA outlines the creation of individualized education programs (IEPs) for students with disabilities, to be implemented at the local level. This legislation provides information about rights for children with disabilities and their parents, such as the right to an initial educational evaluation; the right to an

IEP team consisting of parents, teachers, and other stakeholders; and the right to IEP team meetings (20 U.S.C. 1414). For more information, the IDEA website, https://sites.ed.gov/idea/, links to the Department of Education's Office of Special Education and Rehabilitative Services (OSERS), with reports, publications, policy, newsletters, topical listservs, and other resources. The IDEA website is useful in a wide range of libraries but especially public and school libraries, where parents and educational staff can learn more about IEPs and how they may apply in a given situation.

The ADA applies to K–12 education, small businesses, and a host of other organizations. This is documented in the *Code of Federal Regulations* as "Nondiscrimination on the Basis of Disability by Public Accommodations and in Commercial Facilities" (28 C.F.R. Part 36). However, ADA accommodations are also common in public and private colleges and universities, where services received under IEPs in K–12 education may not apply. Although the Department of Justice ultimately enforces the ADA, it is possible to find education-specific information on the law, along with many other education-related topics, through the Education Resources Information Center (ERIC).

ERIC, https://eric.ed.gov/, is the Department of Education's citation and abstract database of journal literature, reports, and other education-focused scholarship. As with PubMed, ERIC contains selected full-text. However, unlike PubMed, the Department of Education does not have an open access mandate in the way the NIH does, so although ERIC is comprehensive, researchers must often find the full-text from another source.

ERIC uses a single box for both basic and advanced search, employing fields, filters, quotes, and other limiters on one line. Researchers can search for peer-reviewed and/or full-text articles by checking the boxes. Once a relevant article is found, they can use the descriptors, or subject terms, to find more articles. It is worth noting that ERIC covers education in foreign countries in addition to education in the United States. In the case of the ADA, it is possible to compare efforts to accommodate students with disabilities in different countries. ERIC is free to use but is most useful in an academic setting, where patrons may have access to the cited paywalled journal citations they come across.

The National Center for Education Statistics (NCES), https://nces.ed.gov/, is a clearinghouse for a range of educational statistics, surveys, and assessments. The Center's data covers all levels of education from preschool to postsecondary. It is possible to find information on students with disabilities across a wide range of instruments, but there are two key surveys that stand out.

The NCES's *Condition of Education*, https://nces.ed.gov/programs/

coe/, is an annual snapshot of the state of education in the United States. Its Students with Disabilities page, https://nces.ed.gov/programs/coe/indicator/cgg, contains detailed statistics about students with disabilities from ages 3 to 21, such as a breakdown of what disabilities are most common among students served by the Individuals with Disabilities Education Act (IDEA). To make it as readable as possible, NCES alternates text with charts and graphs and allows users to manipulate the findings by race/ethnicity, sex, disability type, and other categories.

A more concise version of the *Condition of Education* can be found in *Fast Facts*, available from the "Menu" button on the NCES home page. For example, *Fast Facts* frames this issue in a question-and-answer format, asking "How many students with disabilities receive services?" and answers the question with text and tables. There are many more surveys, charts, and graphs at NCES, but these two products will meet the needs of most patrons with questions about disabilities, while researchers will have the opportunity to delve into copious amounts of data on this topic.

Workplace Discrimination Information

The two federal entities which enforce federal workplace anti-discrimination laws are the Equal Employment Opportunity Commission (EEOC) and the Department of Labor.

Pertinent to people with disabilities, the EEOC enforces Title I of the Americans with Disabilities Act of 1990 (ADA) and sections 501 and 505 of the Rehabilitation Act of 1973 (RHA) (U.S. Equal Employment Opportunity Commission, n.d.). The EEOC also enforces federal anti-discrimination laws against employers who do not receive federal financial assistance, whereas the Department of Labor's programs only enforce anti-discrimination laws against employers receiving federal assistance.

Within the Department of Labor, the Office of the Assistant Secretary for Administration and Management's Civil Rights Center enforces the aspects of Title II of the ADA which relate to the "programs, services and regulatory activities connected to labor and the workforce" (U.S. Department of Labor, n.d.). Many types of complaints relating to employment discrimination based on disability can be filed through the Department of Labor's Civil Rights Center. However, the Department of Labor only handles discrimination complaints against employers who receive federal assistance. The Civil Rights Center website, https://www.dol.gov/agencies/oasam/centers-offices/civil-rights-center, is user-friendly and jargon-free. Halfway down the landing page, a menu to the left of the screen includes a link to a page titled "Resources for Individuals with Questions about Filing a Discrimination Complaint." This same menu includes links to pages about Reasonable Accommodations for Programs for Employees and Applicants with Disabilities, the Architectural Barriers Act, and Notification of Equal Employment Opportunity Violations.

The Office of Federal Contract Compliance Programs, https://www.dol.gov/agencies/ofccp, is responsible for enforcement of Title I of the ADA as it concerns federal contracts. These are some highlights of the legislation that the Department of Labor is tasked with enforcing, and an exhaustive list can be found on the Department's website. Patrons seeking to file a disability discrimination complaint against a company that contracts with the federal government may do so through the Office of Federal Contract Compliance. The link to the complaint page is easily found on the Office's home page, and this complaint page is easy to follow, jargon-free, and includes complaint forms and filing instructions available to download in PDF format in twelve different languages.

As far as datasets are concerned, the main source of departmental data of interest to librarians is provided by the Department of Labor's Bureau of Labor Statistics (BLS). The main source of labor information relating to people with disabilities is furnished by the Bureau of Labor Statistics, https://www.bls.gov/. The "Data Tools" tab on the BLS home page is where librarians will find almost any federal data needed. Users can find labor data by industry, by location, by a convenient menu of frequently requested data tables; or through an application programming interface (API). This is a customizable program that allows developers to create their own applications using BLS data.

An overall search of the BLS website for the keyword "disability" yields thousands of results, giving a sense of the overall wealth of employment information relating to people with disabilities within the BLS website. The resources range from recent press releases on labor force characteristics, data on the employment status of people with disabilities, information about employee access to disability insurance plans, and many other topics in between. Disability data within the context of employment is located within the Current Population Survey Labor Force Statistics, https://www.bls.gov/cps/lfcharacteristics.htm. Articles relating to employment of people with disabilities also appear within BLS publications, such as *Spotlight on Statistics*, and these often discuss the impact of current events on labor market trends. For example, the October 2021 edition, https://www.bls.gov/spotlight/2021/labor-market-characteristics-of-people-with-a-disability/home.htm, describes the impact of the 2020 Covid pandemic and recovery on the labor market outlook for people with a disability.

Conclusion

Along with key pieces of legislation, this essay discussed federal resources for people with disabilities in healthcare, education, and employment. It is important for librarians to be aware of these resources because to serve marginalized populations and to "advance racial and social justice" are core tenets of librarianship (American Library Association 2021). Additionally, many libraries are undertaking diversity, equity, and inclusion (DEI) efforts to improve the patron and employment experience (Anaya and Maxey-Harris 2017) and addressing the needs of persons with disabilities should be part of those initiatives. Having knowledgeable librarians on staff who are well versed in federal information about disability is an excellent place to start.

References

American Library Association. 2021. "Code of Ethics." Last amended June 29, 2021. https://www.ala.org/tools/ethics.
Anaya, Toni, and Charlene Maxey-Harris. 2017. "SPEC Kit 356: Diversity and Inclusion." Association of Research Libraries. https://publications.arl.org/Diversity-Inclusion-SPEC-Kit-356/.
Center on Education Policy. 2020a. *For the Common Good: Recommitting to Public Education in a Time of Crisis.* Washington, D.C.: George Washington University. https://files.eric.ed.gov/fulltext/ED606967.pdf.
Center on Education Policy. 2020b. *History and Evolution of Public Education in the US.* Washington, D.C.: George Washington University. https://files.eric.ed.gov/fulltext/ED606970.pdf.
Institute on Disability. 2020. *Annual Report on People with Disabilities in America.* Durham: University of New Hampshire. https://disabilitycompendium.org/annual report.
National Institutes of Health. 2021. "NIH Public Access Policy Details." NIH Public Access Policy. https://publicaccess.nih.gov/policy.htm.
Schomberg, Jessica, and Wendy Highby. 2020. *Beyond Accommodation: Creating an Inclusive Workplace for Disabled Library Workers.* Sacramento: Library Juice Press.
U.S. Department of Labor. n.d. "Laws and Regulations." Accessed February 11, 2022. https://www.dol.gov/general/topic/disability/laws.
U.S. Equal Employment Opportunity Commission. n.d. "What Laws Does EEOC Enforce?" Accessed February 10, 2022. https://www.eeoc.gov/youth/what-laws-does-eeoc-enforce.

PART V

Military

From Service Records to Special Collections

General and Specialized Military Resources

HEATHER SEMINELLI *and* LAUREN B. DODD

Disclaimer: The views expressed in this essay are those of the authors and do not reflect the official position or policy of the United States Military Academy, Department of Defense, Department of the Army, or the U.S. Government.

Introduction

The U.S. Military Academy Library, Archives, and Special Collections supports the staff, faculty, and cadets of the U.S. Military Academy (USMA) and maintains Record Group 404, which are the official records of the USMA, maintained on behalf of the National Archives and Records Administration (NARA). Our collection is particularly strong in the areas of military history and the history and story of USMA, West Point, and our graduates. However, that does not always make us the best source for all military-related history, and we receive daily requests that are redirected to other excellent government resources.

Over the years, we have gathered a multitude of external resources that are better suited for military-related research. These include federal agencies, state and federal museums or historical sites, libraries and archives that support all services, private and nonprofit organizations, and databases.

Military data sources are useful for a variety of topics of interest for users such as genealogical information, military history, awards, historical sites, military leadership, veteran's history projects, oral histories, and many other subjects. These sources can help users find information that will assist in getting copies of their services records, find out when and where family members served, research military vehicles, or learn about the fort that used to be nearby. There are a multitude of publications created by the military that may be of general interest. These resources are excellent additions to any librarian's toolkit. They are divided into specific categories such as service records, genealogical information, and Army resources. We have also shared the specific resources USMA publicly provides to support military-related research.

Service Records, Genealogical Information

Many patrons are interested in learning more about the service of their relatives. The National Archives and Records Administration (NARA) is the official repository for records of military personnel who served and were discharged from the U.S. Air Force, Army, Marine Corps, Navy, and Coast Guard. These administrative records include information such as enlistment, duty stations, assignments, training, awards, and separation information. Military service records become archival and may be released publicly based on a rolling date of 62 years since the individual left the service (NARA 2016b). Non-archival records, such as the DD Form 214 Report of Separation, can be obtained by the veteran and their next of kin (NARA 2016a). Service medical records can also be very important for veterans and their families. The National Personnel Records Center has millions of health and medical records of discharged and deceased veterans. They also store retiree medical treatment records and the records of dependents treated at naval medical facilities at https://www.archives.gov/personnel-records-center/military-personnel. Information from the records is made available upon written request (with signature and date) to the extent allowed by law.

Military appointments and service records are available through Ancestry.com®. While this is a subscription service, many local public libraries subscribe to this resource. In addition, patrons who are eligible to access military Morale, Welfare, and Recreation (MWR) facilities can access the Department of Defense (DoD) MWR Libraries online and have access to Ancestry.com® online. Eligibility includes Active duty; National Guard; Reserves; immediate family of Active duty, National Guard, or Reserves service members; as well as additional categories (Department of Defense 2022). The patron can log in using their DoD Identification Number and Date of Birth to gain access to the MWR Digital Library at https://www.dodmwrlibraries.org. Additional information about those who served in the Civil War, both Union and Confederate, is available in the Civil War Soldiers and Sailors System (CWSS), https://www.nps.gov/civilwar/soldiers-and-sailors-database.htm. This database includes the history of Union and Confederate regiments, descriptions of significant battles, and prisoners of war and cemetery records.

The Ancestry.com® U.S. Military Collection includes millions of U.S. military records, covering almost 400 years of American wars and conflicts. Patrons can view items such as draft registration cards, soldier pensions, enlistment records, and muster rolls from the American Revolution through the Vietnam wars at https://www.ancestry.com/cs/militaryrecords. Another useful collection available from Ancestry.com® is the "U.S., Veterans' Gravesites, ca. 1775–2019," available at https://www.ancestry.com/search/collections/8750/. This is a compilation of burial records from a variety of sources and cemeteries. These records provide information on the burials of U.S. veterans and their dependents who are buried in the various Veterans Affairs (VA) National Cemeteries, state veterans' cemeteries, or other military cemeteries. This information is compiled from multiple sources but may include the name of the deceased, birth date, death date, interment date, burial location/site, cemetery name, cemetery address, relationship to veteran, veteran service dates, military rank, and military branch (Ancestry.com (R) 2020).

Free resources that can be used to find information on burials and cemeteries for servicemembers include "Find a Grave®," the Veterans Affairs (VA) Gravesite Locator, and the American Battle Monuments Commission. "Find a Grave®" has photos of the gravesites, information about the individuals buried in cemeteries, and includes federal cemeteries. This website is maintained by volunteers and may not be as complete or up to date as some of the other official resources. Find a Grave® is available at https://www.findagrave.com/. The Veterans Affairs Nationwide Gravesite Locator includes the burial location of veterans and their family members in VA National Cemeteries, state veterans' cemeteries, other military and Department of the Interior cemeteries, as well as for veterans buried in private cemeteries when the grave is marked with a government grave marker (1997 and later). The database of burial information is updated daily. Some search results may contain more information than others because the burial records are compiled from multiple sources. This resource is available at https://gravelocator.cem.va.gov/ngl/index.jsp. The American Battle Monuments Commission manages the cemeteries and memorials that are overseas. More than 200,000 Americans who died during World War I, World War II, Korea, or Vietnam are buried overseas, and this website has burial and memorialization information for those servicemembers. The Commission's website is available at https://www.abmc.gov/.

Army Resources

The U.S. Army supports several educational and record centers, each with a unique mission and informational resources. The U.S. Army Center of Military History (CMH), which reports to the United States Army Training and Doctrine Command (TRADOC), is responsible for the appropriate use of history throughout the United States Army. The CMH website, https://history.army.mil/, contains a wealth of resources that "provides all levels of the Army, as well as other services, government agencies, and the public, with a growing awareness of history that goes well beyond publications alone." Highlights of the online collection include Women in Army History, *Army History* magazine, resources to research by conflict (e.g., World War II) and time period, and the U.S. Army History and Heritage Podcast. Of particular interest to patrons will be the fact that "CMH's art and documents collections, library, and reference services are available to private researchers … [CMH] historians, curators, and archivists advise researchers on military history and stand ready to share their expertise concerning the location of sources" (U.S. Army Center of Military History, n.d.).

A highlight of the CMH website, and one shared often with our external researchers, is the Force Structure and Unit History Branch, https://history.army.mil/unitinfo.html. This includes the "Force Structure Support" for both historical and current TOE (tables of organization and equipment) units as well as historical information on Army Structure. The "Organizational History" includes lineage and honor for active TOE Army units, as well as awards and campaign streamers.

The U.S. Army Heritage & Education Center, https://arena.usahec.org/web/arena, is a part of the U.S. Army War College, located at Carlisle Barracks, Pennsylvania. It is "the nation's best resource for the study of strategic leadership, the global application of landpower, and the heritage of the U.S. Army, in honor of Soldiers, past and present" (U.S. Army Heritage & Education Center, n.d.). Members of the public may ask a question via the AHEC website and will also find a FAQ that may provide a quick answer to an inquiry at https://usawc.libanswers.com/. The AHEC also provides a list of useful museums and resources at https://usawc.libguides.com/c.php?g=657420&p=4615556.

The U.S. Army Institute of Heraldry, https://tioh.army.mil/, provides information on United States heraldic entitlements, how they are displayed, and how and why they are worn. Per its website, heraldic services include "decorations, flags, streamers, agency seals, coats of arms, badges, and other forms of official emblems and insignia" (The Institute of Heraldry, n.d.). The Institute of Heraldry is an excellent and comprehensive resource for learning more about items such as mottos and military, civilian, and government agency decorations and medals. The FAQ pages include U.S. flag etiquette, Army organizational flags, guidons and streamers, insignia and decorations, general information, service flags and service lapel buttons, and how to request Army medals.

The U.S. Army Records Management and Declassification Agency, https://www.rmda.army.mil/, maintains Headquarters, Department of the Army (HQDA) level responsibility for the entire spectrum of the Army's interrelated records management programs, including Army Records Management, Army Freedom of Information, Army Privacy, Civil Liberties, Army Office for Unit Records Response, and Declassification of Army Records. Members of the public can submit Army Electronic Freedom of Information Act (FOIA) requests through this website, and search through an electronic FOIA library of agency records that have already been made publicly available at the main website and also the Army's FOIA Library, https://www.rmda.army.mil/readingroom/.

Army Military Research and Education Support

Libraries that support the Army's education mission also have resources that are of interest to the public, such as bibliographies, reading lists, oral histories, and digitized repositories of publications and papers written by students. The U.S. Army Combined Arms Center (CAC), https://usacac.army.mil/, delivers professional military education and functional training through twenty branch and seven non-branch schools, the Center for Army Lessons Learned, and the Army University Press. The website contains Army Strategic Documents and interactive Army leadership resources. Other advanced schools include the U.S. Army Command and General Staff College, https://armyuniversity.edu/cgsc/cgsc, and the NCO Leadership Center of Excellence (NCOLCOE) Digital Library, https://cgsc.contentdm.oclc.org/digital/collection/p15040coll2/search/searchterm/. The NCOLCOE contains oral histories, World War II Operations Documents, Fort Leavenworth History, and paper and theses from the advanced schools.

The U.S. Army Corps of Engineers (USACE) Digital Library, https://usace.contentdm.oclc.org/, includes USACE Publications from districts, but some collections also contain materials by other governmental agencies written about USACE. Interesting resources available include Fish and Wildlife Reports with annual fish counts, photographs of the Civil War and Alaska Highway construction, and histories related to districts nationwide from "A city for the nation: The Army engineers and the building of Washington, D.C., 1790–1967" to "A mission in the desert: Albuquerque District, 1935–1985."

U.S. Army Training and Doctrine Command (TRADOC), https://www.tradoc.army.mil/, provides specialized libraries that support branch training locations across the Army. There are basic branch libraries, such as the Aviation Technical Library or the Maneuver Support Center of Excellence, that support engineers, military police, and the chemical corps. Specialized schools such as the Defense Language Institute also have academic libraries to support learning. The full list of TRADOC Libraries is available at https://www.benning.army.mil/Library/TRADOC-libraries.html.

U.S. Military Academy Resources

The U.S. Military Academy was founded in 1802. The U.S. Military Academy (USMA) Library, https://library.westpoint.edu/asc, is home to the Archives and Special Collections. The Archives collection is comprised of the historical administrative records of the Academy. These materials constitute Record Group 404 of the National Archives and Records Administration of the United States and are maintained at West Point. The Special Collections are comprised of a variety of materials from a variety of sources and includes materials related to graduates, West Point, the Academy, the Hudson Valley, and Army figures. The USMA Library also has a large collection of digitized resources for the public to access and learn more about the Academy and its graduates.

The Association of Graduates (AOG) maintains records of graduates of the Academy. One way the AOG traces this legacy is through the West Point *Register of Graduates & Former Cadets*, which traces its legacy to the post–Civil War era when George W. Cullum, Class of 1833, compiled the *Register*. This resource can be used to search for individual entries recording the names, classes, and careers of every West Point graduate from 1802 to the present. There have been various iterations of this resource throughout the years that are digitized and available to access.

Biographical Register of the Officers and Graduates of the U.S. Military Academy at West Point, N.Y.

The official record of cadets begins from the founding of the Academy. The following digitized versions are available:

◊ Biographical register of the officers and graduates of the U.S. Military Academy at West Point, New York, from its establishment, in 1802, to 1890, https://usma.primo. exlibrisgroup.com/permalink/01USMA_INST/1fetnvl/ alma991014653979005711.

◊ Biographical register of the officers and graduates of the U.S. Military Academy at West Point, New York, from its establishment, in 1802, Supplement. Coverage through the Class of 1950. https://usma.primo.exlibrisgroup.com/permalink/01USMA_ INST/11tghq3/alma991001066989705711.

◊ Volumes one through nine are also available through the HathiTrust, https://catalog.hathitrust.org/Record/000883632.

Official Register of the Officers and Cadets of the U.S. Military Academy at West Point, N.Y.

Although content changes substantially during the 148 years of its publication, a list of the academic and military staff and the order-of-merit lists for each class are included in all editions. The staff list includes information on the individual's rank, unit, or branch, and period of service at USMA. The order-of-merit list includes such data on each cadet as his date of admission, age, source of appointment, rank in respective studies, demerits accumulated, and contains remarks on cadets not examined, discharged, or turned back to a lower class. Registers from 1818 to 1966 are digitized as part of the digital collection of the USMA Library, https:// usmalibrary.contentdm.oclc.org/digital/collection/p16919coll3/search.

Howitzer Yearbooks

There are two versions of what would be thought of as yearbooks throughout USMA's history. Cadets created class albums between 1857 and 1909. USMA has examples from every year except for 1858 and 1860. They vary in composition because individual cadets purchased the photographs they wanted as part of their albums. Class albums from the classes of 1862 and 1898–1902 are available digitally at https://usmalibrary. contentdm.oclc.org/digital/collection/clalbums/search. The yearbook of the United States Corps of Cadets published by the first class of cadets. Digitized *Howitzers*, ranging from 1897 to 1949, are available through the USMA Library Digital Collection at https://usmalibrary.contentdm.oclc. org/digital/collection/howitzers/search.

Obituaries

The West Point Association of Graduates (AOG) publishes "memorial articles" in memory of deceased graduates and former cadets. Articles are published in an annual issue of *TAPS* magazine and can be found online. Search for obituaries using the "Deceased Graduate Search" function on the memorials page at https://www.westpointaog.org/memorials. Earlier obituaries are also published in the *Annual Reunion of the AOG, 1870–1916*, and the *Annual Report of the Association of the Graduates of the United States Military Academy at West Point, New York, 1917–1941.* Not all obituaries from these earlier works are included on AOG's current website. https://usma.primo.exlibrisgroup.com/permalink/01USMA_INST/11tghq3/alma991013679159705711 (*Annual Reunion*); https://usma.primo.exlibrisgroup.com/permalink/01USMA_INST/11tghq3/alma991012452489705711 (*Annual Report*).

Some obituary information is included with the biographical sketches from the *Biographical Register of the Officers and Graduates of the U.S. Military Academy at West Point, N.Y., from its establishment, in 1802, to 1890* and the *Biographical Register of the Officers and Graduates of the U.S. Military Academy at West Point, N.Y., from its establishment, in 1802, Supplement* (coverage through the Class of 1950); both are available digitally. https://usma.primo.exlibrisgroup.com/permalink/01USMA_INST/1fetnv1/alma991014653979005711 (*Biographical Register*); https://usma.primo.exlibrisgroup.com/discovery/fulldisplay?context=L&vid=01USMA_INST:Scout&docid=alma991001066989705711 (*Biographical Register/Supplement*).

Archives Record Group 404

The Archives include many series of Academy publications, such as the cadet yearbook, *Howitzer*; the post newspaper, *Pointer View*; and the *Annual Report of the Superintendent.* The annual reports by the Superintendent cover the state and accomplishments of the U.S. Military Academy. Among the subjects covered are personnel, academic departments, courses of study, expenditures, buildings and grounds, athletics, official visitors, and major events. Often included as appendixes are reports of the Adjutant, Surgeon, Treasurer, Librarian, Quartermaster, Dean, Commandant of Cadets, and other Academy officials. Normally prepared in June after the end of the academic year, Academy officials submitted reports to the Secretary of War and, after 1947, to the Secretary of the Army. Beginning in 1890, the Government Printing Office or the U.S. Military

Academy Press issued these reports as separate publications. There are no reports for the years 1874–76. https://usma.primo.exlibrisgroup.com/permalink/01USMA_INST/11tghq3/alma991002013499705711 (*Annual Report of the Superintendent*)

After the centennial celebration of the U.S. Military Academy, the Academy created the *Centennial of the United States Military Academy at West Point, New York*, 1802–1902. This includes information such as the textbooks used, graduates, bibliographies of West Point (1694–1902), of the U.S. Military Academy (1776–1902), and of the writings of graduates of USMA in the first 100 years. https://usma.primo.exlibrisgroup.com/permalink/01USMA_INST/1fetnvl/alma991011129199705711

Curriculum

Digitized descriptions of the Academic Program at USMA, also known as The Redbook, can be found for the years 1946–2014 by searching the USMA Library online catalog. The current version of the Redbook is publicly available at https://www.westpoint.edu/academics/curriculum. The *Official Register of the Officers and Cadets of the U.S. Military Academy at West Point, N.Y.*, include curriculum information starting in the mid-nineteenth century. Registers from 1818 to 1966 are digitized as part of the Digital Collections of the USMA Library and may be found at https://usmalibrary.contentdm.oclc.org/digital/collection/p16919coll3/search.

News and Photographs

The USMA Library has digitized copies of *Pointer View* newspapers from 2004 to 2010 via our online library catalog and in our digital collections at https://usmalibrary.contentdm.oclc.org/digital/collection/ptview/search. The USMA Public Affairs Office (PAO) also maintains digital copies of the years 2006–2023 on its website at https://www.westpoint.edu/about/public-affairs/pointer-view-archives. PAO's Flickr page is also an incredible resource for thousands of photographs of USMA, from approximately 2009 to present, https://www.flickr.com/photos/west_point/. The USMA Library also hosts significant collections of historical photographs online, such as the Photographs of West Point by the Army Signal Corps, https://usmalibrary.contentdm.oclc.org/digital/collection/signalcorp/search, and the Photographs of West Point by William H. Stockbridge at https://usmalibrary.contentdm.oclc.org/digital/collection/stockbridge/search.

Military Museums

Each of the military branches maintain museums dedicated to preserving the unique histories of the places, people, and activities the museums historically and currently conduct. Many of these museums also include libraries or archival collections.

The U.S. Army has a variety of museums honoring branches, training locations, and units. To find the wide variety of museums located all over the country, visit the U.S. Army Center of Military History's Find an Army Museum site, https://history.army.mil/museums/directory.html. Army museums include museums for all branches, many posts, and special museums such as National Guard Memorial Museum (Washington, D.C.), The National Infantry Museum (Columbus, Georgia), U.S. Army Museum of Hawaii (Fort DeRussy, Hawaii), U.S. Cavalry Museum (Ft. Riley, Kansas), White Sands Missile Range Museum (White Sands Missile Range, New Mexico), West Point Museum (West Point, New York), Airborne and Special Operations Museum (Fayetteville, North Carolina), U.S. Army Heritage and Education Center (Carlisle Barracks, Pennsylvania), and the National Museum of the United States Army (Fort Belvoir, Virginia).

The U.S. Navy has a variety of museums throughout the country. More information is available at https://www.history.navy.mil/visit-our-museums.html. Navy Museums include the National Museum of the U.S. Navy (Washington Navy Yard, D.C.), National Naval Aviation Museum (Pensacola, Florida), National Museum of the American Sailor (Great Lakes, Illinois), U.S. Navy Seabee Museum (Port Hueneme, California), Submarine Force Museum (Groton, Connecticut), Naval War College Museum (Newport, Rhode Island), and U.S. Naval Academy Museum (Annapolis, Maryland).

The U.S. Marine Corps has Recruit Depot Command Museums at Parris Island (South Carolina) and San Diego, but the Corps' major museum is the National Museum of the Marine Corps (Triangle, Virginia). More information on Marine Corps history is available from the Research Division of the Marine Corps University at https://www.usmcu.edu/Research/History-Division/.

The U.S. Air Force also has museums at posts across the country; more information is available at https://www.nationalmuseum.af.mil/Visit/Questions/Aviation-Museums/. Air Force Museums include the National Museum of the Air Force (Wright-Patterson Air Force Base, Ohio), as well as smaller post museums such as the Air Force Armament Museum (Eglin Air Force Base, Florida), Air Force Flight Test Center Museum (Edwards Air Force Base, California), and Peterson Air and Space Museum (Colorado Springs, Colorado).

General Interest and Research

In addition to official records, NARA also has a variety of military records, from photos to documents to searchable databases available. There are online collections related to Vietnam, Korean War, World War II, World War I, Spanish-American War, Civil War, and the Revolutionary War available online at https://www.archives.gov/research/military/veterans/online.

Conclusion

As illustrated in this essay, the Army, the Department of Defense and other military branches, the National Archives and Records Administration, and many more government entities share a wealth of freely accessible resources for military questions about topics such as history and genealogy. The United States Military Academy Library and its Archives and Special Collections also has digitized and shared information specific to USMA graduates on its website. These military resources are often little-known, under-utilized, and will be of use to a variety of patrons in any type of library.

REFERENCES

Ancestry.com®. 2020. "U.S., Veterans' Gravesites, ca.1775–2019." U.S., Veterans' Gravesites, ca. 1775–2019. November 12. Accessed February 7, 2022. https://www.ancestry.com/search/collections/8750/.

Department of Defense. MWR Libraries. 2022. "DoD MWR Libraries." Accessed May 10, 2022. https://www.dodmwrlibraries.org/.

National Archives and Records Administration. 2016a. "Request Military Service Records." January 27, 2016. Accessed February 7, 2022. https://www.archives.gov/veterans/military-service-records.

National Archives and Records Administration. 2016b. "About Military Service Records and Official Military Personnel Files (OMPFs, DD Form 214)." August 15. Accessed February 7, 2022. https://www.archives.gov/veterans/military-service-records/about-service-records-0.

The Institute of Heraldry. n.d. "The Institute of Heraldry | Home." Accessed May 10, 2022. https://tioh.army.mil/.

U.S. Army Center of Military History. n.d. "U.S. Army Center of Military History." Accessed May 10, 2022. https://history.army.mil/.

U.S. Army Heritage & Education Center. n.d. "Explore the USAHEC Collections." Accessed May 10, 2022. https://arena.usahec.org/web/arena.

Using Government Sources to Support Military Queries in Academic Libraries

MICHELLE SHEA

Introduction

Military research in an academic library can be conducted by veteran students, active-duty community members, faculty with a vested interest, and families seeking genealogical information. These individuals will likely request both subscription-based and free sources for data, but ultimately government databases, websites, and documents may be the best options for their needs. As academic librarians, we can consolidate much of this information through curated digital guides and knowledgeable staff who answer queries in-person and online. Research can include any of the branches—such as the Army, Navy, or Marines—and may be most common in areas where bases or outposts are located across the world.

Some military-related government information is available as physical or digital records at libraries. This includes information for finding military records, locating service-based scholarships, gathering data on military operations, determining what research will be funded by the military, locating ongoing projects within the reserves, filing VA paperwork for health needs, determining employment opportunities, and other common questions. Other electronic content may be limited to those with special login credentials, as issued by military entities, but that is beyond our scope. As government websites and databases have a surplus of knowledge, this essay will focus on just publicly available resources that provide answers to specific information needs.

Libraries must have staff who are prepared to serve all learners, so additional staff knowledge and training can benefit veterans and active-duty students. In this essay, librarians will learn how to find resources for common requests and search branch-specific government websites for research starting points.

Connecting Veterans with Information

At the Texas A&M Central Texas library, we have a high percentage of military-affiliated students due to our proximity to Fort Hood, a major army base. As a result, our librarians get many questions related to financial aid, military records, Veteran Affairs (VA) paperwork, and employment opportunities. To prepare for these queries, we must stay current on government information sources, which come from military branches and federal websites. The best way to stay informed is to check credible government links for updates, at least once a semester, and to speak with representatives from one's campus office for military or veteran services. Much of the information relates to forms that students will need to submit to ensure eligibility for education benefits, such as tuition or transition assistance. We typically will direct individualized questions of this nature to our departmental contacts; however, we can at least show students the government pages that host updated data and eligibility criteria. Students can then use those resources to become more informed before talking with a representative.

Librarians should also be aware of local resources, including services and organizations, which might benefit their populations. This could include military and government libraries, affiliated museums, and veteran offices that provide social and emotional services. Our library and museum contacts communicate through local consortium meetings, but we also reach out to them when we get patron requests linked to their holdings. For military offices located farther away, it can be helpful to do a web search for keywords using Google's "advanced search" option, while also limiting the domain to .gov or .mil. Many military departments will have some general knowledge posted online, but individuals with veteran credentials can login to military servers to complete required documentation or look up personal details. This is particularly true when dealing with health benefits or portals secured for personal information. Additionally, military sites may list specific contacts. Those individuals can often provide guidance over the phone, email, or in person, based on their proximity to the questioner and their availability.

Scholarships and Financial Aid

Military-affiliated individuals often visit libraries with a clear purpose, so our job is to discern these needs and direct people accordingly. In the sources below, information will be given on the types of resources that are available to potential, current, or past service members. Website URLs and brief descriptions will outline what librarians might find and how they can begin to investigate content to make better recommendations.

For military-affiliated students starting or continuing in college, it can be essential to locate scholarships and financial aid to pay for schooling. There are many places to find funding online, both through financial government websites and individual branch portals. To start, it is recommended that students check Federal Student Aid, https://studentaid.gov/, sponsored by the U.S. Department of Education. This is a broader resource that covers checklists, forms, and deadlines for common government financial aid programs. Of note, there is an "Understand Aid" category near the top with a subcategory of "Aid for Military Families" that gives more specific suggestions. This includes links to scholarship pages, VA education benefits, and loan deferment options for students in all stages of the process. In most cases, veteran students or children of soldiers who died in the line of duty must complete federal financial paperwork, such as FAFSA® (Free Application for Federal Student Aid), https://studentaid.gov/h/apply-for-aid/fafsa, to determine eligibility for either Pell or service grants. This applies only if the student is seeking financial-based need grants. Other options focused on merit and current or past service are available elsewhere.

Some students are interested in the Reserve Officers' Training Corps (ROTC) for scholarships, which are given based on a willingness to enlist after degree completion and other special conditions, such as language proficiency or specific school attendance. Students who are selected may be in high school, college, or in the service. In the Army, this program allows for coverage of all tuition and fees, as well as stipends for some books and living expenses that increase slightly as students near graduation (U.S. Army, n.d.). ROTC programs have a longer military commitment and are best for students who want to gain early career experience and are prepared to move or train at different bases around the country. Each ROTC branch webpage has details on which colleges have programs for their recruits, so students interested in a particular force may want to consult these lists first and think about their proximity and desire to attend different schools. For example, in the Navy, expectations generally include physical training, classes on military topics, and special camps or programs to gain practical experience over the summer (Naval Service Training Command Officer Development, n.d.).

For active-duty service members and some reservists, military tuition assistance programs exist for all the branches. As reported by the Department of Defense website, https://www.todaysmilitary.com/, in these programs, troops can receive benefits that cover around $250 per credit hour with a cap between $3750 and $4500 depending on the branch (Department of Defense 2022a). This amount should cover a large portion of tuition and fees per semester for state schools and a smaller portion for private institutions, but it is only available for those who are currently enlisted. The maximum hours per semester also varies, as the Air Force allows fifteen course hours from the start (Absher 2021a), while the Marines require students to register for no more than three to six hours at a time (Absher 2021b). Students must know the rules that align with their specific branch to maintain tuition assistance coverage; however, all programs require passing grades or repayment is expected. This stipulation may incentivize servicemembers to only take a course load that is manageable for a balanced life, including jobs, families, and college attendance. Although each branch has different requirements regarding service expectations, coverage limits, and application methods, all who use tuition assistance must agree to stay with the military for the duration of their education and a set period beyond it.

Finally, those who have already served may have access to education bills that dictate eligibility based on the time of military service. Many veterans currently have access to GI Bills, such as the post–9/11 GI Bill and the Montgomery Bill. Specifically, the VA offers a useful GI Bill Comparison Tool that simultaneously contrasts schools to show tuition benefits, housing or book allowances, credit for past military experience, and any special programs that might influence one's choice of attendance. Some schools also have Yellow Ribbon programs to cover remaining balances for private or graduate schools, although individual campuses may have limits on how many students per academic year will be granted these funds. Details can be found at https://www.va.gov/education/about-gi-bill-benefits/, a webpage of the U.S. Department of Veterans Affairs.

Military and Civilian Jobs for Soldiers

After completing an education, either at the high school or college level, military service personnel often begin or continue the job search. Librarians at public and academic libraries may be asked to provide guidance on where to look for employment. This could include new troops who want to build their skills, long-term military staffers who are advancing the ranks, and veterans searching for civilian jobs. It is important to understand that military-affiliated individuals will have unique circumstances, such as physical abilities or specialized knowledge, which might make their search more complicated or personalized. While librarians are not expected to have the same expertise as an education training center or recruiter, we can direct patrons to government and military sources that get people started on the right path.

Investigations into future careers can start as early as high school for students who may be considering the military or adjacent professions. The Department of Defense created a portal, the Armed Services Vocational Aptitude Battery (ASVAB) Career Exploration Program (CEP), https:// www.asvabprogram.com, which is free for schools to utilize. In ASVAB CEP, students in 10th grade and above can use the OCCU-Find feature, described at https://www.asvabprogram.com/media-center-article/49, to see job categories with bright outlooks. They can also explore growing military and branch-adjacent military careers that align with interest and skill areas. Typically, librarians should direct students with these questions to their school counselor, who can request the testing for their campus. For those who want to prepare for the ASVAB test, the Army sponsors a free website, https://march2success.com/, which hosts test prep information. These resources show that the military has a vested interest in promoting their programs and resources to high school students, even if test takers opt not to join the armed forces, since awareness may boost later interest or spark ideas about careers that support military work in a civilian capacity. Post-secondary options also exist for those who want career advice outside of high school.

For current troops, a major career-building option is apprenticeships that provide on-the-job training to prepare for future work. The United Services Military Apprenticeship Program (USMAP) is sponsored by the Department of Defense and allows servicemembers to earn certifications to prove professional competency. The Navy and Marine Corps created the program after starting training programs, which later expanded across many of the armed forces (U.S. Department of Labor, n.d.a.). For those who have at least twelve months left of active duty, it is possible to select a trade area to complete between 2000 and 6000 hours of work in a field that overlaps with civilian duties. For example, in the Coast Guard, apprentices can learn to be electricians, power-plant operators, riggers, or welders with similar tracks available to the other branches (Department of Defense 2022b). This type of training can make a transition out of the military smoother and improve professional opportunities beyond the specific skill sets learned as an enlisted troop.

To support veterans who are already leaving the force, transition assistance programs exist to provide employment workshops, sponsored by the Department of Labor, and career-seeking advice (U.S. Department of Labor, n.d.b.). In these seminars, participants will learn about career clusters, such as architecture or business management, and determine personality types and aptitudes. As reported in the Department of Labor's "DOL Career and Credential Exploration (C2E): Participant Guide," other helpful sites include CareerOneStop, https://www.careeronestop.org/, and the Veterans' Employment and Training Service at https://www.dol.gov/agencies/vets (U.S. Department of Labor 2021). On these pages, veterans can look for jobs within and beyond the government. Some positions also give priority to applicants with military service, as indicated by icons and verbiage on job postings. The Department of Veterans Affairs has a Veteran Readiness and Employment Program (VR&E), https://www.va.gov/careers-employment/vocational-rehabilitation/programs/, which includes reemployment support, training for outside jobs or self-employment, vocational training, and independent living. If veterans ask for employment assistance, the resources within these training packets and the workshops are a good place to start. Some libraries also offer business or career preparation centers, so those might be worth recommending, depending on expressed interests.

Military specific sites exist for those who want to try civilian careers within the armed services. The website Feds Hire Vets®, https://www.fedshirevets.gov/, links to a "Job Seekers" webpage that discusses some federal jobs giving preference to veterans based on a points system. This preference will not automatically result in veteran employment, but it will weigh the scales in favor of one who has existing experiences or credentials aligned with a job posting. One hiring website, USAJOBS, https://www.usajobs.gov/, is a great centralized place where military personal can find civilian employment. There are also specific portals for the Army Civilian Service, https://armycivilianservice.usajobs.gov/, the Civilian Marines, https://usmc.usajobs.gov/, and limiters for categories such as "National Guard & Reserves," "military spouses," and "veterans." A few branches have their own career portals, but they often have duplicate postings. While searching for employment websites, a good determiner of authority is to check if the publishing entity is a government department, military branch, or approved affiliate on the "about" pages or in the bottom footer area of websites.

Research on Military Topics

Military-affiliated individuals often want to know more about research topics, grant programs, and statistics conducted by one of the armed force branches. For each of these purposes, librarians can recommend sources with peer-reviewed, or government-backed, information that is credible and somewhat timely. Operational information is usually released on a delay for security reasons, so data may be a few years old. Even so, researchers can still gather facts and draw conclusions about how the military is managed.

Databases for military research are created by vendors, such as EBSCO and ProQuest, as well as governmental branches. In our collection, we subscribe to the *Military and Government Collection* and the *Military Database*, but some academic and public librarians may have access to different resources. The benefit of subscription databases is that many public domain, primary source documents, and ongoing research items are available in one space. For example, in the *Military and Government Collection*, there are hundreds of journals and magazines that can be read as HTML documents, downloaded as full-text PDFs, or linked from other databases through discovery searches (EBSCO, n.d.). It is most efficient to search by publication name when attempting to locate a specific article, but strategic keyword searching for any one branch, military topic, or government organization can also yield valuable results. In these databases, scholarly articles by academic publishers can be found in journals such as *Military Medicine, Presidential Studies Quarterly*, and *The Journal of Military History*. Items published by government institutions, federal departments, and military branches are often in the public domain when the information is not confidential. Military publications range from the Marine Corps' *Journal of Advanced Military Studies (JAMS)* to the Navy's *Naval War College Review. JAMS* and *Naval* are open access journals and are available at https://www.usmcu.edu/Outreach/Publishing/Marine-Corps-University-Press/MCU-Journal/ and https://digital-commons.usnwc.edu/nwc-review/, respectively.

Sometimes military research involves exploring grant opportunities to fund current or prospective projects. Many federal endowments can be found on https://www.grants.gov/, which has allotted money to distribute from the Department of Defense (DoD), Department of Homeland Security (DHS), Department of Veteran Affairs (VA), and others (Grants.gov, n.d.). Just for the DoD, grants may cover science and technology, behavior health, outreach, and weapons research. There are many options for those who want to propose new ideas that could benefit military work. On grants.gov, under the "Search Grants" tab, you can limit results by agency, topical category, or funding type to customize the suggested opportunities, which are given posted and closing dates for planning purposes. Each record page has details on the paperwork needed to apply, as well as the government contacts who can provide clarification.

Financial information can be found in a few places. For data on government budgets, researchers can explore https://www.usaspending.gov/, which has details on defense contracts and other Department of Defense agency awards. Comprehensive budget information for the entire department can be found at the Office of the Under Secretary of Defense (Comptroller) website, https://comptroller.defense.gov/, under the "Budget Materials" heading. The fiscal year reports include data on key programs and financial statements. To see narrower and more detailed information on military spending, some branches maintain Financial Management and Comptroller webpages with data spreadsheets. This includes the Air Force at https://www.saffm.hq.af.mil/, the Army at https://www.asafm.army.mil/Budget-Materials/, and the Navy at https://www.secnav.navy.mil/fmc/fmb/Pages/Fiscal-Year-2024.aspx. While the Coast Guard and Marines do publish their financial standards, they are less overt about where their full budget is located. Some government entities, like the Government Accountability Office, https://www.gao.gov/, have a website with some spending details sorted by agency, which can shed light on fiscal management. The Comptroller of the Department of Defense's centralized page, https://comptroller.defense.gov/Budget-Materials/, that links to many of the budget landing pages.

For statistics, the DoD's Military OneSource website, https://www.militaryonesource.mil, is an excellent place to find surveys and reports. For example, demographics on service families can be found at https://www.militaryonesource.mil/data-research-and-statistics/reports/. This information is accessible by scrolling to the bottom of the homepage and locating the "Data, Research, and Statistics" header where all the links are collated. For most other general statistical military requests, a source to check is the Defense Manpower Data Center (DMDC), https://dwp.dmdc.osd.mil/dwp/app/main. On the homepage, under "DoD Data/Reports," there is a "Statistics & Reports" section to find numbers for "military casualties" and "military training and readiness reports," as well as surveys on equity and gender concerns. These reports are open to the public. Any statistics that are more specific, such as those focused on aspects of housing or transportation, could be researched from a list of federal departments at https://www.usa.gov/statistics.

Military Documentation and Service Benefits for Veterans

Veterans or their spouses may visit libraries to look at military records, which are often stored on microfiche or microfilm. These are small images that can be expanded to a larger size when using a microform reader machine. Sometimes, patrons will have a fiche or film item ready for us to set up, but at other times they need help requesting a copy from their military branch. In the first case, our librarians will provide basic training on how to magnify images and print records. For the latter circumstance, we would recommend visitors search the National Archives and Records Administration (NARA) website, if the service dates were more than 62 years in the past, or contact the post they served at for guidance. In many cases, recently discharged veterans can access records online through the "Department of Veterans Affairs and Department of Defense eBenefits portal." Patrons can reference NARA's "Veterans' Service Records" website, https://www. archives.gov/veterans/military-service-records, for more information.

After acquiring proof of military service, many veterans can apply for varied benefits, including health, retirement, and housing options. For health needs, the Department of Veterans Affairs (VA) determines health care eligibility based on criteria, such as having served as an active-duty troop or leaving the force with a positive record if injured or disabled. Those who qualify may get some health coverage, caregiving assistance, prescription refills, medical supplies, and appointments with VA workers. More information is available at https://www.va.gov/health-care/ eligibility/. The VA also has programs oriented at different populations, including women and minorities, for both physical and mental care. Current troops will want to visit the Military Health System's website "Military Health Topics," https://www.health.mil/Military-Health-Topics, which has toolkits on support, conditions, and health care access. For retirees, there is a legacy pension and blended retirement system (USA. gov 2022), as well as tools at Military Compensation, https://militarypay. defense.gov, for benefit links, retirement calculators, and related information. While active-duty members or veteran students can use housing stipends within the GI Bill for education, other honorably discharged members are also eligible for home loans to support life after the military. For those interested in purchasing a home, the VA's Home Loan's website at https://www.benefits.va.gov/homeloans/ discusses how a VA loan has advantageous features such as lower interest rates, closing costs, and down payment amounts. Being a former serviceperson qualifies patrons for many special programs, so it is helpful when librarians can point to government departments or organizations that help reduce living expenses.

Conclusion

In this essay, an overview of common government and military sources is given. The websites listed are not comprehensive, but they do highlight .gov and .mil pages that may be most pertinent to student queries. In practice, librarians may want to consult some of these sources as a first line of inquiry and then use patron feedback to narrow down results to other subpages or categories. The process should typically involve determining the information need, uncovering whether the person wants facts related to a specific branch or organization, and then locating any publicly available data. It could also involve helping patrons determine if they require special permissions or credentials to access certain sites. At times, it may be most logical to direct someone to the contacts listed on a government page for more personalized help, but this should occur only after a solid reference consultation. This would include guidelines on where to find starting point information. Scholarship, employment, research, and documentation are all valid reasons for military-affiliated patrons to visit the library. Some libraries may find it beneficial to curate these links and sources in one place, perhaps on a library website; however, it is also feasible to train library staff in the basics and create guides or visual aids that can be distributed in-person to students or visitors. The goal is to offer multiple modes of instruction and information gathering to suit all kinds of purposes, so that government articles, statistics, and websites can be found when needed to minimize frustration and improve utility for all involved.

References

Absher, Jim. 2021a. "Air Force Tuition Assistance." September 30. https://www.military.com/education/money-for-school/air-force-tuition-assistance.html.
Absher, Jim. 2021b. "Marine Corps Tuition Assistance." September 30. https://www.military.com/education/money-for-school/marine-corps-tuition-assistance.html.
Department of Defense. 2022a. "Paying for College." Accessed June 7, 2022. https://www.todaysmilitary.com/education-training/paying-college.
Department of Defense. 2022b. "United States Military Apprenticeship Program (USMAP): Coast Guard Trades." Accessed June 7, 2022. https://usmap.osd.mil/coastguardRatings.htm.
EBSCO. n.d. "Military & Government Collection." Accessed June 7, 2022. https://www.ebsco.com/products/research-databases/military-government-collection.
Grants.gov. n.d. "Grant-Making Agencies." Accessed June 7, 2022. https://www.grants.gov/web/grants/learn-grants/grant-making-agencies.html.
Naval Service Training Command Officer Development. n.d. "NROTC Preparatory Programs." Accessed June 7, 2022. https://www.netc.navy.mil/Commands/Naval-Service-Training-Command/NROTC/Program-Info/.
U.S. Army. n.d. "Army ROTC Scholarships." Accessed June 7, 2022. https://www.goarmy.com/careers-and-jobs/find-your-path/army-officers/rotc/scholarships.html.
U.S. Department of Labor. n.d.a. "United Services Military Apprenticeship Program." Accessed June 7, 2022. https://www.apprenticeship.gov/case-studies/united-services-military-apprenticeship-program.
U.S. Department of Labor. n.d.b. "Veterans' Employment and Training Service: Transition Assistance Program." Accessed June 7, 2022. https://www.dol.gov/agencies/vets/programs/tap.

U.S. Department of Labor. 2021. "DOL Career and Credential Exploration (C2E)." January 2021 Edition. https://www.dol.gov/sites/dolgov/files/VETS/files/TAP-C2E-Participant-Guide.pdf.

USA.gov. 2022. "Military Pay and Pensions." Last updated April 19, 2022. https://www.usa.gov/military-pay.

PART VI

Native Americans
and the Federal Government

Native American History from Government Documents and Maps

BRANDON R. BURNETTE

Introduction

Finding Native American historical information from government documents can be intimidating. This essay will demonstrate where to find historical information from titles that are available online as well as specific websites. There are examples on how to use these online resources. Many of these titles are also available from the HathiTrust, https://www. hathitrust.org/, and the Internet Archive, https://archive.org/.

The materials pertaining to Native Americans that are discussed in this essay such as treaties, land cessions, and maps are important for understanding the history of the relationship between the white man and the Native Americans. Treaties affirm the sovereignty of American Indian nations by allowing tribal governments to maintain a nation-to-nation relationship with the United States government. Land cessions and maps are important in the understanding of where Indian nations once lived and where they were transferred.

The library at Southeastern Oklahoma State University has a total of four subject guides on Native American resources on the webpage titled Government Information Subject Guides, https://www.se.edu/library/ government-information-resources/subject-guides/. The links to the resources within this essay can be found within the Native American Historical Resources subject guide. Since most of the subject guides are in alphabetical order, it is necessary to scroll down the webpage to find the Native American Historical Resources subject guide.

The Native American Historical Resources subject guide has several sections. The first section has several websites that include *The North American Indian* by Edward S. Curtis, an American photographer in the early twentieth century who concentrated on photographing the Native American people, and George Catlin—The Complete Works, a nineteenth-century American painter who specialized in portraits of Native Americans. The Legislative Branch section has congressional and legal materials and links from the Library of Congress. The Executive Branch section includes links from the Departments of Agriculture, Commerce, Defense, Education, and Interior. The Independent Agencies section has links from the National Archives and Records Administration, National Endowment for the Humanities, and the Smithsonian Institution. The last section is specific to Oklahoma.

Bureau of American Ethnology

In 1879, the Smithsonian Institution established the Bureau of Ethnology for the purpose of managing the archives, records, and materials from the Department of the Interior relating to Native Americans; in 1897, the name changed to the Bureau of American Ethnology. The Bureau of American Ethnology published five series of reports: Annual Reports, Bulletins, Contributions to North American Ethnology, Introductions, and Miscellaneous Publications (Hodge 1907, 171, 173). If you are interested in learning about North, Central, and South American Indians on subjects such as anthropology, history, language, mythology, and music, these five series are an excellent set of materials to explore. A list of titles for each of these five series is available from the Smithsonian Institution's List of Publications of the Bureau of American Ethnology website, https://www.sil.si.edu/DigitalCollections/BAE/Bulletin200/200title.htm. The Biodiversity Heritage Library (BHL) has digitized all five series, and the links are accessible from the Smithsonian Institution section of the Native American Historical Resources subject guide. After choosing a volume to read within the BHL website, click on "View Volume" and then, next to "Fit to Height," click on the plus sign twice. The document will zoom in at 50 percent magnification.

The *Annual Reports of the Bureau of American Ethnology to the Secretary of the Smithsonian* is one of two major series within the Bureau of American Ethnology: Annual Reports #1–15: https://www.biodiversitylibrary.org/bibliography/38077 and Annual Reports #16–81: https://www.biodiversitylibrary.org/bibliography/37968. It contains reports from the director of the Bureau of American Ethnology as well as accompanying papers on subjects such as Native American culture, art, and pottery. These are available through the Forty-Seventh Annual Report. The Forty-Eighth Annual Report contains an index for the first forty-seven annual reports. Only the director's report is available for the Forty-Ninth through the Eighty-First annual reports.

If you are interested in learning about the history of the Cherokee Nation and the treaties with the United States, there is an accompanying paper from the 1883–84 Fifth Annual Report published in 1887 titled "Cherokee Nation of Indians: A Narrative of their Official Relations with the Colonial and Federal Governments," written by Charles C. Royce. This paper describes the treaties from 1785 to 1868 between the Cherokee Nation and the United States government, the historical data of the events that led up to the negotiations, and the subsequent period connected with the results of these treaties. Of particular importance is a section found on page 264 titled "Cherokees contemplate removal to Columbia River." In the 1830s, the Cherokees considered leaving their homeland in the east and moving across the country adjacent to the mouth of the Columbia River on the Pacific Coast. The Secretary of War discouraged the idea because they may be surrounded by hostile tribes and be too remote for the United States military to support and protect them (Smithsonian Institution 1887).

The other major series, which began in 1887 and has 200 volumes, is the *Bulletins*: Bulletins #1–24: https://www.biodiversitylibrary. org/bibliography/37878; and Bulletins #25–200: https://www. biodiversitylibrary.org/bibliography/37959. The *Bulletins* have papers with similar subjects just like the *Annual Reports of the Bureau of American Ethnology*. These *Bulletins* have many titles on the history of Native American tribes. John R. Swanton, an anthropologist for the Bureau of American Ethnology, wrote several bulletins that include Native American history. These titles include *Bulletin* numbered 43, the *Indian Tribes of the Lower Mississippi Valley and Adjacent Coast of the Gulf of Mexico*, published in 1911. *Bulletin* numbered 73, published in 1922, is titled *Early History of the Creek Indians and their Neighbors*. Published in 1942, *Bulletin* numbered 132 is titled *Source Material on the History and Ethnology of the Caddo Indians*. The *Indians of the Southeastern United States*, published in 1946, is *Bulletin* numbered 137. Published in 1952, *The Indian Tribes of North America* comes from *Bulletin* numbered 145.

Treaties

One of the most important set of documents on Native Americans is Kappler's *Indian Affairs: Laws and Treaties*. This is available from the

Oklahoma State University Library Digital Collections, https://dc.library. okstate.edu/digital/collection/kapplers. Charles J. Kappler, who served as a clerk to the Senate Committee on Indian Affairs, compiled and edited the first five of seven volumes of this set. Volume two has treaties and agreements from 1778 to 1883. To find a specific treaty, such as the Treaty with the Mandan Tribe, 1825, scroll down on the right-hand side of the page and click on it. The entire treaty can be read by using the provided tool to enlarge the document. Once open, the zoom tool can be used to modify the magnification, print it, or download it.

The Oklahoma State University Library created the database Tribal Treaties Database, https://treaties.okstate.edu/. As of this writing, this database is in public beta. There are several ways to find a treaty on this website besides using the search box. The "Treaties" link displays a list of ten treaties per page. The "Tribes" link allows for the option to find treaties for present-day (Federally recognized) tribes and from tribes as they originally appeared in Kappler's *Indian Affairs: Laws and Treaties* by using the term "Original Signatories." After clicking on a treaty, the entire treaty can be read as well as the annotated notes beside it. Each treaty has a link to the original treaty from the National Archives website. It also has a link to the published version of the treaty from Kappler's *Indian Affairs: Laws and Treaties* from the Oklahoma State University Library Digital Collections.

The Treaties: Database of US-Indian Treaties and Historical Narratives, http://portal.treatysigners.org/us/Site%20Pages/TreatyPage. aspx, which is part of the U.S. Treaty Signers Project, is a special initiative of the Indian Land Tenure Foundation (ILTF). This website has information on 386 treaties and agreements between the United States and Native American tribes and historical overviews that present six distinct eras in treaty-making. For example, by choosing the 1819 Indian Removal Act (1830) era and scrolling down to the last section, Pre-Removal: Western Land, 1824–1828, there is a link for Shawnee 1825. The treaty records for each of the treaties contain: date and place where the parties signed the treaty, name(s) of indigenous nation(s) involved in the treaty, and the names of U.S. treaty signers. There were 2,300 men who represented the United States in treaty negotiations that signed Indian treaties. Treaty records also include links to the text of the treaty from Kappler's *Indian Affairs: Laws and Treaties* and land cession maps.

Due to the partnership between the National Archives and the Indigenous Digital Archive (IDA) project of the Museum of Indian Arts and Culture in Santa Fe, New Mexico, 374 of the original ratified treaties between the United States government and Native American tribes have been digitally scanned and are accessible on the IDA Treaties Explorer website, https://digitreaties.org/treaties/. For example, to find the 1825 treaty with the Shawnee tribe, click on the "Treaties" button. There are search boxes underneath the word Treaties. Search for the word "Shawnee" in the title search box. It will be important to limit by the date— Later than: 01/01/1825 and Earlier than: 01/01/1826. A drop-down menu appears that provides the options for All, Treaties, and Accompany Document. Choose "Treaties" and click the go button. There will be three items pertaining to registered Indian treaty number 143. The original copy of the treaty is "Treaty Between the United States and the Shawnee Indians Signed at St. Louis." Clicking on the treaty allows for viewing the document in two ways. To take a closer look at the document, use the plus sign on top of the image or click on the download button on the bottom left-hand corner of the box. Underneath the image of the treaty, it gives information on which land cession numbers that accompany the 1825 Shawnee treaty: 125, 126, 318, 319, and 320. Click on one of the numbers and it retrieves a map of what the land cession currently looks like. By scrolling down the bottom of the page, the user will see a map named for cession numbers 125 and 126: Missouri 2. The link to the source URL retrieves this specific map on the Library of Congress website. These types of maps come from Charles C. Royce's *Indian Land Cessions in the United States.*

Land

Charles C. Royce compiled the *Indian Land Cessions in the United States* (Library of Congress: https://memory.loc.gov/ammem/amlaw/lwss-ilc.html; Internet Archive: https://archive.org/details/annualreportofbu182smit/page/n5/mode/2up), published in 1899 within part two of the *Eighteenth Annual Report of the Bureau of American Ethnology to the Secretary of the Smithsonian, 1896–97.* This volume begins with the introduction "Right to the Soil Dependent on Discovery" and has information on the Indian policies of the Spanish, French, English, and the United States as well as the original thirteen original colonies. It also has the schedule of Indian land cessions (pages 648–949), a list of land cessions by tribes (pages 951–964), and sixty-seven cession maps. The schedule of Indian land cessions includes the date of the land cession, starting in the year 1784 and lasting through 1894; the name of the tribe(s); the description of the cession or reservation; historical data and remarks; and the designation of cession on a map. The numbers on a cession map represent the Indian land cession number for each tribe. These cession maps, which are in color, can be seen in greater detail from the Library of Congress website, https://www.loc.gov/item/13023487/, and the USGenWeb Archives website, http://usgwarchives.net/maps/cessions/.

Land Tenure History, https://iltf.org/land-issues/history/, is part of the Indian Land Tenure Foundation's website. This webpage begins with the history of allotment for Native Americans, which is a parcel of land divided among individual tribal members. It gives descriptions of historical allotment legislations from the General Allotment Act of 1887, also known as the Dawes Act (Pub. L. 49-105), through 2004, and it has brief descriptions of United States Supreme Court cases, listed in reverse order by the year, from 2009 to 1810.

Another website on allotment is the Native American Documents Project, https://easchwartz.us/nadp/. This website includes reports from the Commissioner of Indian Affairs from the 1870s, allotment data, legislation, and readings for further study of allotment. If you are interested in learning more about allotment, E.A. Schwartz, an associate history professor from California State University San Marcos, wrote the article "What Were the Results of Allotment?" on the results of the Allotment Act, which includes several tables with a comparison of tribal land for the years 1887 and 1904.

Maps

The U.S. Forest Service of the United States Department of Agriculture's Tribal Connections is an online interactive mapping tool, https://usfs.maps.arcgis.com/apps/webappviewer/index.html?id=fe311f69cb1d4 3558227d73bc34f3a32. According to the U.S. Forest Service Tribal Relations webpage, https://www.fs.usda.gov/working-with-us/tribal-relations, this interactive map shows the connection between national forests and grasslands, tribal trust lands, and tribal lands ceded as part of a treaty. Using the zoom feature allows for viewing land cessions and land cession numbers. For example, clicking on land cession number 202 within the states of Arkansas and Louisiana, which relates to the Caddo Tribe, displays links to the schedule of Indian land cessions from the Internet Archive, the text of the treaty from the HathiTrust, and cession maps from the Library of Congress website.

An excellent source to find maps pertaining to Native Americans is the Library of Congress's website Native American Spaces: Cartographic Resources at the Library of Congress, https://guides.loc.gov/native-american-spaces/introduction. The "Cartographic Resources" section has nine different topics. One of the topics is "Indian Lands, Village Sites,

Tribal Range, Place Names, and Communication Routes." On this webpage is a map drawn by Father P.J. De Smet titled "Map of the Upper Great Plains and Rocky Mountain Region, 1851." This map shows territories of several Native American tribes. To get a closer look at the map, click on the map itself or click on the hyperlinked author and title of the map. Click on the map and locate six square boxes in the upper right-hand corner. These boxes are tools used to "go home" (starting point), zoom in and out, rotate clockwise, toggle to the full page, and use the scissors to clip the map. Using the zoom in and the rotate right buttons allows for viewing the finer details of the map.

The Oklahoma Digital Maps Collections, https://library.okstate. edu/search-and-find/collections/digital-collections/oklahoma-digital-maps-collection/, also has maps pertaining to Native Americans. To look for maps, click on the View the Collection box to view the map collection. Keyword searching is available to search the entire map collection. For example, prior to Oklahoma becoming a state, a proposal had been made for a new state to be created from Indian Territory called the State of Sequoyah. Use the search box on the right-hand side of the page to search "State of Sequoyah." Three maps with the title of the State of Sequoyah will be displayed. After clicking on one of these three maps, the map details can be displayed by using the "expand" tool located in the upper-right hand corner of the map.

Reports of Indian Affairs

The University of Wisconsin Digitized Collections had digitized the *Annual Report of the Commissioners of Indian Affairs*, https://search. library.wisc.edu/digital/A3YVW4ZRARQT7J8S, from 1826 to 1917 and 1921 to 1932. These annual reports include reports by the Commissioner of Indian Affairs, reports by agents from different states and territories, and statistical information. From the published reports from 1851 to 1906, you can choose a specific year, and this will include a detailed table of contents for each year. After that, once you choose a specific section, you can click on the PDF button to download each section. Specific sections for each report can be downloaded in PDF format. Each year, the Commissioner of Indian Affairs would write about different issues. For example, in the 1877 report written by Ezra Hayt (2–3, 6, 9–17, 21–23), https://search.library. wisc.edu/digital/AK2JSOKHFOADSK9C, he wrote of a need for laws committed to address crimes by or against Indians within the boundaries of an Indian reservation, and the need for an Indian police to preserve order within Indian reservations. Hayt also wrote on Indian removal to Indian

Territory for Colorado and Arizona Indians, the Nez Perce War, the Sioux War, and the removal of the Poncas.

Legislative and Executive Documents

The *American State Papers*, which has a total of 38 volumes and legislative and executive documents from 1789 to 1838, comes from the Library of Congress American Memory website A Century of Lawmaking for a New Nation: U.S. Congressional and Debates, 1774–1875, https://memory.loc.gov/ammem/amlaw/. This series is arranged into ten topical classes. For example, class two is titled Indian Affairs, https://memory.loc.gov/ammem/amlaw/lwsplink.html#anchor2. It is divided into two volumes and these volumes are considered to be volume seven and volume eight of the *American State Papers* series. The Indian Affairs documents cover the years 1789 to 1827, and it contains communications from the president of the United States, the secretary of war, and reports from congressional committees. Both volumes have an index, but volume one is more extensive than volume two. The indices start on page i in each volume. Only volume two has a table of contents. Topics such as treaties, trade, and civilizing the Indians can be found in some of these reports. One such example is titled Trade and Intercourse, which is report number 142. It starts on page 26 of volume two. Page one of the table of contents lists the report under the section "Communications from the Secretary of War" as report number 142, "On the trade and intercourse with the Indians, March 14, 1816." In the "Notes" on page 66, it discusses the fur trade factory system.

> The factories ... are trading-houses fixed at certain points under the protection of a fort, and more or less distant from the Indian villages. Though living at a considerable distance from those houses, Indians are obliged to go to them to trade. They get in exchange for their furs goods at a reasonable price.

The American Indian and the Alaskan Native Documents in the Congressional Serial Set: 1817–1899 database, https://digitalcommons.law.ou.edu/indianserialset/, contains documents and reports published by the U.S. House of Representatives and the Senate in the nineteenth century. This comes from the University of Oklahoma College of Law Digital Commons. If you are interested in reading congressional reports on organizing Indian Territory in the 1870s, use the search the term "Oklahoma Territory" within the search box and then select from the KEYWORD section on the left-hand side of the webpage, "Indian Territory—Government." If you choose the March 1876 document "Province of Oklahoma," click on the Download link, which is next to the PDF icon, and the document will appear.

Indian Education and Civilization: A Report Prepared in Answer to Senate Resolution of February 23, 1885, https://catalog.hathitrust.org/ Record/100208234, by Alice C. Fletcher is an 1888 special report from the Bureau of Education. Chapters one through three have a historical account of Native Americans and Europeans from the sixteenth through the eighteenth century, while chapter four is titled "Administration of Indian Affairs." Chapter six addresses Indian education, but the main content of the report, beginning with chapters 5 and 7–21, focuses on Indian reservations. The chapters on reservations have information such as treaties, executive orders, acts of Congress, establishment of the reservations, population of tribes, location of reservations, and government rations. For example, on page 486, the Winnebago Reservation has 108,924 acres of land with a population of 1,572. They did not receive government rations, but they established an Indian police force.

Southeastern Native American Documents

The Digital Library of Georgia has an online collection, Southeastern Native American Documents, 1730–1842, https://dlg.usg.edu/collection/ dlg_zlna. This website has documents pertaining to the Cherokee, Chickasaw, Choctaw, Creek, and Seminole Nations. For example, searching for Creek Nation, one of the documents retrieved is "A talk of the Headmen and Warriors of the Lower Creek Nation, 1786 Apr. 23." Clicking on the title allows for taking a closer look at the document. Located on this page are two tabs: Metadata and Text. Two of the things the Metadata tab includes are the subject heading(s) and a description of the document. The Text tab contains the text of the document. This document, written by Lower Creek leaders to the governor of Georgia and state commissioners, expresses their discontent with encroachments by white settlers across the Oconee River, Georgia.

Indian Law

The *Handbook of Federal Indian Law, with Reference Tables and Index*, https://thorpe.law.ou.edu/cohen.html, by Felix S. Cohen (1941) is a unique book on Indian laws. Chapter one begins with definitions of the terms "Indian" and "Indian country," while chapter two focuses on the development and the policies of the Office of Indian Affairs. On page twelve, chapter two, Cohen refers to an 1826 report written about appropriating money to support Indian schools:

> the vast benefits which the Indian children are deriving from these establishments; and which go further, in my opinion, towards securing our borders from bloodshed, and keeping the peace among the Indians themselves, and attaching them to us, than would the physical force of our Army....

Some of the other chapters include "Indian Treaties," "Federal Indian Legislation," "The Scope of Federal Power over Indian Affairs," and "Federal Services for Indians." There are also chapters for specific states: New Mexico, Alaska, New York, and Oklahoma.

Census Reports

In 1894, the Census Office published *Report on Indians Taxed and Indians Not Taxed in the United States (Except Alaska)*, https://babel. hathitrust.org/cgi/pt?id=uc1.31822038213948&view=1up&seq=7&s kin=2021. This report begins with the "Introduction" chapter that has Indian census information since the 1700s. Other chapters include: "Historic Review of Indians in the United States (Alaska Excepted)"; "Policy and Administration of Indian Affairs (from 1776 to 1890)"; a statistical section called "Population, Educational, Land, and Vital and Social Statistics of Indians"; "Condition of Indians Taxed and Indians Not Taxed by States and Territories"; and "Indian Wars and their Cost, and Civil Expenditures for Indians." On page 50 of the "Historic Review of Indians in the United States (Alaska Excepted)" section, it describes how having horses changed the landscape for the Indians by not having to rely on canoes.

> The Spaniards brought the modern horse to America. Some of the horses escaped in the southwest and ran wild in bands. The Indians soon captured and adopted them, and so after a time the canoe was partially abandoned, and as a result the roaming plains Indian followed. The new means of locomotion, the horse, became the Indians inseparable companion. The interior of the country was thus easily explored.... The horse, enabling the Indian to follow the buffalo for food and clothes, and the claiming of the lands by the tribes encouraged his nomadic habits and paved the way for his continued unsettled life.

During the 1890s, the Census Office published four extra census bulletins on Native Americans, https://www.census.gov/library/ publications/1890/dec/bulletins.Demographics.html. The bulletins cover a variety of information about each tribe, such as education, form of government, statistics, photographs, illustrations, and maps. These four bulletins all have indexes. The titles for these bulletins are: *Eastern Band of Cherokees of North Carolina*; *The Five Civilized Tribes in Indian Territory: The Cherokee, Chickasaw, Choctaw, Creek and Seminole Nations*; the *Moqui Pueblo Indians of Arizona and Pueblo Indians of New Mexico*; and the *Six Nations of New York: Cayugas, Mohawks (Saint Regis), Oneidas, Onondagas, Senecas, Tuscaroras*. For example, to find out how the Iroquois Confederacy started, use the index from the *Six Nations of New York* bulletin, authored by Thomas Donaldson (1892), page 86, and find the entry "Hiawatha initiates the Iroquois confederacy, 20." On page 20 is the section "the Words of Hiawatha."

> We have met, members of many nations, many of you a great distance from your homes, to provide for our common safety. To oppose these foes from the north by tribes, and alone, would prove our destruction. We must unite as a common band of brothers, and we shall be safe…. You five great and powerful nations must unite and have but one common interest, and no foe shall be able to subdue us. If we unite, the "Great Spirit" will smile upon us. Brothers, these are the words of Hiawatha.

In 1915 and 1937, the Bureau of the Census published the *Indian Population in the United States and Alaska, 1910*, https://www.census.gov/library/publications/1915/dec/aian.html, which is part of the thirteenth census (1910), and the *Fifteenth Census of the United States: 1930, The Indian Population of the United States and Alaska*, https://www.census.gov/library/publications/1937/dec/1930sr-aian.html. Both publications contain twelve different types of statistics; nine of them are similar: population, full-bloods and mixed-bloods, age distribution, linguistic stocks and tribes, martial condition, school attendance, illiteracy, inability to speak English, and occupations. The thirteenth census publication includes 110 tables, but it also has statistics on sex distribution, fecundity and vitality, and Indians taxed and not taxed. The fifteenth census, which has seventy-three tables, includes statistics on the composition of the Indian population of selected counties and thirty-two selected cities, including twenty from the state of Oklahoma (table 54 from chapter nine), Indian farm operators and farms operated by Indians, and the Indian population of Alaska.

In *Indian Population in the United States and Alaska, 1910*, to find out the number of full-blooded and mixed-blooded Indians from a specific tribe, go to table 14, page 32 of the chapter "Proportion of Mixed-Bloods." The table is titled Distribution of Indians According to Purity of Blood, for each Principal Stock, Tribe, and State: 1910, pages 32–34. For example, the Pawnee tribe, which is of Caddoan Stock, has a total of 633 members. The number of full-blooded tribal members totaled 544, while the census counted 77 members as of mixed-blood and twelve members did not report being full-blooded or of mixed-blood.

In the *Fifteenth Census of the United States: 1930. The Indian Population of the United States and Alaska*, to find out how many Indians who are unable to speak the English language, go to table 52 titled Inability to Speak English in the Indian Population 10 years old and over, by Sex, by Stock, Tribe, and Blood: 1930. It starts on page 161 of chapter eight. The Blackfeet tribe, which is of Algonquian Stock, had a total of 2,188 tribal members with 267, or 12.2 percent unable to speak English. This table also documents 804 tribal members that are full-blooded members, with 244, or 30.3 percent unable to speak English. This table is split up by sex as well.

Conclusion

There are several ways in finding Indian treaties, including the original version of those treaties. Finding out about land cession maps, Commissioner of Indian Affairs reports, and congressional documents pertaining to Native Americans, especially before the twentieth century, are helpful to understand what happened in the past between the white man and Native Americans.

These sources will enrich anyone doing research on Native Americans. Granted there are other websites where Native American materials can be found, many of them are available from Southeastern Oklahoma State University's Native American Historical Resources subject guide, https://www.se.edu/library/government-information-resources/subject-guides.

References

Donaldson, Thomas. 1892. *The Six Nations of New York: Cayugas, Mohawks (Saint Regis), Oneidas, Onondagas, Senecas, Tuscaroras*. Washington, D.C: United States Census Printing Office. https://www2.census.gov/library/publications/decennial/1890/bulletins/demographics/indians-the-six-nations-of-ny.pdf.

Hodge, Frederick Webb, ed. 1907. *Handbook of American Indians North of Mexico*. Smithsonian Institution, Bureau of American Ethnology Bulletin 30. Washington, D.C.: Government Printing Office. https://www.biodiversitylibrary.org/item/87747#page/9/mode/1up.

Smithsonian Institution. Bureau of Ethnology. 1887. *Fifth Annual Report of the Bureau of Ethnology to the Secretary of the Smithsonian Institution 1883–84*. Washington, D.C.: Government Printing Office. https://www.biodiversitylibrary.org/item/88787#page/7/mode/1up.

Appendix: Additional Resources

American State Papers: Indian Affairs 2:66. Accessed April 19, 2022. https://memory.loc.gov/cgi-bin/ampage?collId=llsp&fileName=008/llsp008.db&recNum=73.

A Century of Lawmaking for a New Nation: U.S. Congressional and Debates, 1774–1875.

Indian Land Tenure Foundation. n.d. "About the US Treaty Signers Project." Accessed April 4, 2022. http://portal.treatysigners.org/us/SitePages/AboutILTF.aspx.

Kappler, Charles J., comp. and ed. 1903. *Indian Affairs: Laws and Treaties Vol. 2 (Treaties).* "Treaty with the Mandan Tribe, 1825." Accessed April 4, 2022. Washington, D.C.: Government Printing Office. https://dc.library.okstate.edu/digital/collection/kapplers/id/29480.

Museum of Indian Arts and Culture, https://www.indianartsandculture.org/.

Researching Indian Treaties and Other Related Documents

An Annotated Bibliography

CONNIE STRITTMATTER

Introduction

Native Americans and the United States have had a strenuous relationship over the past 250 years. Insight into this history can be found in treaties and their related documents. Through this lens, one can see how relationships between these two entities changed over the course of time. The relevance of these documents is not for legal scholars alone. Researchers in Native American studies, political science, government, and other disciplines can benefit from the valuable information contained in Indian treaties. Unfortunately, these resources often go unused due to the difficulty of researching legal documents.

The purpose of this essay is to provide a brief overview of the United States and Indian negotiations and the resources available to locate these documents. This essay begins by discussing the types of documents used in the United States/Indian relations from 1776 to the early 1900s. It is followed by exploring the United States policy and agenda during three distinct time periods during U.S./Indian relations. This is followed by a discussion of the nuances of Indian treaties such as the canons of treaty construction and treaty abrogation. The final section lists and annotates resources that can be used to locate Indian treaties and related documents.

Indian Treaties and Related Documents

From 1776 through 1871, the United States and Indian negotiators used treaties as the primary negotiating tool. Treaties are "agreements formally signed, ratified, or adhered to between two nations or sovereigns" (Garner 2009, s.v. "treaty" 1640). In the United States, the president, with the advice and consent of the Senate, has the power to enter into treaties (U.S. Const. art. II, §2) although the actual negotiations are often delegated to a representative.

When an agreement is reached, the executive branch transmits the text of the treaty to the Senate for consideration. Two-thirds of the Senate must vote in favor of a treaty before it can be ratified by the president. By constitutional definition, treaties are supreme law of the land and hold the same weight as statutes and cases.

Between 1778 and 1871, the United States and tribal nations entered into over 360 treaties (Prucha 1994, 1).* In the first edition of the seminal work by Cohen (1941), he identified five major components of treaties:

- *International Status of the Tribe* stipulated that the United States and the tribal nation would cease war and strive for perpetual peace (38–40).
- *Dependence of Tribes on the United States* required that an Indian nation place itself under U.S. protection. This stipulation played a crucial role in the transition from U.S. perception of Tribal nations as independent nations to wards of the state. This section also established trade regulations and the right of travel and passage over land (40–43).
- *Commercial Relations* delineated the boundaries and cessation of lands by Indian nations to the United States. Although the Indian nations ceded land to the United States, the treaty often included a stipulation that Indian nations would retain their hunting and fishing rights on these lands. This section also included any payments made or services provided to the Indian nation in exchange for land (43–44).
- *Jurisdiction* covered civil and criminal jurisdictions. Different treaties used different criminal jurisdictions. Some used traditional practices and stated that the physical location of the crime determined jurisdiction. In later years, the jurisdiction agreements changed and became more stringent toward Indians. All crimes, regardless of whether committed on Indian land or U.S. land, had federal jurisdiction and ignored local jurisdiction (45).

---

*There are discrepancies about the actual number of treaties between Indian nations and the United States. Debates include whether to count treaties entered into prior to the Revolutionary War, treaties between the Confederacy and Indian nations during the Civil War, and treaties omitted from Kappler's *Indian Affairs: Laws and Treaties.*

- *Control of Tribal Affairs.* The federal government did not impose limitations on a tribal nation's ability to self-govern (46).

Treaty-making between the United States and Indian nations officially ended in 1871 per the Indian Appropriations Act of 1871 (16 Stat. 566):

> No Indian nation or tribe within the territory of the United States shall be acknowledged or recognized as an independent nation, tribe, or power with whom the United States may contract by treaty.

Although the statute no longer permitted the United States to enter into future treaty negotiations with Indian nations, a further provision preserved the legality of previous treaties negotiated prior to 1871 (16 Stat 566).

The law grandfathered in previously ratified treaties. Any treaty promulgated prior to March 3, 1871, remained in force. Congress passed the law primarily for two reasons. The first reason is linked to two constitutional rules—treaties need the advice and consent of the Senate and budget requests must be initiated in the House of Representatives. Since many treaties included payment to an Indian nation in exchange for land, the treaties required members of the House of Representatives, without being consulted in the actual treaty negotiation, to initiate monetary requests for Indian treaties (Goldberg 2008, 26).

The second reason is related to the long-established principle of the sovereignty of Indian nations. A growing sentiment within the United States viewed Indian nations as not being independent but rather wards of the United States. If not a sovereign nation, they should not have the privilege of negotiating treaties (Prucha 1994, 289).

These two issues led to the end of treaty making with Indian nations. However, this did not end Indian and U.S. relations. After 1871, the U.S. employed agreements, legislation, and executive orders when negotiating with Indian tribes. While used to an extent prior to 1871, their prevalence increased significantly after abolishing treaty making with the Indian nations.

- Agreements had been primarily used from 1871 to 1911 (Prucha 1994, 313). They are similar to treaties with the only difference being that both the House and Senate approved them. Agreements could be initiated by Congress, the executive branch, or a tribe and primarily dealt with land cessation and the redrawing of boundaries.
- Statutes are initiated at the congressional level. Initially, many of these laws passed and were implemented upon tribal consent. This

process soon deteriorated, and more often than not, laws affecting Indian nations passed without consulting the affected tribe (Prucha 1994, 326).
 • Executive orders are rules the president issues that have the force of law but do not require the consent of Congress (Garner 2009, 651). The president used these orders heavily to establish the reservation system and often set aside designated land for the creation of new reservations or added land to an existing one (Prucha 1994, 329).

The tools used for Indian relations reflect the diminishing negotiating power that Indian nations had with the United States. When using treaties and agreements, Indian nations at least had a seat at the negotiation table. As statutes supplanted treaties and agreements, consultation with tribes diminished and the president, at his leisure, issued executive orders and pronouncements with no input from Congress or tribes. The shift to these documents, which reduced tribal nations' abilities to negotiate with the United States, aligned with the changing U.S. policy and agenda toward Indian relations.

United States Policy

From 1778 to 1869, the United States used treaties to obtain as much Indian land as possible for as little cost as possible and with few fatalities of its citizens (Goldberg 2008, 13). However, from the 1770s to the early 1900s, the U.S. went through three distinct time periods in which the desired outcomes for U.S./Indian negotiations changed.

1778 to 1810s—Create Allies, Keep Peace, and Obtain Permission to Cross Indian Land

From the Revolutionary War to the early stages of the new republic, Britain and France challenged the United States to prove its strength as a nation. Britain's and France's presence in North America long exceeded U.S.'s presence and both countries established relationships with native tribes. As the U.S. embarked upon a revolution, the new country negotiated treaties with Indian nations to:

 • Gain allies—The U.S. sought to create allies with Indian nations to help the country fight the war against the British.
 • Keep peace—If unable to create allies, the U.S. at least sought neutrality and peace with Indian nations to avoid fighting an additional war on the Indian front.

• Obtain permission to cross Indian land—Indian lands predominated the Northeast where the Revolutionary War occurred. The U.S. negotiated to have troops cross Indian land unimpeded.

The first treaty negotiated by the U.S. took place with the Delaware Indians in 1778 and is referred to as the Treaty of Fort Pitt or the Treaty with the Delawares. The treaty achieved U.S. goals of maintaining peace, establishing the Delaware Indians as an ally,* and obtaining permission for free passage of U.S. troops through Delaware land. The free passage article is significant because it acknowledged the sovereignty of the Delaware Tribe by recognizing it as the property owners who could allow or not allow others onto their territory.

In exchange, the U.S. agreed to build a fort in Delaware country "for the better security of the old men, women and children while their warriors are engaged against the common enemy" (Treaty with the Delawares, art. 3).

In keeping with the ultimate goal of the United States to obtain land to build a larger nation, the U.S. negotiated additional treaties in which, for exchange of land, the U.S. would provide Indian nations with cash payment, livestock, or services.

1812 to mid–1860s—Indian Relocation to Indian Territory West of the Mississippi

The negotiating power of Indian nations achieved its strongest point prior to 1812. Once the War of 1812 ended, U.S. domination in North America increased since Britain and France no longer served as a dominant threat. As a result, native nations lost much of their negotiating leverage and treaty negotiations began to favor the United States and disadvantage Native Americans.

With a growing population and citizens' increased desire for land, the United States actively negotiated treaties for native lands east of the Mississippi (Cohen 2012, 41). In an attempt to encourage native nations to enter into these agreements, President Andrew Jackson signed the Indian Removal Act of 1830 (Pub. L. 21-148), which allowed negotiators to offer native tribes land west of the Mississippi in exchange for their current land (Cohen 2012, 44).

The Act placed Native Americans in difficult positions. If they stayed on their existing land east of the Mississippi, they may have to submit to state laws and lose their existence as a nation. Relocation to the West did

---

*The treaty states: "If either of the parties are engaged in a just and necessary war with any other nation or nations, then each shall assist the other in due proportion to the abilities till their enemies are brought to reasonable terms of accommodation" (7 Stat. 13).

not ideally serve the tribes because they may lose sacred land or receive land that was not conducive to their hunting and gathering lifestyle.

While the tribes supposedly volunteered to move west, they faced immense pressure to sign these treaties (Cohen 2012, 44). Tribes reacted differently to the relocation efforts by the United States government. The Choctaws acknowledged their removal as inevitable and entered into treaty negotiations. The 1830 Treaty at Dancing Rabbit Creek resulted in the Choctaws ultimately ceding all eleven million acres of their land in exchange for land in present day Oklahoma (Treaty at Dancing Rabbit Creek, art. 2; O'Brien 2018, 114).

The Cherokee Tribe resisted U.S. efforts to move them west. They filed several court cases seeking an injunction to prevent the federal government and Georgia from seizing their land (Cohen 2012, 44–45). Ultimately, a minority faction of the Cherokee Tribe entered treaty negotiations against the wishes of the Cherokee National Council. The minority Cherokee political faction and U.S. officials and representatives signed the Treaty of New Echota in December 1835. In the treaty, the Cherokee agreed to cede all their land in exchange for five million dollars and comparable land in the Arkansas Territory. This included present day Arkansas and Oklahoma (Treaty of New Echota, art. 2). Officials from the Cherokee National Council argued that it did not approve the treaty and thereby invalidated the treaty. The Council unsuccessfully nullified the treaty, and the U.S. forcibly removed the Cherokee from their land. This action became known as the Trail of Tears (O'Brien 2008, 118–19; Cohen 2012, 47–48).

During this time, the U.S. forcibly moved most of the Eastern tribes west of the Mississippi. While the initial intent may have been to have the Mississippi River serve as a natural divider between Indian nations and U.S. citizens, the intent did not last long. As the country continued to grow and gold was discovered in the West, the United States began eyeing Indian land west of the Mississippi as well.

Mid–1860s to Early 1900s—Reservation Movement and Acculturation of Indians

From the mid–1860s to the early 1900s, policy shifted again. Interest in exploring and establishing territory in the West increased, and the land set aside for Indians went mostly undeveloped because of their hunter and gatherer culture. To reclaim and develop this land, the U.S. government sought to acculturate Native Americans into U.S. society by encouraging them to forego their hunter and gatherer ways and adopt an agricultural lifestyle instead. The U.S. rationalized that, if Indians became farmers, they would need less land which could then be distributed to white settlers moving west (Kirby 2008, 672). Actions taken during this time, such as the creation of reservations (executive order or statute created 90 of the 162 reservations) (Prucha 1994, 312) and the passage of the General Allotment Act of 1887, significantly reduced the land belonging to tribal nations.

The General Allotment Act of 1887, also known as the Dawes Act (Pub. L. 49-105, 24 Stat. 388), allotted portions of reservation land to individual Indians. In its draft form, the Dawes Act provided an opt-in clause for Indians, but the final version made it mandatory for Indians to participate in the allotment program (Prucha 1994, 328). The Dawes Act had three implications:

1. Individual Indians became property owners. Allotments of 160 acres were given to each head of family and up to 80 acres to other individuals with the exception of married women. The land was held in trust for 25 years to be used exclusively by the allottee and their heirs.

2. Once the allotment was out of trust, Indians became United States citizens and were subject to state and criminal law.

3. Excess Indian land not provisioned to Indians was ceded to non–Indians for settlement (Kirby 2008, 673).

The allotment experiment did not fare well for Indians because, as hunters and gatherers, they did not adapt well to an agrarian lifestyle. In addition, the Indians received mostly poor-quality land, making productive crop yields difficult. Overall, this resulted in the Indians losing much of their land. From 1881 to 1934, Indian land shrunk from 138 million acres to 48 million (Cohen 2012, 73). The Indian Reorganization Act of 1934 (Pub. L. 73-383; 48 Stat. 984) officially ended the practice of allotment.

Canon of Treaty Construction and Abrogating Treaties

Canons of Treaty Construction

Indian nations and the United States approached treaty negotiations in fundamentally different ways. For Indians, the context of the discussions and the formation of relationships formed the crux of the agreement rather than the words written on a piece of paper. Indians often did not know what appeared in the written documents since the U.S. often wrote the treaties in English. Their signatures, often indicated as an "x," indicated their agreement to what they believed to be in the treaty based upon the discussions with the U.S. negotiators. The native perspective differed markedly from the U.S. perspective which relied on the written words within the document (Leeds 2008, 16). As a result, treaty negotiations often benefited the United States and often compromised Native American interests.

To reconcile the disadvantages that Indian tribes endured when negotiating treaties, the federal courts developed, through several court decisions, interpretive rules known as the Canons of Treaty Construction (Clark 2008, 41–43; Canby Jr., 2020, 132–33). The canons recognize the importance of the negotiation process and the historical contexts upon which agreements were made. The canons of treaty construction are:

- Ambiguities must be resolved in favor of the Indians,
- Treaties need to be interpreted as Indians would have understood them, and
- Treaties must be construed liberally in favor of the Indians [Clark 2008, 41–43; Canby Jr., 2020, 132–33].

Winters v. United States (207 U.S. 564) exemplifies how the Supreme Court construed the canon. Members of the Fort Belknap Indian Reservation ceded land that bordered a stream. The settlers diverted water from the stream to their land stating that the land would not have been wanted if the water rights did not accompany it. The tribes claimed that they would not have agreed to cede the land and the water rights since diverting the stream impacted the habitability of the Fort Belknap Indian Reservation (Canby Jr., 2008, 132–33). Since the agreement did not explicitly state to whom the water rights belonged and both arguments were equally plausible (ambiguity canon), the tribes understood the agreement to mean that they only ceded the land and not the water rights (interpreted as Indians would have understood them). The Supreme Court ruled in favor of the Indian tribes (treaties and agreements should be construed liberally in favor of the Indians) (Canby Jr., 2020, 133). The scope of the canons of treaty construction has been expanded to not just include discrepancies within treaties but also to federal statutes as well (Clark 2008, 43).

Abrogating Treaties

Although treaties often had clauses stating that the negotiated agreements last in perpetuity, many treaties or parts of treaties are no longer in effect because they have been abrogated by the U.S. Since treaties, like federal statutes, are the law of the land, they carry no more weight than federal statutes. Since a federal statute can repeal or amend another federal statute, it can also repeal or amend a treaty (Canby Jr., 2020, 142).

Two Supreme Court cases, *The Cherokee Tobacco Case* (78 U.S. 616) and *Lone Wolf v. Hitchcock* (187 U.S. 553), set this precedent. In these cases, the Supreme Court stated that Congress had the authority to nullify Indian treaties when necessary to implement or carry out national policy (Clark 2008). *Lone Wolf v. Hitchcock* has been strongly criticized and, more recent cases like *Menominee Tribe v. United States* (391 U.S. 404), have attempted to temper the sweeping power that the Supreme Court gave Congress in the *Lone Wolf* ruling (Royster 2009, 771).

In essence, the courts have ruled that if Congress clearly states, through statutory language, that the law is changing the terms of a treaty, that section of the treaty is abrogated. Expressed abrogation is not open to judicial interpretation (Canby Jr., 2020, 144). However, not all statutes that contradict a treaty provision will nullify the treaty. If enacted legislation does not clearly indicate the impact of the law on a treaty, the validity of the law and its impact on a treaty can be decided by the courts. By looking at the legislative history and congressional deliberations when passing the law, the courts will determine whether Congress considered the implications that the law would have on existing treaties. For the statute to be constitutional, Congress must consider how the new law will affect the treaty and still choose to pass the law. This is known as implied abrogation. If there is no clear evidence that Congress considered the impact of the law on a treaty, the Court can rule the statute unconstitutional (Canby Jr., 2020, 145).

Sources for Treaty Research

Below is a list of primary resources that contain the text of treaties, executive orders, and other documents. The annotated bibliography is not a comprehensive list of resources available for Indian treaty research but rather highlights unique and prominent sources for locating treaties.

- *American State Papers: Indian Affairs.* 1832. Washington, D.C.: Gale and Seaton. Also available at http://memory.loc.gov/ammem/ amlaw/lwsplink.html#anchor2.
  The two volumes that comprise Indian Affairs includes congressional documents, letters, and other documentation related to United States relationship with Indian tribes from 1789 to 1827. Each volume contains a subject index.
- Bernholz, Charles D. 2003. *Kappler Revisited: An Index and Bibliographic Guide to American Indian Treaties.* Kenmore, NY: Epoch Books.
  The index and bibliographic guide produced by Bernholz attempts to remedy some of the weaknesses in Kappler's

> *Indian Affairs* which includes the omission of seven ratified
> treaties signed before 1778, the absence of treaty titles, and
> the lack of standardization when referring to various tribes.
> The bibliographic guide describes the resources that appear
> in Bernholz's updated table. He includes a list of government
> publications and treatises related to Indian policy. Part two of
> this guide provides tables that list in which resource each treaty
> can be located and an index by tribal name. This is a useful
> reference tool to locate materials related to U.S./Indian treaty
> negotiations.

- Bernholz, Charles D., Brian L. Pytlik Zillig, Laura Weakly,
  and Zacharia A. Bajaber. n.d. "Early Recognized Treaties with
  American Indian Nations." Accessed February 2, 2022. Retrieved
  from http://treatiesportal.unl.edu/earlytreaties/.

  > The University of Nebraska–Lincoln, Center for Digital
  > Research in the Humanities has made digitally available nine
  > treaties that do not appear in Kappler or the *Statutes at Large.*
  > These treaties were ratified between 1772 and 1805 and appear in
  > *Ratified Indian Treaties, 1722–1869,* which the U.S. Department
  > of State published in 1966. The texts of these treaties are
  > reproduced in html format. Scanned images are also available.

- Deloria, Vine, Jr., and Raymond J. DeMallie, comps. 1999.
  *Documents of American Indian Diplomacy: Treaties, Agreements,
  and Conventions 1775–1979.* Norman: University of Oklahoma Press.

  > Deloria and DeMallie's two volume treatise serves as a
  > supplement to volume two of Kappler's *Indian Affairs: Laws
  > and Treaties.* It provides a comprehensive picture of Indian
  > relations in North America by including the text of treaties
  > negotiated by the states, Confederate states, Republic of Texas,
  > and foreign nations. This set also contains a new chronological
  > list of treaties which removes treaties that were not fully ratified
  > and includes treaties omitted in Kappler and those agreements
  > that should be accepted as ratified treaties. Volume two
  > includes the text of treaties rejected by Congress or an Indian
  > nation, unratified treaties, and land grants to private parties.
  > The authors introduce each chapter with an explanation of its
  > purpose before outlining the treaties and their text.

- *Executive Orders Relating to Indian Reservations 1855–1922.* 1975.
  Wilmington, DE: Scholarly Resources. Also available at https://
  catalog.hathitrust.org/Record/102138624.

  > Locating the text of executive orders prior to their publication
  > in the *Code of Federal Regulations* in 1938 can be challenging.

This two volume set, originally published by the Government Printing Office in 1912 and 1922, contains the text of executive orders about Indian reservations from 1855 through 1922. Instead of being arranged chronologically by issue date, the orders are arranged by state and then alphabetically by tribe within that state.

- Kappler, Charles J., ed. 1904. *Indian Affairs: Laws and Treaties.* Washington, D.C.: Government Printing Office. Also available at https://dc.library.okstate.edu/digital/collection/kapplers.
  More commonly known by the editor's name and originally published in 1904, Kappler's has been updated to include treaties, laws, proclamations, executive orders, and cases that relate to Indian relations with the United States from 1778 to early 1971. The text of treaties can be found in volume two, which is arranged chronologically and includes a thorough index. Kappler used the *Statutes at Large* when compiling the volume on treaties. While users researching Indian treaties tend to gravitate to volume two, treaty information can be found in additional volumes of this set. Volume four includes a list of treaties construed by the U.S. Supreme Court as well as the text of additional treaties. Volumes three and five contain unratified treaties.
- *The Public Statutes at Large of the United States of America* (vol. 7). 1846. Boston, MA: Charles C. Little and James Brown. Also available at http://memory.loc.gov/ammem/amlaw/lwsllink.html.
  Volume seven of the *Statutes at Large*, the official compilation of United States law, contains ratified treaties between the United States and Indian nations from 1778 to 1842. The texts of treaties are arranged chronologically. Access points to this volume are the table of contents and index. Treaties ratified between 1843 and 1871 appear in volumes nine through sixteen. It should be noted that seven treaties ratified between the British and an Indian Nation do not appear in the *Statutes at Large*. In addition, two other treaties that appeared in the *American State Papers* are omitted from this set.
- Royce, Charles C., comp. 1899. "Indian Land Cessions in the United States, 1784–1894." Published in the *Eighteenth Annual Report of the Bureau of American Ethnology to the Secretary of the Smithsonian Institution, 1896–1897 in Two Parts—Part 2*, directed by J.W. Powell. Washington, D.C.: Government Printing Office. [U.S. Serial Set 4015] Also available at http://memory.loc.gov/ammem/amlaw/lwss-ilc.html, and https://archive.org/details/annualreportofbu182smit/page/n5/mode/2up.

This report identifies land ceded by Indian nations through treaties, executive orders, and laws from 1784 to 1894. The volume contains a 116 page introduction by Cyrus Thomas that discusses policy towards Indians from early Colonial times to the late 1800s. The rest of the 500-page report includes two tables and 67 maps. Table one, Schedule of treaties and acts of Congress authorizing allotments of land in severalty, lists acts which enabled Congress to seize land. The table includes the tribe's name, *Statutes at Large* cite, and date of the treaty or law. The second table, Schedule of Indian Land Cessions, includes the date, location of negotiation, treaty/agreement citation, tribe, description of the land cession or reservation, and maps. The online version allows researchers to browse by date, tribe, or state.

- United States. 1873. *A Compilation of All the Treaties between the United States and the Indian Tribes: Now in Force as Laws.* Washington: Government Printing Office. Also available at https://catalog.hathitrust.org/Record/000560008/Home.

    This 1,000-plus page compilation was prepared under the direction of Congress. The volume, which contains the full-text of treaties, is arranged alphabetically by the Indian tribe. There is no index or other access point.

- University of Wisconsin Digital Collections. n.d. *Documents Relating to Native American Affairs.* Accessed February 2, 2022. Retrieved from https://search.library.wisc.edu/digital/ATreatiesMicro.

    Documents Relating to Native American Affairs (formerly known as *Documents Relating to Indian* until the mid–2010s) is a sub-collection of *The History Collection* created by University of Wisconsin Digital Collections. This digitized collection consists of *Documents Relating to the Negotiation of Ratified and Unratified Treaties with Various Indian Tribes, 1801–1869,* annual reports by the Commissioner of Indian Affairs, and Bureau of Indian Affairs documents. While the text of the treaties is not always available, the value of this collection is the records, letters, and proceedings related to United States treaty negotiation with Indian nations. Researchers can either search the full-text of the documents or browse the documents. This collection includes ratified treaties 30 through 374. For each treaty, there is a list of documents related to the negotiations.

- Vaughan, Alden. T. 1974. *Early American Indian Documents, Treaties & Laws 1607–1789.* Washington, D.C.: University Publications of America.

Most Indian treaty resources present information from the mid–1770s to the 1870s. This twenty volume set is unique because it provides coverage back to the 1600s. This includes accompanying documents such as letters, conferences, and reports that provide insight into the negotiations of treaties and the enactment of agreements and laws. Each volume has several chapters, including a short essay that provides the context for each chapter's primary source materials.

Conclusion

The relationship between the United States and Native Americans is complicated and often divisive. As a new nation, the United States took actions to benefit its interests at the expense of native nations that inhabited the land long before the colonists arrived on North American soil. The impact of its actions and negotiations is evident today.

Embarking upon treaty research is not an easy task. Yet, treaties and other agreements can provide insight into the changing relationship between the United States and Native Americans, which began peacefully but progressed to Native American cessation of land to ultimately the creation of reservations and attempts at acculturation. Primary sources and legal treatises and articles on Indian treaties are plentiful, but resources for novice legal researchers are limited. This essay attempts to fill a void in the literature by providing a basic introduction to the phases of Indian and U.S. relations, the tools used to negotiate agreements, and an annotated bibliography of primary source materials.

References

Canby, William C., Jr. 2020. *American Indian Law in a Nutshell*, 7th ed. St. Paul: West Publishing.

Clark, C. Blue. 2008. "Relevant Court Cases Related to Treaties." In *Treaties with American Indians: An Encyclopedia of Rights, Conflicts, and Sovereignty*, edited by Donald L. Fixico, 39–47, Vol. I. Santa Barbara, CA: ABC-CLIO.

Cohen, Felix S. 1941. *Handbook of Federal Indian Law with Reference Tables and Index*. Washington, D.C.: United States Government Printing Office.

Cohen, Felix S. 2012. *Cohen's Handbook of Federal Indian Law*. Newark: LexisNexis.

Garner, Bryan A., ed. 2009. *Black's Law Dictionary*, 9th ed. St. Paul: West Publishing.

Goldberg, Carole. 2008. "Federal Policy and Treaty Making: A Federal View." In *Treaties with American Indians: An Encyclopedia of Rights, Conflicts, and Sovereignty*, edited by Donald L. Fixico, 13–26, Vol. I. Santa Barbara, CA: ABC-CLIO.

Kirby, Annie. 2008. "General Allotment Act (Dawes Act), 1887." In *Treaties with American Indians: An Encyclopedia of Rights, Conflicts, and Sovereignty*, edited by Donald L. Fixico, 672–73, Vol. II. Santa Barbara, CA: ABC-CLIO.

Leeds, Stacy. 2008. "Indian Treaty Making: A Native View." In *Indian Treaties in the United States: An Encyclopedia and Documents Collection,* edited by Donald L. Fixico, 5–19, Vol. I. Santa Barbara, CA: ABC-CLIO.
O'Brien, Greg. 2008. "Indian Removal and Land Cessions, 1830–1849." In *Treaties with American Indians: An Encyclopedia of Rights, Conflicts, and Sovereignty,* edited by Donald L. Fixico, 83–93, Vol. I. Santa Barbara, CA: ABC-CLIO.
Prucha, Francis Paul. 1994. *American Indian Treaties: The History of a Political Anomaly.* Berkeley: University of California Press.
Royster, Judith V. 2009. "Treaty Abrogation." In *Encyclopedia of United States Indian Policy and Law,* edited by Paul Finkelman and Tim Alan Garrison, 770–71. Washington, D.C.: CQ Press.
Treaty with the Delawares, Sept. 17, 1778, 7 Stat. 13.
Treaty at Dancing Rabbit Creek, Sept. 27, 1830, 7 Stat. 333.
Treaty of New Echota, Dec. 29, 1835, 7 Stat. 478.
United States. *Constitution—Presidential Power,* art. II, §2.

PART VII

Science

Finding Current and Historical Weather Data

CLAUDENE SPROLES *and* ANGEL CLEMONS

Introduction

The federal government performs the majority of weather data collection and forecasting in the United States. Most forecasts from entities such as the Weather Channel, local news broadcasts, and newspapers are based on National Weather Service (NWS) data. This paper covers the primary websites for gathering current, future, and past weather information distributed by the government.

The National Weather Service has origins dating back to 1870 when the United States formed the Weather Bureau "to provide for taking meteorological observations at the military stations in the interior of the continent and at other points in the States and Territories ... and for giving notice on the northern (Great) Lakes and on the seacoast by magnetic telegraph and marine signals, of the approach and force of storms" (U.S. National Weather Service 2004). While originally placed under the administration of the Secretary of War, the Department of Commerce has administered the organization since 1940. In 1966, it became a part of the Environmental Science Services Administration, which changed its name to the National Oceanic and Atmospheric Administration (NOAA) in 1970. At that time, and as we know it today, the Weather Bureau became the National Weather Service. Its current mission is to "provide weather, water, and climate data, forecasts and warnings for the protection of life and property and enhancement of the national economy" (U.S. National Weather Service, n.d.).

The NWS is comprised of nine National Centers for Environmental Protection (NCEP) and 122 Weather Forecast Offices (WFO) spread over six regions. The NCEPs are divided by areas of interest and include aviation weather, climate prediction, environmental modeling, central operations, hurricanes, ocean prediction, storm prediction, space weather prediction, and weather prediction.

The National Weather Service website, https://www.weather.gov, is the vehicle NWS uses to disseminate its weather data. The site is arranged into seven primary areas: "Forecast," "Past Weather," "Safety," "Information," "Education," "News," and "About." Types of forecast data provided include local, graphical, aviation, marine, rivers and lakes, hurricanes, severe weather, fire weather, sun/moon, long range forecasts, climate prediction, and space weather. For example, the "Past Weather" section includes data on monthly temperatures, record setting temperatures, and astronomical data. The "Safety" section includes resources and information on how to deal with twenty different weather emergencies including tsunamis, wildfires, rip currents, drought, and lightning. The general "Information" section covers a variety of topics from what to do if you receive a wireless emergency alert to damage/fatality/injury statistics.

The "Forecast" section of weather.gov provides the most comprehensive data about current weather. The user will find information about short and medium range forecasts, precipitation amounts, temperatures, surface analysis, predominant weather, sky cover, wind speed and direction, and graphical forecasts for Alaska, Hawaii, and Puerto Rico. Detailed analysis exists within each of these areas and includes graphical depictions which can be manipulated according to dates and times of day.

The national radar, https://radar.weather.gov/, provides an enhanced graphical view of current weather at the national and local levels overlayed onto a map of the United States. The local radar displays weather data from a specific weather station, while the national radar combines all data from local weather stations into one seamless view. Users can choose from six different radar products: QCd base or composite reflectivity, raw base or composite reflectivity, precipitation type, and Echo tops. The radar also displays current storm-based weather alerts if they exist. Users can change the base layer of the map from standard to topographic, satellite, ocean, or dark canvas, and display boundary overlays including air route traffic control centers, counties, county warning areas, states, and river forecast centers.

The NWS also provides data on current "Active Alerts" broken down by areas and type of alert. Users can view warnings by state or latest warnings, both of which update every two minutes. Categories of active weather alerts available include excessive rainfall and winter weather, national river flooding, thunderstorms and tornadoes, hurricanes, fires, tsunamis, drought, space weather, and UV alerts.

Users can access extensive data about past weather for specific areas on the weather.gov website. Data is arranged by NWS Weather Forecast Office areas, then further broken down by city within each area. To access the data, click on any city displayed on the NWS Forecast Offices map at https://www.weather.gov/wrh/climate to be directed to the weather forecast office for that area. Select a location within that area to narrow your search. For example, if one selects the Indianapolis weather forecast office on the main page, you can then narrow your search area to Bloomington, Columbus, or any of the other five dozen smaller cities listed for that forecast office. Next, select the data output desired under the "Product" category. Product search options on the website include daily data for a month, a daily almanac, calendar day summaries, daily/monthly normals, first/last dates, and temperature and accumulation graphs. Choose a date under the options section and then press "Go." The user has the option to enlarge the data or print it, but there is no option to download it currently. Additional data provided here includes daily and monthly climate information, climate prediction and variability, and other sources for certified past weather information.

Hazardous Weather

The National Weather Service is responsible for issuing hazardous weather alerts. For a general overview of current weather watches in the continental U.S., visit the Storm Prediction Center's Current Connective Watches page, https://www.spc.noaa.gov/products/watch/. The NWS homepage, as discussed earlier, lists current warnings in effect at https://www.weather.gov/.

Warning Dissemination

When hazardous weather or emergencies occur, the NWS will release warning and emergency information in a variety of ways:

- Emergency Alert System (EAS), https://www.weather.gov/nwr/eas_description.

The EAS allows government officials to quickly relay critical or emergency information to citizens. These EAS messages are broadcast through outlets such as TV, radio, satellite radio, or cable systems. Examples of EAS alerts include AMBER alerts and severe weather warnings.

- National Warning System (NAWAS), https://www.hsdl.org/?abstract&did=843365.

NAWAS is part of the Civil Defense Warning System, originally designed to warn of nuclear attacks. Administered by the Federal Emergency Management Agency (FEMA), warnings are delivered via an automated telephone system that can warn of natural disasters, as well as other emergencies such as train derailments and plane crashes.

- Wireless Emergency Alerts (WEA), https://www.weather.gov/riw/WEA_Info.

WEAs allow emergency information to be sent to wireless devices such as cell phones. The Alerts are sent to cell towers where they are then pushed to mobile devices. The webpage includes an extensive list of frequently asked questions.

- NOAA Weather Radio (NWR), https://www.weather.gov/nwr/.

NWR continually broadcasts weather information nationally across a large network of over 1,000 radio transmitters. Special equipment is required, such as a scanner, that can pick up its signal. Reports are generated from the nearest NWS office. In addition to weather hazards, the NWR will also broadcast other emergency information such as oil spills or AMBER alerts.

- Integrated Public Alert & Warning System (IPAWS), https://www.fema.gov/emergency-managers/practitioners/integrated-public-alert-warning-system.

Administered by FEMA, IPAWS integrates NOAA Weather Radio, Wireless Emergency Alerts, the Emergency Alert System, and the National Warning System into a single format using the Common Alerting Protocol (CAP) Standards. Authorities create alerts using CAP enabled software that will send emergency information to users' mobile phones.

- NOAA Weather Wire Service (NWWS), https://www.weather.gov/nwws/.

This service consists of an internet and satellite broadcast system to transmit important weather information, as well as alerts from the U.S. Geological Survey Earthquake Center. These alerts are targeted toward emergency management, news outlets, state and local governments, and the public.

- Emergency Managers Weather Information Network (EMWIN), https://www.weather.gov/emwin/.

EMWIN is a data stream for emergency managers and public safety officials detailing the latest watches, warnings, and advisories. Streams are uplinked to weather satellites. This broadcast also requires special equipment to receive the signal.

- NOAAPORT, https://www.weather.gov/noaaport/.

The service is provided by the Advanced Weather Interactive Processing System (AWIPS) Satellite Broadcast Network. NOAAPORT broadcasts a one-way, real-time, satellite data stream of NOAA environmental and hazard data. One must have special software and a receiver to receive data.

Disaster Preparedness

- Ready.gov, https://www.ready.gov/.

FEMA's website is dedicated to helping citizens prepare for dangerous weather or emergencies. Ready.gov is designed to help people monitor their local situations, create an emergency plan, and assemble an emergency supply kit. Also, it supplies information about specific storm threats such as tornadoes, hurricanes, earthquakes, tsunamis, wildfires, power outages, and terrorism attacks. Under the Resources tab, users can locate links to YouTube videos about public service announcements such as disaster tips and National Preparedness Month. A Ready in Your Language website provides links to documents prepared in languages such as Spanish, Chinese, and Korean. The Ready Kids tab provides disaster resources for kids, teens, families, educators, and organizations.

- MedlinePlus—Disaster Preparation and Recovery, https://medlineplus.gov/disasterpreparationandrecovery.html.

MedlinePlus, created by the National Library of Medicine, offers mediated health information for consumers on a variety of topics. The website's Disaster Preparation and Recovery page helps users create disaster plans and emergency responses for individuals. Links to specific disasters, relevant information from other government agencies, disaster-related research, and professionals in the field are provided. It covers topics such as safe drinking water, pet safety, disaster clean-up, and considerations for the elderly.

Hazardous Weather Prediction Centers

- National Centers for Environmental Prediction (NCEP), https://www.weather.gov/ncep/.

The Hazardous Weather Prediction Centers are under the National Centers for Environmental Prediction (NCEP). The NCEP oversees national and global forecasts, guidance, and warnings. The agency governs nine weather centers, including the Weather Prediction Center, the Aviation Weather Center, the Storm Prediction Center, the Space Weather Prediction Center, the Environmental Monitoring Center, the Ocean Prediction Center, the National Hurricane Center, and the NCEP Central Operations.

- Storm Prediction Center (SPC), https://www.spc.noaa.gov/.

The SPC, based in Norman, OK, forecasts severe thunderstorms, tornadoes, hail, wind, winter weather, and fire weather for the continental U.S. The SPC issues watches, forecasts, outlooks, and mesoscale discussions centered around hazardous weather.

- National Hurricane Center (NHC), https://www.nhc.noaa.gov/.

The NHC, located in Miami, Florida, issues watches, warnings, forecasts, and analyses of tropical weather, high seas, marine weather, and storm surge in the Eastern Pacific and North Atlantic basins. In addition to current watches and warnings, the NHC center has the latest satellite imagery, radar, aircraft reconnaissance, and tools to aid in tracking and analysis.

- National Integrated Drought Information System (NIDIS), https://www.drought.gov/.

The NIDIS gathers, coordinates, and integrates drought research. This information is used to develop a National Drought Early Warning System (DEWS). The website supplies information such as current drought conditions, drought impacts, outlooks and forecasts, and historical information. Also, the website contains information by area and educational materials.

- Weather Prediction Center (WPC)—Winter Weather Desk, https://www.wpc.ncep.noaa.gov/wwd/winter_wx.shtml.

The WPC's Winter Weather Desk issues winter weather watches, warnings, and outlooks, including heavy snow and icing warnings. It includes snow and freezing rain probability forecasts, accumulation forecasts, surface low tracking, heavy snow/icing discussions, and recent storm summaries.

Other Natural Disasters

- U.S. Tsunami Warning System, https://tsunami.gov/.

The National Oceanic and Atmospheric Administration (NOAA) operates two tsunami warnings centers, based in Hawaii and Alaska. The centers monitor earthquakes, issue warnings, and predict impacts.

Natural Disasters—Storm Analysis/Histories/Data

- Storm Events Database, 1950–2022, https://www.ncdc.noaa.gov/stormevents/.

This resource documents the significant weather events that caused death, injuries, significant property damage, or disruption to commerce. It records "rare, unusual weather phenomena" and other major weather events, including record temperatures. The data is sortable and downloadable.

Sample questions the database can answer:

Q. How many F5 tornadoes have occurred in Kentucky?
A. 3 (since 1950)
Q. How many people died in wildfires in 2020?
A. 44
Q. How many tsunami events have been reported since 1950?
A. 33
Q. How many people were killed in 1997 Jarrell, Texas, tornado?
A. 27

- Data.gov, https://www.data.gov/.

The amount of data included at data.gov cannot be overstated. Users will find a plethora of weather-related data using keyword searching. This includes posters, aerial photography, satellite data, timeseries, observations, and datasets.

Tornadoes

- U.S. Tornadoes, https://www.ncdc.noaa.gov/societal-impacts/tornadoes/.

Monthly and yearly tornado statistics from 1950 to present, including monthly reports and fatalities. This site is maintained by the National Centers for Environmental Information (NCEI).

- U.S. Tornado Outbreak Interface, https://www.spc.noaa.gov/exper/outbreaks/.

Detailed information about violent EF4 and EF5 tornadoes. Includes information about tracks, conditions, and deaths/injuries. Links to report information for all significant historical tornadoes, including non-government produced histories.

Hurricanes

- NHC Data Archive, https://www.nhc.noaa.gov/data/.

The NHC provides historical information about hurricane seasons as well as individual storms from the Atlantic, and Eastern and Central Pacific. It includes tropical cyclone reports, data archives, tracking maps and data, Geographic Information Systems (GIS) data, as well as monthly, seasonal, and annual summaries.

- United States Geological Survey (USGS)-Hurricanes, https://www.usgs.gov/special-topics/hurricanes.

The United States Geological Survey (USGS) offers data, maps, and research related to hurricane aftereffects. It gives information on coastal change, storm surge, environmental aspects, ecosystem impacts, and provides flood and water level data as well as aerial photography.

Tsunamis

- Tsunami Data and Information, https://www.ngdc.noaa.gov/hazard/tsu.shtml.

Including various data, images, and reports related to tsunamis, such as global tsunami events, tide gauge records, runups, and deposits, the website also contains a tsunami source poster and tsunami images, useful for students writing reports.

- NGDC/WDS Global Historical Tsunami Database, https://www.ngdc.noaa.gov/hazard/tsu_db.shtml.

It contains a database of tsunami events dating back to 2000 B.C., covering all oceans and basins. Information on both the source event and runup, including date, time, event magnitude, deaths, and damage are included.

Earthquakes

- Earthquake Hazards Program, https://earthquake.usgs.gov/.

Earthquake monitoring is conducted by the USGS, as it is not weather related. The Earthquake Hazard's Program's mission revolves around mitigating destruction during earthquakes as well as to further understanding of how and why earthquakes occur. The webpage links to hazards, data, education, monitoring, and research. For example, under Education, the "For Kids" links provide information about the science of earthquakes, science fair project ideas, and how to become an earthquake scientist. There are other links to resource collections such as "Science for Everyone," "Earthquake Topics," and "Earthquake Summary Posters."

• Earthquake Lists, Maps, and Statistics, https://www.usgs.gov/programs/earthquake-hazards/lists-maps-and-statistics.

Information about both United States and global earthquakes, by year, location, or magnitude are detailed on the website. It includes a list of the top twenty largest earthquakes, a photo collection, and notification information.

Volcanoes

• Volcano Hazards Program (VHP), https://www.usgs.gov/programs/VHP.

According to the USGS, there are 161 "potentially active volcanoes" within the United States. The USGS's VHP monitors volcanic activity, performs research, collects data, and issues forecasts and warnings. The VHP works closely with emergency management to mitigate risks during a volcanic event. On the VHP webpages, users can find volcanic updates, hazard assessments, publications, news, and information updates from U.S. volcanic observatories. The webpage links to data, software, and other products to assess ash, gases, lahar, seismic activity, and other phenomena related to volcanic activity. Educational resources include field guides, posters, and teaching materials.

Climatology

Climatology studies the weather conditions of an area over time to ascertain normal conditions for the area, such as average rainfall, snow, and temperature.

• Climate.gov, https://www.climate.gov/.

Climate.gov has more of a public focus. Its mission centers around education and guidance, as well as adaption and mitigation of climatic events. The website features four main parts: News & Features, Maps & Data, Teaching Climate, and the U.S. Climate Resilience Toolkit. The toolkit focuses on policy makers and climate decision making.

- National Centers for Environmental Information (NCEI), https://www.ncei.noaa.gov/.

Located in Asheville, NC, the NCEI was created as a merger of The National Climatic Data Center (NCDC), the National Geophysical Data Center, and the National Oceanographic Data Center. NCEI offers one of the largest environmental data depositories in the world. Its mission is to create "new products and services" that facilitate the use of environmental data. The NCEI archives over 26,000 data sets and other materials. The agency warehouses data on such topics as space weather, coastal indicators, radar meteorology, and severe weather. In addition, it collects and archives station weather data as well as world-wide climate and weather data.

- Climate Prediction Center (CPC), https://www.cpc.ncep.noaa.gov/.

The CPC issues climate forecasts, outlooks, and discussions for temperature, precipitation, drought, and heatwaves, as well as assessment of climate anomalies. Its products cover a variety of time periods, including weekly, monthly, and seasonally.

Other Governmental Sources

- World Meteorological Association (WMO), https://public.wmo.int/en.

Based in Geneva, Switzerland, the WMO serves as the intergovernmental atmospheric science branch of the United Nations. The WMO coordinates data and research related to hydrology, climatology, and climate change. It is part of the Nobel Peace Prize winning Intergovernmental Panel on Climate Change (IPCC). On its website, users can find WMO publications, resources, educational materials, programmes, and projects.

- Environment and Climate Change Canada, https://www.canada.ca/en/environment-climate-change.html.

Weather forecasting, environmental protection, environmental assessment, and environmental enforcement are all under the jurisdiction of Environment and Climate Change Canada. Users can locate information about current weather conditions, ice conditions, pollution, wildlife, and climate change in Canada.

Conclusion

The detailed amount of weather information available from the United States government is extensive. Users can locate current conditions, download forecasts, create disaster plans, learn about natural phenomena, and learn about historic weather events. Additionally, the government provides a wide assortment of K–12 educational resources for both teachers and students. Any research involving weather, climate change, or natural disasters should begin with government resources. Typically, the National Weather Service and its subordinate organizations can provide most weather data that the average weather watcher needs daily. For the more seasoned weather researcher, other organizations exist, both nationally and internationally, to provide data on specific types of weather information. Government data should be users' go-to source for accurate weather data.

REFERENCES

U.S. National Weather Service. n.d. 2019–2022 Strategic Plan. Accessed February 27, 2022. https://www.weather.gov/media/wrn/NWS_Weather-Ready-Nation_Strategic_Plan_2019-2022.pdf.
U.S. National Weather Service. 2004. "History of the National Weather Service." September 30. Accessed May 20, 2022. https://www.weather.gov/timeline.

National Park Service

The Importance of Place

Connie Hamner Williams

Introduction

Walking along the path in Hawaii Volcanoes National Park, hikers must watch their feet as they trek over lava fields on the way up Mauna Loa. The occasional green plant that pushes its way through the rock confirms that the environment is continually changing.

The sky, mountains, and distant sea are breathtaking. Susan Thompson, a longtime hiker in Hawaii relates: "It's the power of the place, the mana ... is absolutely palpable there. Watching new earth being birthed with fire and water ... planet Earth is more than just geology." Worlds away, similar thoughts passed through Mady Cloud's mind when she approached the opening to Yellowstone National Park on Park Road. "Standing upon a bluff on the eastern edge of the road stood a buffalo, majestic and huge. I had an immediate, visceral response to seeing this animal in its natural environment. This was no zoo, no video nor photo; there were no fences or barriers of any kind to separate us. This was a vision of wildness, a primal presence standing before us, an experience we could only get here, in the ancient place that bison have inhabited for centuries" (Susan Thompson and Mady Cloud, author interview, January 4, 2022).

These experiences, grounded firmly in place, mirror each other yet speak specifically to the wonder that each encounter brings throughout the National Park System, universal yet intimate. This idea makes up the backbone of the National Park Service (NPS) and allows both armchair and field travelers the ability to seek out the importance of discovering that things happen in places. These places are important to preserve and protect for all time. Whether you are a teacher, school librarian, library patron, parent, or adventurer, recognizing that events happen in a place allows us to explore that event with the wide lens of perspective, time, and location.

As a hidden gem within government information agencies, the NPS is easily dismissed as a source for information because it is most likely thought to be useful only for travelers looking for their next adventure. However, the NPS has created a portal that invites researchers of all ages to explore science, history, and culture through the places in which events occurred. Each park, historical site, seashore, or monument offers a scientific, cultural, and historic look at the area and its importance to the local community as well as to the nation. It is well worth a look.

National Park System: A Brief History

Beginning with the Yellowstone National Park Protection Act of March 1, 1872, the U.S. Government created Yellowstone as the first national park designed "as a public park or pleasuring-ground for the benefit and enjoyment of the people" (Dilsaver 1994, chap. 1). Cities began to grow; workers headed to newly created factories, which took up much of the local landscape; and at the same time, there was a push to move west, creating towns and highways along the way. As land began to fill, a growing awareness took hold that this land offered much that needed to be protected from this cultural imperative to expand. Over time, other parks and historical sites were added under the Act. By 1916, the government identified many sites as worthy of saving and, it became apparent that the parks needed oversight. Created under the umbrella of the Department of the Interior, the Act created and designed a newly established National Park Service to "promote and regulate the use of the National parks, monuments, and reservations" and to "conserve the scenery and the natural and historic object and the wild life therein and to provide for the enjoyment of the same in such manner and by such means as will leave them unimpaired for the enjoyment of future generations" (16 U.S.C. 1) (Dilsaver, 1994, chap. 1). New parks and sites are still added to the NPS to commemorate and protect as they are recognized to be of value and interest. It may be helpful to patrons and students to understand that the National Park Service covers parks, monuments, historical sites, recreation areas, national seashores, trails, reserves, and partnerships with State Parks. Knowing this aids researchers in their search for the historical and geographical information that can be found on the NPS website.

Searching the NPS Website

Become acquainted with the most recent information at the National Park Service, https://www.nps.gov, by visiting the "News" section for up-to-date news releases and for links to hot topics and social media channels. It provides access to the more timely and seasonal activities offered. The "About Us" site offers information on how the service is organized and a link to the various park units and related areas such as commemorative sites. If there is a special month such as Black History Month, this is the place to locate historical, instructional, and recreational resources for your patrons. Getting the "lay of the land" from this front page makes the site easier to navigate by topic.

Librarians are often asked for travel information. The NPS website can provide ideas on where to go, how to get there, why it is important, as well as the historical and scientific context in these public spaces. Start on the National Park Service homepage, https://nps.gov, as shown in Image 1.

Use the dropdown menu link located at the top of the homepage to find a list of portal choices or scroll down the homepage to find the same options in a visual format. These three portals (Image 2) are the entry points to each topical area. "Plan Your Visit" is the entry to each park, while "Learn and Explore" is the doorway to history, educational

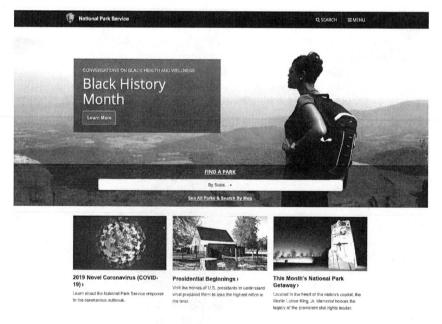

Image 1: Home page of the National Park Service website (https://nps.gov).

Image 2: "Plan your Visit" is your entry to each park, while "Learn and Explore" opens the doors to history and education. "Get Involved" offers activities to enjoy (National Park Service at https://nps.gov).

resources, science, and individual topics. "Get Involved" offers information on jobs, donating, and other action-oriented programs.

The 2020 Covid pandemic mandate to socially distance and recreate outdoors encouraged many to head to their local national park to explore. Crowd limits and opening/closing times may at any time change, so it is important to check the website for current information. Because each National Park site has its own page, visit each individual site, https://www.nps.gov/findapark/index.htm, so that patrons can locate the most up-to-date park visitor's information, virtual visits, webcams, history, and other information specific to that location. It is especially important to check this information as entrance allowance, hiking, camping, or other activities can require reservations or may not be available during specific time periods. Information at each location's site includes local educational programming and on-site visits with classes or other groups. A useful quick list of the National Park System can be seen in its "About Us" link on the homepage, https://www.nps.gov/aboutus/national-park-system.htm.

While the pandemic encouraged many to head outdoors, it also kept many inside. Like many agencies, the National Park Service pivoted its website to include more visual and virtual offerings. The NPS offers virtual "traveling" from home with the use of webcams, images, stories, and maps. Check out each site for virtual visits, and head over to Google Earth for another view of National Parks. Conduct a browser search using the terms "google earth national parks" to reach a variety of park viewing options. Not all parks are represented.

Another National Park resource site to explore is its YouTube channel, https://www.youtube.com/nationalparkservice. Subscribing to this channel opens many audio-visual adventures that provide another virtual platform to not only view the natural wonders found in the parks, but also to participate with Rangers, scientists, teachers, and other park leaders to learn more about the history of heritage sites, engage with virtual field trips, and plan your next outdoor adventure. Offerings include informative videos on the topics covered by their location such as Buffalo Soldiers, the Washington Mall, Denali, and even Sesame Street.

Quick Tips for Searching

Because the National Park Service covers a huge number of sites, use the "search" function on the home page, https://nps.gov, if you want to find a topic within this domain. The results of the search from this portal cover a wide swath of NPS sites that contain that topic. While the first three results may be what you are seeking, take a moment to scroll further to see other options. These can often provide the serendipity that often brings new perspectives from sites that did not float to the top of the queue.

Another way to quickly search a topic that might be contained within the NPS is to utilize a browser search with the topic and domain: topic site:nps.gov. For example, to find information about bears and the NPS, use the search strategy "bears site:nps.gov." For any given research question, there are many avenues to assistance, but a browser search with the patron's topic used as search terms and limiting the search to the nps.gov domain will bring up sites that relate to the topic that reside within the nps.gov domain. A search using just the .gov domain can also bring up nps.gov sites but will do so alongside other government agencies. This is one way to start a search if you do not know for sure where it might reside, but you think that a government resource might be of use. It is often a surprise to discover many interesting topics on the NPS website. These links may not display first in a search, as these are often the larger agencies such as the Library of Congress or the National Archives and Records Administration. Subsequent pages will often surprise you with their wealth of offerings.

Trails and Hiking

Point adventuring patrons to the many trails that can be followed across the country in both rural, wilderness, and urban settings, https://

www.nps.gov/subjects/trails/index.htm. The National Trails System portal site links to downloadable maps of the trails, giving a geographical overview of the trails across the country.

Patrons wanting to find information on interesting backpacking, camping, or hiking can follow these trails for topical adventures and follow in the footsteps of history, for example, the Lewis and Clark Trail or the Trail of Tears.

Trails such as the one from Selma to Montgomery take researchers alongside the marchers of 1965 following U.S. Highway 80 and ending at the Alabama State Capitol in Montgomery. A timeline is included with explanations about events along the way to fill in the story. Trails included in the portal are divided by scenic trails such as the Appalachian Trail, the Continental Divide, and Natchez Trace. Historic trails include the Mormon Pioneer Trail, the California Trail, and the Iditarod. Trace the route of the Pony Express to learn more about the history of postal and other messenger services.

National Recreation Trails are both land-based and water-based for recreational activity. Surprisingly, there is a whole set of water-based trails that include rivers, shorelines and other water areas preserved to keep access and viability of the area open to all. Examples of these trails include the Bayou Teche Paddle Trail, the Black Canyon Water Trail, and the Mohave Water Trail. The uses of these water trail areas by native cultures as well as contemporary issues relating to their use could easily be investigated in a classroom study of water, land, culture, and climate change. Add in creative writing, map reading, and investigating cultural interactions in any of the trails' lessons, and teachers will have opened many possible investigations across many curricular areas.

Patrons wanting to mix history with adventure might like the Heritage Travel information, https://www.nps.gov/subjects/heritagetravel/index.htm. Heritage Travel sites are those that bring a specific historical, scientific, geological, or ecological lens to their created itineraries. These curated trips stand out as guides for travel following a theme or a particular interest. One can investigate identified archeological sites in an urban landscape, visit indigenous landscapes, or explore African American archeology in locations throughout the country. Teachers can use these suggestions as geography lessons by mixing the locations with maps and historical site information.

Historical Markers

Because events happen in places, geography can influence those events. How might the West have influenced voting rights for women, https://www.nps.gov/articles/woman-suffrage-in-the-west.htm? How did discoveries in the Black Hills lead to the Battle at Little Bighorn, https://www.nps.gov/libi/learn/historyculture/battle-story.htm? Might the 1969 Stonewall Uprising in New York City have happened anywhere else, https://www.nps.gov/ston/index.htm?

Searching for historical information using the NPS keyword search function can retrieve research results across the nps.gov domain. This is particularly useful in helping researchers make connections between places, time periods, and people. As an example, using World War II as a topic search retrieves site information on events relating to the war such as the Women at Floyd Bennett Field, https://www.nps.gov/articles/000/-hour-history-lesson-the-world-war-ii-navy-women-of-floyd-bennett-field.htm; Rosie the Riveter Museum, https://www.nps.gov/rori/index.htm; the Springfield Armory National Site, https://www.nps.gov/spar/index.htm; and the Manhattan Project National Historical Park, https://www.nps.gov/mapr/hanford.htm. Each site reflects how these different locations provide a context that can be added together to complete a larger picture. Travelers might take a historical site trip or participate in some armchair historical traveling. Students could use these sites as information for reports and other studies. Comparing and contrasting the sites and the events that happened in those sites can show how a war such as World War II was fought from several fronts.

U.S. history is filled with the conflict from wars conducted both within and outside our borders. There are many sites to be found in the National Park Service dedicated to those wars, battles, and soldiers. For patrons searching genealogy for historical battle information, the *Soldiers and Sailors Database* at https://www.nps.gov/civilwar/soldiers-and-sailors-database.htm can serve as a starting point to discovering the names of soldiers in the Civil War, African American sailors, and Medal of Honor recipients. See Image 3. Library patrons searching their family histories can search their Civil War ancestors by name. Once found, a check of the regiment gives the history and locations of the participants, providing links to home states and relatives. These databases are an index to materials located at the National Archives and Records Administration. This opens another avenue for further exploration. Teachers can use these to help students explore Civil War battles while bringing life to the men and women who participated in them. Following the links for each of these portals retrieves National Park sites and memorials along with the names and battalions.

While not everyone has access to a national park, local history abounds. Of interest to many is the National Register of Historic Places, the official list of historic places deemed worthy of preservation, https://

BROWSE PEOPLE

Soldiers >

Search the service records of over 6 million men, blue and gray, who served in the Civil War.

Sailors >

See a list of 18,000 African American sailors that served in the Civil War.

Regiments >

Search unit histories of over 4,000 Union and Confederate regiments.

Cemeteries >

The National Park Service manages 14 National Cemeteries, all but one of which is linked to a Civil War battlefield park.

Battles >

Of the 10,500 armed conflicts that occurred during the Civil War, nearly 400 were identified as the principal battles.

Prisoners >

Check the lists of the Confederate prisoners held at Fort McHenry and the Union troops kept at Andersonville prison camp.

Image 3: Soldiers and Sailors Database provides information about soldiers, battles, regiments, and other details from the Civil War (National Park Service at https://nps.gov).

www.nps.gov/subjects/nationalregister/index.htm. Introduce this page to patrons wanting to know more about the historic homes and buildings in their locale and to students researching their local area for stories of the past. Teachers can pair this page with other NPS pages such as the Heritage Travel sites or Find a Park to help complete the context as students investigate locations nearby.

Not all things about National Parks are about hiking or "running through fields" however, as Katherine Rivard's blog post points out, https://www.nationalparks.org/connect/blog/bibliophiles-guide-finding-your-park. There are National Park sites such as the Adams National Historical Park and Frederick Douglass National Historic Site that include the libraries of their previous owners. Many of these libraries can be visited today at the sites, and images of the libraries themselves are available on their websites. The rooms are shared as they were lived in by their respective owners. This blog post by Rivard brings up another excellent source of information about the parks: blogs. Blog posts can be found throughout the NPS and partner sites. They are excellent resources for discovering interesting and quirky tidbits, as well as highlighting people, historical events, and resources that are easily missed within a large agency site like the NPS.

Data

Data relating to the science and social science activities that are accomplished within the National Parks can be found throughout the nps. gov site. Each park, historical site, or monument website includes a "by the numbers" listing of important statistics relating to that specific site. Other data can be accessed through the NPS "Data Store," https://irma. nps.gov/DataStore/. This page includes links to reports on park use, scientific trends, plus data on the geology and ecology of the different sites. Historical data highlighting inventories of cultural sites and potential sites, data using maps to locate administrative boundaries, and ecological boundaries of species and plants are useful for a variety of inquiry investigations. This portal is useful for librarians to direct patrons, students, and researchers to statistics relating to climate change, park resources, visitor statistics, and the links to cultural resources can be of special use to architects, house owners, and historians. These cultural resources include reports documenting historic landmarks, the furnishings within those landmarks, and cultural landscape reports.

Teaching and Lesson Plans

NPS offers many ways on how teachers or parents can locate lessons, resources, and ideas that will engage their students. This will encourage them to dig into compelling and meaningful research across any curricular subject area and understand their event in the place it happened.

Teaching Based on Standards

Using nps.gov to teach meets many teaching standards such as the Next Generation Science Standards (NGSS) for K–12; the College, Career, and Civic Life (C3) Framework for Social Studies State Standards, and the Common Core State Standards Initiative for English Language Arts & Literacy in History/Social Studies, Science, and Technical Subjects. All the content standards ask students to know and understand the nature of information: how to find it, how to evaluate it, and how to create with it. Once learned, they ask students to head out into the world and participate, whether this is engaging in civic action, creating art, developing science experiments, designing and/or fixing automobiles, or any number of projects that engage students in the world.

All these standards ask for question-building, exploration, analysis, and reflection. Cross-curricular subjects merge social science topics with science, adding context as students build content understanding within both fields. Adding art or music history into any project rounds out that context while meeting not only core content standards, but art and/or visual performing arts standards. Using the visual and other information from the NPS website or visiting sites in person opens many possibilities to foster question building. Engaging students with a compelling image sparks questions that can be used to guide student research. One strategy is using the Question Formulation Technique (QFT) from the Right Question Institute, https://rightquestion.org. Using this strategy as one example of student engagement, giving students the image displayed at https://www.nps.gov/places/milk-bottle-grocery.htm, from which they formulate their questions, begins an exploration into Route 66. Layer that with the map, https://rt66.me/more-route66/, *and with the questions created, students jump right into geography and the many other possible topics which can encompass this one route including* music, art, architecture, food, the American landscape, and the impact of automobiles on American culture.

To find lessons created by NPS educators, start with the Educator's portal, https://www.nps.gov/teachers/index.htm. While this page directs teachers to the many possible lessons, curriculum topics, and instructional ideas using NPS materials and sites, it is only the beginning. By using the search boxes on the top of this page, teachers can find many programs of interest. Search by subject, grade level, or Common Core Standard. Be sure to investigate many grade levels, as many subjects as lessons can be modified to fit classroom or home interests and teaching goals. Check out the NASA/NPS partnership Junior Ranger Spaceflight Explorer program. In this program, students complete activities that teach about space and spaceflight while working toward earning Junior Ranger Badge. Other programs and lesson materials, including virtual field trips, images, or maps, can be utilized in a variety of learning environments.

Teaching with Historic Places

The NPS's "Teaching with Historic Places" resources, https://www.nps.gov/subjects/teachingwithhistoricplaces/index.htm, is the "umbrella" concept that covers the distinct tools of discovery. This includes lessons, programs, and resources that ground instruction in the concept of 'place.' While much of this is centered on classroom activities and instruction, they also provide families or home-schooling groups with activities that can be used before traveling to any park, whether in-person or virtually. This collection takes teaching to the next level by utilizing a variety of materials that bridges the connections between place, people, objects, and events across time. Lessons are included for those shorter

teaching times called "(H)our History," https://www.nps.gov/subjects/
teachingwithhistoricplaces/-h-our-history-lessons.htm. These lessons
include small less-than-an-hour activities within a series such as Civil
Rights, the legacy of slavery, and activities that teach engaged citizenship. They can be taught as stand-alone lessons or as a series with each one
building upon the other. School and public librarians might consider programming or other outreach with any of these activities.

Teaching with Traveling Trunks

A classroom teacher can order these trunks which are filled with artifacts relating to STEM topics including bats, fossils, and sharks. History
lessons include Victorian Architecture, a "traveling Haversack" filled with
artifacts from the American Revolutionary War period. This is hands-on
learning at its best. Each includes a teacher's guide and lesson ideas,
https://www.nps.gov/teachers/teacher-resources.htm?#fq%5B%5D=Type_
Group%3A%22Materials+For+Loan%22. While many of the trunks can be
ordered by mail, some must be picked up in person, so check with your
local National Park or historic site to see what items they may have that
can be shared via these traveling trunk programs.

Teaching with Curiosity Kits

Curiosity kits are an NPS treasure for student discovery, located at
https://www.nps.gov/subjects/teachingwithhistoricplaces/curiosity-
kits.htm. This multi-sourced collection covers wide-ranging topics, people, and places from Alice Paul to Black Baseball History and to less
well-known people like Dr. Mabel Ping-Hua. The kits include primary
sources and lesson ideas that can spur questions. These resources can be
paired across NPS portals, grade levels, and curricular areas.

The "Places of...." Series, https://www.nps.gov/articles/000/places-of-
series.htm, takes researchers into the places of importance about a subject
such as Ida B. Wells-Barnett. Students researching the "Hidden Figures"
women can identify the location of the research facility that employed
each of them and link to the articles that explain further their important
history.

Students throughout the country are often assigned "State Reports"
in which they investigate one State, identifying its flag, animal, history,
and geography. Using National Park Service resources, students can
dig deeper into their assigned state to research the ways that geography
affected the culture of native peoples, attracted colonists, and created the
local environment that defines each state. Not only can students identify

and understand why the chosen landmarks honor the past and what happened in that place, they are developing critical thinking skills, backed up by evidence as to why these events and these people merged in time while becoming important cultural memory landmarks. Once a State is chosen, the link to it becomes a portal to affiliated sites which leads to deeper discovery and a myriad of ways to understand their State today. This type of learning activity bumps up the traditional report assignment by allowing students access to a wider variety of content and context, giving them an opportunity to think deeper about how their State interacts as part of the entire nation.

Youth Activities

Librarians can direct parents, home-schoolers, youth leaders, and kids themselves to the invitation by the National Park Service to participate in a variety of activities designed specifically for young people to interact with nature, https://www.nps.gov/subjects/youthprograms/index.htm. Local scouting organizations can partner with NPS to join their Resource Stewardship Scout Ranger program. This project includes volunteer service at national parks nearby. The National Park's "Every Kid Outdoors" gives free passes to 4th graders and their families who complete a short activity; and Junior Rangers is a program conducted in all the parks where young people complete activities and share their answers with a park service Ranger to receive a Junior Ranger patch and certificate. For older youth, the Youth Conservation Corps provides work experience with education in land and resource stewardship. Direct interested youth to the "Work with Us" site, https://www.nps.gov/subjects/youthprograms/jobs-and-internships.htm, to view opportunities such as internships. Youth interested in an internship are encouraged to contact the park that interests them to get current information on openings and job descriptions. Youth between the ages of 15–18 can apply for the Youth Conservation Corps, while recent graduates from high school, trade school, or college can apply for the Pathways Program, which offers federal employment opportunities.

Climate Change, Science, and Nature Studies

Understanding weather changes, geology, and preserving native habitats are some of the initiatives that make up the NPS. Clicking on the link titled "Explore Nature," https://www.nps.gov/nature/index.htm, introduces researchers to a variety of options that highlight work the NPS accomplishes, including inventorying and monitoring weather, species, air, vegetation, geology, and park resources. Providing data that can be used by scientists and other researchers worldwide helps to create laws, protocols, and other measures to help mitigate changes to the environment. Social science and science interact through human presence, and the NPS provides some solutions to consider through its Environmental Stewardship program. Investigating its website on climate change, https://www.nps.gov/subjects/climatechange/index.htm, explores the science behind climate change, how it is observed in the parks, and how the effects might be slowed down. Citizens are invited to participate through the NPS's Citizen Science programs and the many youth programs offered. These can be an integral part of our children's lives. To locate the many topics covered, click on the link "Topics" where one discovers the full range of subjects that NPS shares. Topics such as biodiversity, bison, condors, the air, glaciers, mountains, energy, and natural phenomena invite all to explore and understand the complexity that nature offers.

For studying nature, invite students and young children to listen to the sounds of nature through the sound gallery. Using it as a compelling way to start the discussion of any natural habitat, the *sound gallery*, https://www.nps.gov/subjects/sound/gallery.htm, provides sounds including chickens, bison, honey bees, an avalanche, crickets, and alligators. There are many more nature and human generated sounds that will engage and enlighten. During lunchtime, these can be used in the school library as a nudge for further exploration or for an "entry activity" as students settle into class. These sounds delight and invite discussion.

One partner that is important to mention is the National Parks Foundation, https://www.nationalparks.org. As the charitable arm of the NPS, its goal is to raise money to support Park projects. The website, however, includes useful and informative information on sites that is not covered in the nps.gov domain by covering the blogs, images, and program information, taking on another lens from which to view the park.

Conclusion

The National Park Service is not often thought of as a location for historical or in-depth scientific information. This essay reminds users that location or place provides a context and a concept for teaching and learning about history and science. By providing online and in-person programs, data-rich information, solutions-oriented discussions, and educationally engaging lessons all packaged up in the wild variety that Nature presents, the NPS leads the way to citizen participation in creating solutions for a sustainable and healthy future.

References

Dilsaver, Lary M., ed. 1994. *America's National Park System: The Critical Documents.* Lanham, MD: Rowman & Littlefield. Accessed January 2, 2022. https://www.nps.gov/parkhistory/online_books/anps/anps_1c.htm.

Appendix: Additional Readings

Fester, James. 2021. "7 Tips for Exploring Environmental Science Through Project-Based Learning." Edutopia. April 14. Accessed December 15, 2021. https://www.edutopia.org/article/7-tips-exploring-environmental-science-through-project-based-learning.
U.S. Department of the Interior. National Park Service. 2018. "Quick History of the National Park Service." Last updated May 14, 2018. Accessed December 9, 2021. https://www.nps.gov/articles/quick-nps-history.htm.

Appendix: Teaching Standards

Next Generation Science Standards (NGSS) for K-12, https://www.nextgenscience.org.
College, Career, and Civic Life (C3) Framework for Social Studies State Standards, https://www.socialstudies.org/standards/c3.
Common Core State Standards Initiative for English Language Arts & Literacy in History/Social Studies, Science, and Technical Subjects, http://www.corestandards.org/.

Government Information Resources from the U.S. Department of Energy

MARK LOVE

Introduction

The U.S. Department of Energy (DOE) contains a multitude of online resources on all types of energy produced within the United States. There is a wealth of information on all sources of clean energy and fossil fuels. Students, researchers, industry professionals, and members of the public can find information on wind and solar energy, electricity, nuclear power, petroleum, and natural gas. This will assist users in exploring an industry that plays an important role in the U.S. economy. Users can find resources on the current administration's energy policies and the current state of energy production in the United States. Statistics and research reports related to energy industries and energy production are available.

Students and industry professionals looking for the latest research reports related to effective methods of oil and gas production can find them through the DOE's repository of scholarly information, OSTI.gov. Consumers looking for information on installing solar panels on their homes can look to the valuable resources on the DOE's Energy Saver site, https://www.energy.gov/energysaver/energy-saver. Students and members of the public interested more about the latest trends and projections for gasoline prices can check out the DOE's Energy Information Administration website, https://www.eia.gov/.

U.S. Department of Energy

Officially formed in 1977, the U.S. Department of Energy (DOE) traces its roots back to the Manhattan Project and the development of the atomic bomb during World War II. The Atomic Energy Act of 1946 created the Atomic Energy Commission, which managed the production of this new form of energy and focused on producing nuclear weapons. The energy crisis of the 1970s and the shift to using nuclear power for non-military uses prompted President Jimmy Carter and Congress to create the current U.S. Department of Energy in 1977 (U.S. Department of Energy, n.d.). Since the 1990s, the DOE included a focus on the production of clean energy, as well as fossil fuels and nuclear power.

The official website of the U.S. Department of Energy, Energy.gov, established in the late 1990s, is the starting point for researching energy issues. The homepage, as shown in Image 1, highlights the priorities of the current presidential administration concerning energy policymaking and the energy industry. Prominently featured on the home page is information about the clean energy corps, https://www.energy.gov/CleanEnergyCorps. The DOE refers to its staff as the clean energy corps, and this page serves as a tool to recruit employees to work on the Department's clean energy initiatives. This could serve to help those job hunting in this and related fields.

The DOE's homepage includes information on the current administration's energy policymaking priorities. The DOE's efforts to combat climate change are available at https://www.energy.gov/combating-climate-crisis, and the DOE's push to create clean energy union jobs, https://www.energy.gov/creating-clean-energy-union-jobs.

The website is organized into four main sections: Science & Innovation, Energy Economy, Security & Safety, and Save Energy, Save Money. Under Science & Innovation, for example, there are links to resources on

Image 1: Home page of Energy.gov.

the various types of energy produced in the United States: fossil fuels, nuclear, renewable or clean energy, and electricity.

Clean Energy

The clean energy resources cover solar, wind, water, geothermal, bio-energy, nuclear, and hydrogen. These links refer users to the site for the Office of Energy Efficiency & Renewable Energy (EERE), https://www.energy.gov/eere/wind/wind-energy-technologies-office. This could come in handy for people planning to build a new structure to meet city and state planning standards and regulations. Contractors looking for more information about designing energy-efficient buildings to meet these new standards can find resources at https://www.energy.gov/eere/energy-efficiency.

The public can access pages that provide basic information defining each type of energy and how it benefits society. The section on solar energy includes a Homeowner's Guide to Going Solar, https://www.energy.gov/eere/solar/homeowners-guide-going-solar, and a guide to the basics of solar energy for communities, https://www.energy.gov/eere/solar/community-solar-basics. For wind energy, there is an explanation of how wind turbines work, https://www.energy.gov/eere/wind/how-do-wind-turbines-work, and how wind research and development benefits the public, https://www.energy.gov/eere/wind/offshore-wind-research-and-development.

The site for EERE contains research reports and data on clean energy that will be of interest to scholars, industry professionals, and policymakers. The site's section on funding and grant opportunities, https://www.energy.gov/eere/funding/eere-funding-opportunities, is a valuable resource for industry professionals. Professionals can learn how to apply for grant funding and access a list of approved projects. The EERE Publication and Product Library, https://www1.eere.energy.gov/library/default.aspx, provides a database containing a multitude of resources, including research reports, maps, statistics, presentations, guides, technical information, and newsletters. For example, researchers looking for information on bioethanol and biodiesel can find multiple research reports on the topic. Contractors looking for information on codes, standards, laws, and taxes for solar panels and solar-powered buildings can find reports, guides, and fact sheets discussing this topic.

Fossil Fuels

The resources for fossil fuels cover the types of oil and gas produced in the United States and the methods of production, https://www.energy.

gov/science-innovation/energy-sources/fossil. Image 2 displays this web-page. The fossil site contains links to basic facts about oil and gas production. There are links to research reports, as well as data and statistics. For example, under the section devoted to carbon storage research, there are links to research reports and statistics, https://www.netl.doe.gov/coal/carbon-storage/publications. For example, users looking for information on offshore drilling can find research reports published from 2010 to the present and datasets (e.g., Energy Data Exchange) at https://edx.netl.doe.gov/offshore/research-portfolio/. Those interested in learning about current federal regulations for natural gas can find valuable resources provided by the Office of Fossil Energy and Carbon Management at https://www.energy.gov/fecm/regulation.

Energy.gov » Science & Innovation » Energy Sources » Fossil

Fossil energy sources, including oil, coal and natural gas, are non-renewable resources that formed when prehistoric plants and animals died and were gradually buried by layers of rock. Over millions

Image 2: Energy.gov's Fossil Fuels page.

Security and Safety

The Security and Safety section focuses on the DOE's efforts at securing the nation's energy infrastructure. As we witness news events, we realize this is a critical responsibility. For nuclear security, the National Nuclear Security Administration (NNSA), https://www.energy.gov/nnsa/national-nuclear-security-administration, is a valuable source to learn about DOE's efforts to secure the nation's nuclear weapons arsenal. Information on securing and managing the nation's nuclear power plants is available from the Office of Environmental Management (EM), https://www.energy.gov/em/office-environmental-management. This includes information on nuclear cleanup sites. For cybersecurity, the Office of Cybersecurity, Energy Security, and Emergency Response (CESER), https://www.energy.gov/ceser/cybersecurity, provides details on how the DOE partners with private industry to secure the technology linked to the variety of energy facilities in the U.S. The cybersecurity of all electronic systems tied to critical energy infrastructures such as power grids and oil and gas refineries is critically important to U.S. national security. For example, CESER posts five cybersecurity priorities "to address the evolving cyber risk landscape to the energy sector." CESER is the agency within DOE that helps to coordinate the DOE's efforts to secure the computer applications vital to the nation's energy supply.

Energy Saver

The Energy Saver site, https://www.energy.gov/energysaver/energysaver, is of great interest if a patron is looking for information on how to save energy and money. The site provides five sections: Services, Heat & Cool, Weatherize, Design, and Electricity & Fuel.

The Services section provides useful information about do-it-yourself projects, https://www.energy.gov/energysaver/do-it-yourself-energy-savings-projects, including step-by-step instructions on home improvement projects that will help consumers save energy. For example, consumers can learn about how to insulate hot water pipes to help prevent freezing in winter. The section includes the Energy Saver Guide, with tips on how consumers can save on energy costs and use clean, renewable energy to power their homes. Versions are available in English and Spanish.

The Home Comfort section, https://www.energy.gov/energysaver/home-comfort, includes tips on ways to save money when consumers heat and cool their homes, along with ways to use renewable energy for heating and cooling.

The Weatherization section includes information on Air Sealing and describes ways consumers can prevent air leakage from their homes and save money on their energy costs. Energy-saving insulation tips are provided.

The Design section provides information on designing or remodeling homes; the result is to use renewable energy sources and reduce costs. This section includes information on landscaping and how tree placement can aid in saving energy costs and making homes more energy-efficient. This section might be of interest to students looking for science fair projects on energy savings at home.

The Electricity & Fuel section, https://www.energy.gov/energysaver/save-electricity-and-fuel, contains information on buying energy-efficient appliances, lighting, saving money on gas, and buying fuel-efficient cars.

STEM Research

The DOE website, https://www.energy.gov, contains a section of educational resources for Science, Technology, Engineering, and Math (STEM), https://www.energy.gov/doe-stem/doe-stem, with a particular emphasis on how STEM applies to energy sources and production. There are resources for students and teachers from kindergarten through 12th grade, including activities, lesson plans, and study guides, https://www.energy.gov/kindergarten-high-school. For college students, there is a section of resources on workshops, programs, and internships for students with STEM majors that have an interest in the energy industry, https://www.energy.gov/college-continued-learning. On this website, students can learn about the DOE Scholars Program. Students or recent graduates can tap opportunities to learn about DOE functions and prepare them to seek entry and mid-level positions with the DOE or DOE-supported positions with other organizations. Teachers can access an interesting selection of materials at https://www.energy.gov/teachers. This includes study guides and activities. Other training resources for working in the energy industry are available at https://www.energy.gov/workforce.

Energy Explained

For students or members of the public with limited knowledge of the types of energy and how they are used, the DOE's Energy Explained site is a valuable resource, https://www.eia.gov/energyexplained/. The site contains a thorough explanation of non-renewable resources such as oil and petroleum products, natural gas, and nuclear energy as well as renewable sources such as hydropower, wind, geothermal, and solar. It provides an extensive examination of how energy is used in the United States: https://www.eia.gov/energyexplained/use-of-energy/.

Energy Kids

The DOE provides a multitude of educational resources for teachers and students to learn more about energy and its importance to society. The Energy Kids site, https://www.eia.gov/kids/, provides resources on the types of energy and how they are used that are geared toward younger audiences. Under Games & Activities, the site includes puzzles, popular words and their meanings that are used in the energy industry, science fair experiments (PDF format) for kindergarteners through the 12th grade, and other educational activities. A teacher's guide, https://www.eia.gov/kids/for-teachers/teacher-guide/, is an excellent resource for teachers that includes lesson plans and classroom activities on topics such as creative writing and a website scavenger hunt.

National Science Laboratories

The Department of Energy operates a network of science laboratories around the United States, https://www.energy.gov/national-laboratories. Seventeen national laboratories serve as research centers for exploring scientific issues related to climate change and various types of energy. Each laboratory has a website with information on the research being performed. Check each lab's website for career opportunities, educational information, and potential visitor information.

The Oak Ridge National Laboratory, located in Tennessee, provides scientific support to the Department of Energy through the lab's discoveries and technical breakthroughs. The website (Image 3) provides information about the lab's research efforts and areas, about different types of opportunities to visit, and about job openings, internships, and postdoctorial opportunities. Access to the lab's research library, https://www.ornl.gov/content/research-library, includes a searchable catalog and access to the full-text of technical reports related to the lab's research. The website provides access to information about educational programs. These programs allow students and faculty to participate in programs and internships to learn more about the scientific research being performed at the lab. The lab's Small Business Programs Office, https://smallbusiness.ornl.gov/, provides information on how small businesses can partner with the lab on construction and other projects related to the work being

Image 3: Home page of Oak Ridge National Laboratory.

performed at the lab. For example, the website details business opportunities such as projects dealing with construction and scientific instruments.

U.S. Energy Information Administration

The website (Image 4) for the DOE's U.S. Energy Information Administration (EIA), https://www.eia.gov/, contains valuable resources for researchers and industry professionals. It is an excellent source of information and statistics on the energy sector's role in the economy and energy production for fossil fuels, clean energy, and nuclear power. The site is divided into three main sections: Sources & Uses, Topics, and Geography. Under Sources & Uses, for example, the EIA provides resources on prices and production for each type of energy produced in the United States. Petroleum & Other Liquids includes recent data on prices and production and analysis and projections for the petroleum industry. Under the Data tab under Petroleum & Other Liquids, users can find data on current petroleum prices and current oil production statistics. Under the Analysis & Projections tab, future projections on pricing, production, and other economic and industry data can be found. Likewise, the Renewable & Alternative fuels section provides data and statistics on prices and production. Current prices and production statistics are provided for biomass, geothermal, hydropower, solar, and wind. An analysis of the current state and future projections of the U.S. renewable energy industry is provided.

The Geography section of the EIA site, https://www.eia.gov/maps, contains valuable resources with maps and other state and international energy data. This includes maps that display the pricing, production, and consumption for each type of energy in the U.S. and internationally. For example, users can locate a map to display the top one hundred oil fields in the United States, based on reserves, and the EIA's U.S. Energy Atlas

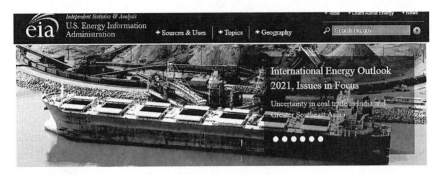

Image 4: U.S. Energy Information Administration home page.

eia | energy information and resources | U.S. Energy Atlas   Maps   Data   Feedback   EIA.gov

The U.S. Energy Atlas is a comprehensive reference for data and interactive maps of energy infrastructure and resources in the United States.

Check back in for further updates as we continue to expand and enhance EIA's data and mapping capabilities.

In the meantime, you can help us improve by submitting your feedback.

Image 5: U.S. Energy Atlas home page.

(Image 5), an interactive mapping tool with up-to-date maps displaying energy infrastructure resources and energy disruptions due to hurricanes, wildfires, and floods. State energy production and consumption maps are available by type of energy produced or consumed. Users can click on a state, for example, Louisiana, and display data (e.g., statistics and charts), https://www.eia.gov/beta/states/states/la/overview. Users can also see where a particular state such as Louisiana ranks in terms of such factors as production, consumption, and expenditures, https://www.eia.gov/beta/states/states/la/rankings.

The Office of Scientific and Technical Information (OSTI), https://www.osti.gov, is the best resource for finding technical reports and scholarly information produced by the DOE (Image 6). Basic keyword and advanced searching, such as looking for a particular publication, are available from the home page. Search results include journal articles, technical reports, datasets, and conference proceedings. For example, a keyword search for petroleum retrieves (as of this writing) over 190,000 items. Full-text copies are available for many of these DOE-funded publications. For those publications in which the full-text is not available, links to ordering information are provided, as well as the full citation so that users can request the item through their local library's interlibrary loan system. Under "Search Tools," users can use DOE Pages and locate DOE-produced scholarly journal articles. Many of these articles have the full-text of the article available. DOE Data Explorer is a database that allows users to search for datasets for research projects performed by DOE employees or for research funded by the DOE. Each item provides a summary of the research project with links to view the dataset or to download.

Industry professionals and policymakers will note with interest OSTI's link to DOE ScienceCinema, https://www.osti.gov/sciencecinema/. This database contains videos on energy-related topics. Basic keyword searching and advanced searching options are available. Although many of these videos are geared toward these two groups, teachers, educators, and the public can find informative videos on topics. For example, searching for "clean energy" retrieves about one hundred results. Results include

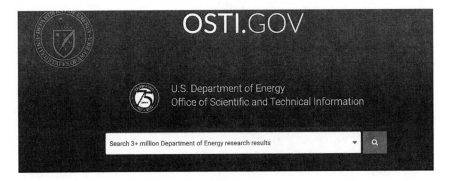

Image 6: Home Page of OSTI.gov.

a video about the "Clean Energy Geek Squad" and videos that are part of the DOE's Energy 101 series. An excellent example for students is the video "Clean Energy Manufacturing Boosting U.S. Competitiveness," https://www.osti.gov/sciencecinema/biblio/1214771.

Conclusion

The U.S. Department of Energy provides valuable resources for researchers, industry professionals, scholars, teachers, students, and members of the public through energy.gov and its related websites. Researchers and members of the public can find detailed information on the types of energy produced in the United States, including fossil fuels and clean energy. Users can find a treasure trove of data, reports, statistics, and other useful information from the Energy Information Administration and OSTI.gov. Teachers and students can find a multitude of educational resources through the DOE's STEM Rising, Energy Kids, and Energy Explained sites. The Energy Saver site is an invaluable resource for consumers interested in saving money and becoming more energy efficient. For users searching for information on energy-related topics, the DOE provides access to a top-notch collection of resources to meet their information needs.

REFERENCE

U.S. Department of Energy. n.d. "A Brief History of the Department of Energy." Accessed February 16, 2022. https://www.energy.gov/lm/doe-history/brief-history-department-energy.

Science Images and Where to Find Them

NATHAN A. SMITH

Introduction

The United States government has been, and remains, an authoritative resource for researchers in many disciplines. This is especially true for scientific researchers where, according to the National Science Board, the U.S. government provided over 20 percent of funding for research and development projects for the years 2000–2019 (National Science Board 2022, 17). An immeasurable benefit of government-funded research is that a good portion of it automatically falls under the public domain once it is published, with the caveat that not *all* publications are unrestricted in their use. It is always a good idea to look for the copyright symbol (©) or a notice stating how the images can be legally used. This includes any graphics such as tables or charts, images such as photographs or illustrations, and even videos from born-digital publications.

Federal government websites, however, can be as confusing to navigate as a labyrinth, and sometimes it seems they are designed and built by Daedalus himself. Some agencies have links directly to their visual resources on their homepage, while others have links buried in seemingly unrelated pages. Some agencies do not have public-facing visual resources pages at all and instead direct researchers to their social media accounts.

It is, therefore, no surprise that researchers come to librarians for help in locating government resources to complete their dissertations, presentations, projects, and reports. While many of our questions come via Ask a Librarian, the Library of Congress also gets phone calls, emails, and even mailed letters. The requests can range from international baccalaureate students looking for images related to HELA cells to doctoral candidates asking for images related to historical influenza outbreaks.

This essay contains information on finding visual resources such as illustrations, photographs, and videos from U.S. government agencies. These resources are grouped by overarching scientific disciplines. Authentic researcher questions, without personally identifiable information, will be used for demonstrative purposes. The images used in this essay are ones suggested to researchers for use in their projects or publications, along with a few fascinating facts discovered while researching appropriate resources.

There are hundreds of agencies and no conceivable way to cover them all, so this essay limits these to ones recommended most frequently to researchers. A full list of government agencies can be found in the Index of U.S. Agencies and Departments at https://www.usa.gov/. While the Library of Congress (LOC) and the National Archives and Records Administration (NARA) are not discussed, keep in mind they are fantastic repositories with many resources to offer.

Agricultural Resources

On May 15, 1862, Congress passed the Homestead Act of 1862 (Pub. L. 37-64; 12 Stat. 392) establishing the Department of Agriculture (USDA):

> ...the general designs and duties of which shall be to acquire and to diffuse among the people of the United States useful information on subjects connected with agriculture in the most general and comprehensive sense of that word, and to procure, propagate, and distribute among the people new and valuable seeds and plants (387).

While it can be near impossible for home gardeners to obtain seeds, the USDA still provides seeds *gratuit* to verified plant breeders and professional scientific researchers via the Agricultural Research Service's U.S. National Plant Germplasm System, https://www.ars-grin.gov/npgs/.

In addition to the USDA's Media Digital page, https://www.usda. gov/media/digital, one can find great visual resources via its social media accounts, particularly Flickr, https://www.Flickr.com/photos/usdagov, Instagram, https://www.instagram.com/usdagov, and YouTube, https:// www.youtube.com/c/UsdaGov. The USDA's National Agricultural Library (NAL) has wonderful online resources, which include the beautiful USDA Pomological Watercolor Collection, https://search.nal.usda. gov/discovery/collectionDiscovery?vid=01NAL_INST:MAIN&collecti onId=81279629860007426, and the Historic Poster Collections, https:// www.nal.usda.gov/exhibits/speccoll/exhibits/show/poster-collections.

Researcher Question: *I'm giving a presentation on how the mechanization of equipment altered farming in America. Where can I find images of farm equipment, both manual and mechanized?*

As with other aspects of industrialization, a dramatic shift in farming practices occurred during the late nineteenth century, but the public still considered farming to be one of the best ways to secure a successful life (Hurt 1994, 165-66) with upwards of half the population leading such lifestyles. The passage of the Morrill Act (Pub. L. 37-108), also known as the Land-Grant College Act of 1862, further emphasized this view. This act provided "Public Lands to the several States and Territories which may provide Colleges for the Benefit of Agriculture and Mechanic Arts." However, according to the USDA, the number of those leading a farm lifestyle has dwindled to a mere 2 percent today. Additionally, automated harvesters have allowed a single farmer to become effectively self-sufficient, cultivating entire acres of land single-handedly (Hurt 1994, 343).

Image 1 from the USDA National Agricultural Library, https://nal.usda.gov/, shows a farmer sitting on a horse-drawn rake, used to clean fields after harvests to prepare them for the following planting season. The design may be a bit different today, but the user can see a clear evolution from this one to the rakes of today that are pulled by tractors.

Image 1: Unknown photographer, *Field Cleaning. Raking the Stalks After Cutting*, undated (Special Collections, USDA National Agricultural Library. https://www.nal.usda.gov/exhibits/speccoll/exhibits/show/manuscript-collections/item/12334).

Energy Resources

U.S. energy agencies such as the Department of Energy (DOE) rely heavily on their social media presence to disseminate visual resources. The Energy Information Administration (EIA) uses both Flickr, https://www.flickr.com/photos/eiagov/, and YouTube, https://www.youtube.com/eiagov. Likewise, the Nuclear Regulatory Commission (NRC) directs the user to its Flickr and YouTube accounts via its Photos & Video webpage, https://www.nrc.gov/reading-rm/photo-gallery/index.html. The EIA provides images and videos on topics such as petroleum production and prices as well as infographics on data from the Residential Energy Consumption Survey. The NRC provides resources that vary from images of American crocodiles at the Turkey Point Nuclear Power Plant to infographics on NRC facility security components.

The Department of Transportation (DOT), which in 2022 announced a $5 billion project for building a national electric vehicle charging network (U.S. Department of Transportation 2022), has an entire webpage devoted to social media accounts, https://www.transportation.gov/social, where the user can find visual resources via its Flickr, Instagram, and YouTube pages.

Researcher Question: *Are there any pros and cons right now with renewable energy? Are there any statements on how it could affect the future?*

Though the debate on whether renewable energy is good or bad seems

Image 2: U.S. Department of Energy, *Electricity Generating Turbines Being Tested by SNL in Bushland, Texas,* 2013 (U.S. Department of Energy Flickr. https://www.flickr.com/photos/departmentofenergy/10346406375/).

to rage everywhere, it can be a challenge to gather authoritative resources of substance. There are real concerns regarding renewables, such as nuclear reactor meltdowns like Fukushima (Peake 2018, 575), while others seem unreasonable given the benefits, such as wind turbines not being aesthetically pleasing (Madrigal 2011, 248). One beneficial aspect of renewable energy is that it can stabilize global energy costs because it does not rely on current inflation and resource availability, a stark contrast to the energy crisis of the 1970s.

Image 2, from the DOE's Flickr website, https://www.flickr.com/photos/departmentofenergy/10346406375/, shows the "unaesthetic" wind turbines in action. Surprisingly enough, these are located in Texas, the state with the largest crude oil production by far of any other, accounting for more than 40 percent in 2021 (U.S. Energy Information Administration 2022).

Environmental Resources

Whether users are looking for resources on environmental science, such as natural disasters or made-man disasters that have environmental ramifications, there are many U.S. government agencies that can help. As a chemistry librarian, I can spend hours, if not days, on the website of the U.S. Chemical Safety and Hazard Investigation Board (CSB). In its Media Room, https://www.csb.gov/media-room/, the user will find images of current and past chemical incidents and animations and recorded statements in the Video Room, https://www.csb.gov/videos/. While the CSB does not keep a comprehensive database of incidents, a more complete picture can be cobbled together by combining the data from other entities such as the EPA's "Open Data" webpage, https://www.epa.gov/data, and the Occupational Safety and Health Administration (OSHA) "Data & Statistics" webpage, https://www.osha.gov/data.

The National Oceanic and Atmospheric Administration (NOAA) has a presence on Instagram, https://www.instagram.com/noaa/, YouTube, https://www.youtube.com/usnoaagov, and its other social media pages. The user will find resources such as images taken at the Mauna Loa Observatory, where air samples are taken so climate scientists can study greenhouse gas data, and videos of satellite imagery of hurricanes taken by NOAA's GOES-16 satellite. Its "Tools and resources" webpage, https://www.noaa.gov/tools-and-resources, provides curated collections for weather & climate, fisheries, education, satellites, and oceans & coasts.

Another fantastic resource is the U.S. Geological Survey (USGS), https://www.usgs.gov. While there is an option to select Maps, https://

www.usgs.gov/products/maps, which has great visuals, its Multimedia Gallery, https://www.usgs.gov/products/multimedia-gallery, is phenomenal. The gallery has stunning visuals that come in a variety of forms such as static images, stereograms, live webcams, and slideshows. The webpage showcases topics such as volcanic eruptions, estuaries, and the work of graduate students in environmental science.

Researcher Question: *I am doing comparison research on glaciers. Where can I find pictures of the same glaciers taken over a long period of time?*

The effects of climate change can be seen in many places, from longer droughts leading to increased forest fires to extreme weather events such as stronger hurricanes that penetrate far inland and flood larger areas than ever before. Glacial retreat is yet another yardstick due to the glaciers' sensitivity to climate change (Black 2013, 763). The USGS Repeat Photography Project, https://www.usgs.gov/centers/norock/science/repeat-photography-project, catalogs changes in glacier mass by taking photographs where previous historical photographs had been taken and comparing the two images. When modern photographs are side-by-side with photographs from as far back as 1887, there is a clear minimization of glacial extent.

Image 3 from the USGS Northern Rocky Mountain Science Center, https://www.usgs.gov/centers/norock, shows Grant Glacier, which is located within Flathead National Forest near Glacier National Park in Montana. The image on the left was taken in 1902 while the image on the right was taken in 1998, clearly illustrating the extent of glacial retreat.

Image 3: Elrod, M., photographer. *Grant Glacier—1902*. Northern Rocky Mountain Science Center. https://www.usgs.gov/media/images/grant-glacier-1902. Holzer, Karen, photographer. *Grant Glacier—1998*. (Northern Rocky Mountain Science Center. https://www.usgs.gov/media/images/grant-glacier-1998).

Health and Medical Resources

The U.S. budget for fiscal year 2022 included over $1 trillion for the Department of Health and Human Services (HHS). The HHS oversees the massive National Institutes of Health (NIH), which is comprised of twenty-seven institutes and centers (U.S. Department of Health and Human Services 2022). From the NIH's homepage, https://www.nih.gov/, the user can access visual resources by way of the News & Events tab and clicking on Images and B-roll. However, this webpage will redirect the user to the NIH's Flickr webpage, https://www.flickr.com/photos/nihgov/albums, to view the resources.

Two agencies under the umbrella of NIH that have great visual resources are the National Human Genome Research Institute, https://www.genome.gov/image-gallery, and the National Institute of General Medical Sciences (NIGMS), https://images.nigms.nih.gov/Pages/Home.aspx. Both agencies provide images and videos on mapped gene locations and equipment used in DNA sequencing to microsporidia invading roundworm cells and antigen protein structures. For resources from the Food and Drug Administration (FDA), https://www.fda.gov/, the user will be directed from its Interactive Social Media page, https://www.fda.gov/news-events/interactive-media, to the FDA Flickr, https://www.flickr.com/photos/fdaphotos/, and YouTube, https://www.youtube.com/user/USFoodandDrugAdmin, accounts where the user will find resources on FDA history, parasitology research, and the Reference Standard Sequence Library for Seafood Identification (RSSL).

For more historical resources regarding health and medicine, the National Library of Medicine (NLM), https://www.nlm.nih.gov/, has fantastic digital collections. These can be accessed using the drop-down Products and Services menu on the homepage and clicking Digital Collections. Most of the items in these collections are digitized books. There are visual resources such as Images from the History of Medicine and the Public Health Film Goes to War.

Researcher Question: *What is a staph infection?*
Staphylococci appeared long before humans and are capable of both aerobic and anaerobic growth. While some species are found on human skin and mucous membranes, others can cause food poisoning via their toxins and even serious disease. For a time, doctors treated staphylococci infections with penicillin, though in the twentieth century, doctors discovered antibiotic-resistant strains of staphylococci, which produced an enzyme that forced hydrolysis of ß-lactam rings (Crossley and Archer 1997, 139). Though treatable, these types of infections are still prevalent,

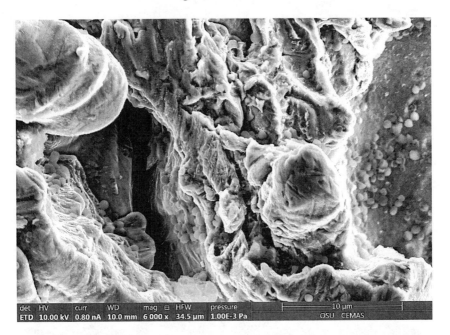

det	HV	curr	WD	mag	HFW	pressure		10 µm	
ETD	10.00 kV	0.80 nA	10.0 mm	6 000 x	34.5 µm	1.00E-3 Pa		OSU – CEMAS	

Image 4: Gupta, Niraj, et al. 2021. *Staphylococcus aureus in the porous coating of a femoral hip stem* (National Institute of General Medical Sciences. https:// images.nigms.nih.gov/pages/DetailPage.aspx?imageid2=6804. This was produced on research that appeared in *Antibiotics*, 10, no. 8 https://www.mdpi. com/2079–6382/10/8/889, though the image itself was not in the article. It is governed by CC BY-SA 3.0 guidelines).

even occurring in hospitals where patients with weakened immune systems are at particular risk (Crossley and Archer 1997, 565).

These opportunistic bacteria can hitch a ride on implants during surgery and cause major infection once they have taken root. In Image 4 from NIGMS, https://www.nigms.nih.gov/, *Staphylococcus aureus* has attached to a femoral hip stem, used in hip replacement surgery. The prefix "staphylo" comes from the Greek for "bunch of grapes," which is apt as one can see from the round cells of bacteria attached to the rougher surface of the stem.

Technology Resources

When one thinks of technology, cloud cities with flying cars or an appliance that can create any recipe displayed on the screen can come to mind. Technology is often characterized as space-age to give it a futuristic quality in the mind of the public, and no agency better exemplifies this than the National Aeronautics and Space Administration (NASA), https://www.nasa.gov. Under the heading Galleries, the user can find fantastical images of faraway stars and galaxies, as well as videos of astronauts, launches, and astronomical education. NASA is a perennial favorite among researchers, even those not in astronomical fields, for vivid visualizations.

The National Institute of Standards of Technology (NIST), https://www.nist.gov, has wonderful visual resources. On its News & Events tab, the user will find the Image Gallery, https://www.nist.gov/image-gallery, which is full of phenomenal resources such as illustrations of vibrating ions and images of carbon nanotubes. Also, from the News & Events tab is the Video Gallery, https://www.nist.gov/video-gallery, with resources in themed collections such as manufacturing and information

Image 5: NASA Jet Propulsion Laboratory/Space Science Institute. 2010. *Bright Spokes, Dark Shadow* (NASA, https://images.nasa.gov/details-PIA12605).

technology. In addition to these, there is the NIST Digital Archives, https://nistdigitalarchives.contentdm.oclc.org/, which contains such gems as oral histories from scientists and staff, artifact images from the NIST Museum and Archives, https://www.nist.gov/nist-museum, and the Gallery of Distinguished Scientists, Engineers, and Administrators.

Researcher Question: *How long have humans known about planetary rings?*

Astronomers have been theorizing about heavenly bodies since at least the invention of writing. Stars and planets were given the names of gods in ancient civilizations and often worshipped as such. Once telescopes had been invented, a whole new world of astronomical study opened wide. Although Galileo saw fuzzy appendages coming out of Saturn, it was Dutch astronomer Christiaan Huygens who determined those appendages were actually rings that circled the planet. Yet, it would not be for another two centuries until James Clerk Maxwell discovered that those rings were not solid, but composed of separate bodies (Lang 2011, 22, 327). Image 5 is Saturn's B ring taken by NASA's Cassini spacecraft, which shows how difficult it can be, even at (relatively) close range, to see these rings as anything but solid.

Today, names such as Saturn, Mars, and the Pleiades have given way to more of a jumble of letters and numbers based on the location of the object, such as the brown dwarf Gliese 229B (GL229B), https://starchild. gsfc.nasa.gov/docs/StarChild/questions/brown_dwarf.html, the discovery of which was published in 1995. The characters that form these odd names are assigned by the International Astronomical Union in Paris, https://www.iau.org/, whose mission is to promote astronomy through international cooperation.

Copyright Law and Citations

Title 17 of the United States Code covers copyrighted material, and this protection was so important that the Framers included it in the United States Constitution under Article I, Section 8:

The Congress shall have Power.... To promote the Progress of Science and useful Arts, by securing for limited Times to Authors and Inventors the exclusive Right to their respective Writings and Discoveries.

Government publications, including images and videos, are usually free of copyright restrictions, but there are some instances when this is not the case. Copyright law (U.S. Copyright Office 2021) has been amended continuously over the years, the latest being an update to "criminal penalties for copyright infringement" as part of the Consolidated Appropriations Act (Pub. L. 116-260, 134 Stat. 1182) enacted by Congress on December 27, 2020, and it can be daunting to get into the weeds regarding special cases and performing due diligence.

Some agencies make this process quite easy. For example, on NIH's Images and B-roll page, the NIH provides a link to Copyright Information, https://www.nih.gov/about-nih/frequently-asked-questions, which details any exceptions to the rule of government publications being part of the public domain. The NIH's National Human Genome Research Institute Copyright Policy webpage, https://www.genome.gov/about-nhgri/Policies-Guidance/Copyright, posts its policy concerning "text, graphics, videos, illustrations, and other information" along with any disclaimers such as copyrighted text. NASA's Media Usage Guidelines, https://www.nasa.gov/multimedia/guidelines/index.html, details its policy on items such as the NASA logo, still images, audio recordings, NASA content used for commercial purposes, and any other restrictions.

Most agencies will have copyright notices of some kind, though they may appear to be nonexistent as in the case of the U.S. Chemical Safety and Hazard Investigation Board (CSB). Images posted by the U.S. government on Flickr, such as the DOE wind turbine image (Image 3), include copyright information by providing a link to the U.S. Government Works webpage, https://www.usa.gov/copyrighted-government-works, and the application of copyright to U.S. government works, especially for copyright exceptions. Instagram is another story, however, and the best way to go about finding the copyright information would be to send a direct message to the account administrator to confirm it is in the public domain.

Helping researchers with proper citations can be tricky, as different scientific fields use different styles. When helping an electrical engineering student, the librarian can provide resources on the style created by the Institute of Electrical and Electronics Engineers (IEEE 1980), https://www.ieee.org/content/dam/ieee-org/ieee/web/org/conferences/style_references_manual.pdf, but if a librarian is helping an author who is writing on a particular variety of an apple, the most likely style resources to provide are the American Psychological Association (APA) and the Council of Science Editors (CSE). Others may need to use Modern Language Association (MLA), Chicago, Turabian, or American Chemical Society (ACS) styles depending on their field of research. Some government agencies extend an olive branch in this regard. For example, the USDA's National Agricultural Library's catalog record for *Malus domestica: Cauley*, https://naldc.nal.usda.gov/catalog/POM00002370, includes a statement of attribution already written and ready for use. Not all catalog records are as clear, and it will be up to the discretion of the researcher to decide how best to move forward.

Conclusion

The U.S. government has a lot to offer and this essay is by no means comprehensive in scope. Many people ask the FDA what products are safe while others ask the USDA what the best proportions are for a balanced meal. Of course, researchers submit Ask a Librarian questions on a variety of subjects depending on their fields of study or interest. There are as many and more fields of inquiry as there are government agencies. Each agency can provide visual resources that could help inform, inspire, and promote a lifelong love of learning to their audience. Whether visual resources are found buried in seemingly unrelated pages, proudly displayed on an agency's homepage, or found on their social media pages, they are a vital aspect of research. The adage that a picture is worth a thousand words can be very true, so be sure to promote the use of freely accessible government resources. These resources can have a huge impact on both the author and the audience and can potentially open new lines of inquiry for current or future projects.

References

Black, Brian C., ed. 2013. *Climate Change: An Encyclopedia of Science and History*, vol. 2. Santa Barbara, CA: ABC-CLIO.

Crossley, Kent B., and Gordon L. Archer, eds. 1997. *The Staphylococci in Human Disease*. Edinburgh: Churchill Livingstone.

Hurt, R. Douglas. 1994. *American Agriculture: A Brief History*. Ames: Iowa State University Press.

Institute of Electrical and Electronics Engineers. 1980. *QRIS: Quick Reference to IEEE Standards*. Piscataway: IEEE Service Center.

Lang, Kenneth R. 2011. *The Cambridge Guide to the Solar System*. Cambridge: Cambridge University Press.

Madrigal, Alexis. 2011. *Powering the Dream: The History and Promise of Green Technology*. Cambridge: Da Capo Press.

National Science Board. 2022. *The State of U.S. Science and Engineering 2022*. https://ncses.nsf.gov/pubs/nsb20221.

Peake, Stephen, ed. 2018. *Renewable Energy: Power for a Sustainable Future*, 4th ed. Oxford: Oxford University Press.

U.S. Copyright Office. 2021. Copyright Law of the United States (Title 17). May. https://www.copyright.gov/title17/.

U.S. Department of Health and Human Services. 2022. HHS FY 2022 Budget in Brief. https://www.hhs.gov/about/budget/fy2022/index.html.

U.S. Department of Transportation. 2022. *President Biden, USDOT and USDOE Announce $5 Billion over Five Years for National EV Charging Network, Made Possible by Bipartisan Infrastructure Law*. February 10. https://highways.dot.gov/newsroom/president-biden-usdot-and-usdoe-announce-5-billion-over-five-years-national-ev-charging.

U.S. Energy Information Administration. 2022. *Oil and Petroleum Products Explained*. Last updated April 7, 2022. https://www.eia.gov/energyexplained/oil-and-petroleum-products/where-our-oil-comes-from.php.

Appendix: Additional Resources

Drexler, Ken. 2021. *Morrill Act: Primary Documents in American History.* Library of Congress Research Guide. Last updated August 17, 2021.

National Archives and Records Administration. 2021. *The Constitution of the United States: A Transcription.* Last reviewed October 7, 2021. https://www.archives.gov/founding-docs/constitution-transcript.

U.S. Senate. n.d. "The Civil War: The Senate's Story." Accessed July 1, 2022. https://www. senate.gov/artandhistory/history/common/civil_war/MorrillLandGrantColle geAct_ FeaturedDoc.htm.

About the Contributors

Emily **Alford** is the head of government information, maps, and microform services at Indiana University Bloomington. She earned an MLIS from Kent State University and a BA in English literature from Miami (Ohio) University. She is a member of the American Library Association and the Government Documents Round Table.

Laurie **Aycock** is the government information librarian and a librarian associate professor at Kennesaw State University Library System in Marietta, Georgia. She holds a BS in biology from University of West Georgia and an MLIS from the Valdosta State University. She is a member of ALA's Government Documents Round Table (GODORT) and serves on its Education Committee.

Ariana **Baker** is the scholarly engagement librarian at Coastal Carolina University in Conway, South Carolina. Her work focuses on instruction, scholarly publishing, open access, and open educational resources. She received a BA in history and an MLIS from Rutgers University.

Kelly **Bilz** is the reference, instruction, and government documents librarian at Thomas More University in northern Kentucky in Benedictine Library. In 2020–2021, she was a librarian-in-residence in the Geography and Map Division of the Library of Congress. She earned her MSLS from the University of Kentucky and a BA in Classics at Ohio University.

Angela L. **Bonnell** is an associate professor and head of government documents at Illinois State University's Milner Library. She earned her MLIS from the University of Wisconsin–Madison, an MS in history from Illinois State University, and a BA in history from Beloit College. She has researched the use of government information in the nineteenth and early twentieth centuries and civic engagement in academic libraries.

Brandon R. **Burnette** is an associate professor at Southeastern Oklahoma State University as the government documents/reference librarian. A graduate of Texas Christian University, he received his MLS from the University of Kentucky. He has published in *DTTP: Documents to the People* and presented on Native American topics for numerous conferences including the American Library Association.

Jennifer **Castle** is a reference and government documents librarian at Tennessee State University. She earned a BA in visual communication (photography) from

Savannah College of Art and Design and a MLIS from San Jose State University. She is the lead editor of the ALA GODORT's *Documents to the People*.

Angel **Clemons** is the electronic resources librarian at the University of Louisville's Ekstrom Library. She earned an MLS from the University of Kentucky and a BA in English from Western Kentucky University. She also has experience in cataloging, serials, collection development, and business reference and teaching.

Jennifer Crowder **Daugherty** is the head of the North Carolina Collection in Academic Library Services at East Carolina University. She holds an MLS from Indiana University Bloomington and a BA in English from Eastern Kentucky University. In 2020, she received a William T. Buice III scholarship for Rare Book School at the University of Virginia.

Tom **Diamond** is the collections and materials selector librarian at Louisiana State University in Baton Rouge. He is a member of the American Library Association, the Business Reference and Services Section (Reference and User Services Association) and the Anthropology and Sociology Section (Association of College & Research Libraries).

Lauren B. **Dodd** is the associate director for Information Services at the United States Military Academy Library, West Point, New York. She served with the U.S. Government/Department of Defense as an academic librarian for the Air Force and as an Army post librarian in Germany. She received her MLIS from the University of Alabama and her BA in English from Mississippi University for Women.

Allison **Faix** is the instruction coordinator at Kimbel Library, Coastal Carolina University, in Conway, South Carolina, where she has worked as a librarian since 1999. She earned her MLIS degree from the University of Pittsburgh and has an MA in writing from Coastal Carolina University.

Isabella **Folmar** is an analyst for the University of South Florida's Institute for School Reform. In her previous positions, she served as the Florida Collection and outreach librarian for the State Library of Florida and reference coordinator for the State Archives of Florida. She received her MSI from Florida State University.

Elisabeth Pearson **Garner** is the government information librarian at the University of North Carolina Wilmington's Randall Library. She received her BA in history education from UNC Wilmington, her MEd in language and literacy education from UNC Wilmington and her MLS from North Carolina Central University. She is the chair of the Government Resources Section of the North Carolina Library Association.

Andrew **Grace** is the federal documents and microforms manager at ECU Libraries. He also acts as the co-chair of the library's Stewardship Committee and the co-chair of the Academic Library Services Paraprofessional Conference. He graduated from East Carolina University with a BSBA.

Dominique **Hallett** is the government information and STEM librarian at Arkansas State University. She earned her MLIS from Louisiana State University, her MA in heritage studies and her BA in political science from Arkansas State University, and she is pursing her PhD in heritage studies at Arkansas State University.

Amy **Laub** is the federal regional depository librarian at the University of Kentucky. She is a member of Depository Library Council and is active in the Kentucky Library Association Government Documents Roundtable and the ALA Government Documents Roundtable, and she serves on ASERL's Collaborative Federal Depository Program Oversight Committee.

Mark **Love** is the government information librarian/assistant professor at Nicholls State University in Thibodaux, Louisiana. He has a MLS from the University of North Texas and an MA in History from Sam Houston State University.

Amanda **McLeod** is the social sciences and government information librarian at Clemson University in R.M. Cooper Library. She received her MSIS from the University of Texas at Austin and her BA in psychology from Winthrop University. Her research interests include collaborative approaches to librarianship and morale and job satisfaction in library workers.

Caterina M. **Reed** is the instructional support associate for acquisitions at Stony Brook University Libraries and serves as the university librarian for Sarasota University. She received an MS in information and library science from the University at Buffalo and holds an MA in English and a BA in comparative literature from Stony Brook University.

Blake **Robinson** is the business librarian and an assistant professor at Rollins College in Winter Park, Florida. He works primarily with students, faculty, and staff in business, economics, and health. Blake holds his MSLIS from Florida State University in Tallahassee, an MA in Arabic and Islamic studies from the University of Sydney, Australia, and a BBA in marketing from the University of Texas at Austin.

Emily **Rogers** is a professor and reference librarian for government information at Odum Library, Valdosta State University, in Valdosta, Georgia. She holds a BA in English from the University of Georgia, an MA in English from the University of Kentucky, and an MSLIS from the University of Illinois. She is active in ALA's Government Documents Round Table (GODORT).

Heather **Seminelli** is the assistant director for communications and assessment at the United States Military Academy Library, West Point, New York. Before becoming a librarian, she served in the Army, assessing training, and flying UH-60 Blackhawk helicopters. She earned her MSLIS from Pratt School of Information.

Michelle **Shea**, MLS, MeD, is an education librarian and co-head of public services at Texas A&M University Central Texas. In her reference work, she often assists military-affiliated families, veterans, and community members. She enjoys writing about library programming, research, and service to diverse patrons.

Nathan A. **Smith** received a BA in history from Virginia Commonwealth University in Richmond and an MLS the Catholic University of America in Washington, D.C. He is a reference and research specialist at the Library of Congress, covering the subject areas of chemistry, the history of science and technology, and mathematics.

Claudene **Sproles** is head of collection management and the government documents librarian at the University of Louisville Libraries. She has been a documents librarian for more than 23 years and has spent her career promoting free and equitable access to government information.

Connie **Strittmatter** is the strategic projects librarian at Fitchburg State University, where she leads the library's assessment initiatives, provides training and educational resources regarding copyright, and serves as the liaison to the business and engineering technology departments. She holds an MLS from Kent State University and an MBA from the W.P. Carey School of Business at Arizona State University.

Connie Hamner **Williams**, MLS, NBCT, is the Petaluma History Room librarian with the Sonoma County Library. She was a teacher librarian with Petaluma City Schools for 28 years. She received her BA in geography and teaching credentials from Sonoma State University and her MLS from Emporia State University.

Nicole **Wood** is the resource management coordinator and the history, philosophy, and government documents librarian at Austin Peay State University in Clarksville, Tennessee. She earned an MSIS from the University of Tennessee, a PSM in environmental informatics from Tennessee Tech University, and a BA in English literature from Trevecca Nazarene University.

Index